Global Perspectives on
Rural Childhood and Youth

Routledge Studies in Human Geography

Global Perspectives on Rural Childhood and Youth

Young Rural Lives

Edited by
Ruth Panelli, Samantha Punch, and Elsbeth Robson

Routledge
Taylor & Francis Group
New York   London

Routledge
Taylor & Francis Group
270 Madison Avenue
New York, NY 10016

Routledge
Taylor & Francis Group
2 Park Square
Milton Park, Abingdon
Oxon OX14 4RN

© 2007 by Taylor & Francis Group, LLC
Routledge is an imprint of Taylor & Francis Group, an Informa business

Transferred to Digital Printing 2010

International Standard Book Number-10: 0-415-39703-0 (Hardcover)
International Standard Book Number-13: 978-0-415-39703-2 (Hardcover)

Library of Congress Cataloging-in-Publication Data

Global perspectives on rural childhood and youth : young rural lives / edited by Ruth Panelli, Samantha Punch, and Elsbeth Robson.
    p. cm. -- (Routledge studies in human geography ; 13)
    Includes bibliographical references and index.
    ISBN-13: 978-0-415-39703-2 (hardback : alk. paper)
    1. Rural children--Social conditions--Cross-cultural studies. 2. Rural youth--Social conditions--Cross-cultural studies. 3. Rural conditions--Cross-cultural studies. 4. Sociology, Rural. I. Panelli, Ruth. II. Punch, Samantha. III. Robson, Elsbeth.

HT453.G56 2007
305.2309173'4--dc22

2006035629

ISBN10: 0-415-39703-0 (hbk)
ISBN10: 0-415-88296-6 (pbk)

ISBN13: 978-0-415-39703-2 (hbk)
ISBN13: 978-0-415-88296-5 (pbk)

Visit the Taylor & Francis Web site at
http://www.taylorandfrancis.com

and the Routledge Web site at
http://www.routledge-ny.com

Contents

Boxes

Figures

xii *Figures*

Tables

Preface and Acknowledgements

The idea for this book emerged during work on the Young Rural Lives special issue of *Journal of Rural Studies* (2002 vol. 18, no. 2). Discussion in the referee processes and editorial writing highlighted the potential for cross-world debate and conceptual work that might complement the specificity of individual researchers' accounts. This dialogue continued via sessions on rural youth at the 2005 RGS-IBG conference in London as we began to discuss case studies and generic conceptual issues. We are grateful to DARG and RGRG of the Royal Geographical Society (with the Institute of British Geographers) who sponsored and supported those sessions, as well as the presenters and audience whose debates and discussions helped shape this book.

Our biggest thanks must go to all the authors who have contributed to writing this book. The diversity and detail of their work with young people has inspired us throughout this project. We are also grateful that they were exemplary at focussing on the agenda of young rural lives and sticking to deadlines despite being spread across several continents and time zones. In addition, we would like to acknowledge all the young people and adults who took part in the varied research projects which made the writing of this book possible.

We have valued the support received from many individuals while completing this volume including Paul Cloke, Jo Little, Richard Welch, and Ian McIntosh. We also gratefully acknowledge permission both: to reprint in shortened form from the *Journal of Rural Studies* (vol. 18), Hunter, K. and Riney-Kehrberg, P. 'Rural daughters in Australia, New Zealand and the United States: An historical perspective' (pp. 135–143), Copyright (2002), with permission from Elsevier; and to reproduce an adapted figure (which appears now as Figure 11.1) from *Geoforum* (vol. 36), Panelli, Kraack, and Little 'Claiming space and community' (pp. 495–508), Copyright (2005), with permission from Elsevier. We also appreciate the Universities of Keele, Otago, and Stirling for supporting our work, and special thanks goes to Richard Welch and Tracy Connolly (University of Otago) for help with artwork and editorial assistance during the final production of this book.

Finally, at Routledge we would like to thank Terry Clague, Ben Holtzmann, and associated staff for their support and guidance in preparing the manuscript for publication.

As co-editors we have found the experience of collaborating across three continents helped give our *global perspectives* reality. Thanks to global communications technology, working closely together has been a pleasurable and rewarding experience despite meeting together face-to-face only once during the preparation of this book.

Ruth Panelli, *Otago, New Zealand*

Samantha Punch, *Stirling, Scotland*

Elsbeth Robson, *Blantyre, Malawi*

1 From difference to dialogue
Conceptualizing global perspectives on rural childhood and youth

Ruth Panelli, Samantha Punch,
and Elsbeth Robson

Adamu (Northern Nigeria)
Robson (2004a: 194)

Adamu is about nine or ten years old, he lives in...Zarewa village.... Adamu wakes up at home in the morning to the sound of the call for prayers so he quickly...washes...in a ritual manner and immediately says his prayers kneeling inside....Adamu eats a bowl [of porridge] before leaving for the farm with his father at about 8am....Adamu and his father spend over two hours working on their family farm before walking back home. On the way...Adamu gathers a bundle of fresh grass from along the path for the sheep and goats tethered in the family compound. When they arrive back home Adamu hauls a bucket of water from the well for them to wash their hands before eating the steamed bean cakes (dan wake) his mother has prepared for them. After...[midday prayers] his mother then sends him on an errand to buy some cooking oil...Adamu then says the afternoon prayers at home before his mother sends him to the grinding

'Butthead' (Southern New Zealand)
McCormack (2000: 137–139, 82)

Butthead [is about nine or ten and lives] on a sheep farm...[His drawing of 'rural New Zealand'] presents an agricultural scene, in which both work and recreation take place. This construction was specialised....For instance, Butthead drew a crop of turnips being grazed by sheep. This area was fenced off from the rest of the scene, which was home to a number of pigs. This extensive knowledge of agriculture was derived from his rich experiences in this arena. Indeed, the farm that he lived on had crops of turnips and farrowing sows at the time of this construction. Butthead also drew his brother riding a motorbike to check the sheep feeding in the crop area. This image illustrated Butthead's understanding of 'rurality' as a site of work, however...his brother is pulling a wheelstand on the motorbike for fun, indicating that 'rurality' was also a site of recreation and pleasure....Butthead [also] drew himself being towed on a sack behind a farm machine with a bowl full of grain for the evening stiff porridge (*tuwo*)...when he gets there he has to wait in line with the other children....The machine is noisy and the dust of the flour is all around, but he sees his friend....Then before the evening prayers he plays for about an hour with other children outside in the street...[Later] he says the final prayers of the day....Until he finally goes to sleep Adamu spends an hour or so playing with other children

vehicle being driven by his father....Butthead also based his constructions on his material experiences. Within the interview session he [explained, "I] go out on the motorbikes to see what the creek's like, if it's risen, and go checking the eeling hole"....[Also] he referred to...'running around in the paddocks', 'getting muddy from working on the farm' and 'working hard at hay making time'.

The conditions and experiences of children and young people who work in rural areas have long been a source of concern for non-governmental organisations as well as academics specialising in development studies and health (e.g. Fyfe 1993; Vlassoff 1985). In contrast, western scholars have paid little attention to these matters until quite recently. This variance can be clearly traced. Studies of young people, such as Adamu in Northern Nigeria, build on a tradition in development geography that has for some time recognized the work and vulnerable positions of children and young people in the Majority world.[1] For it is in the Majority world that the greatest proportion of population, poverty, debt, and child mortality is found (Potter et al. 2004). Recent accounts such as Robson's (2004a) show young people are integral players in the life and work of rural societies, although often their lives are quite different from those of the adults in such settings.

In contrast, geographies of young people in the Minority world have concentrated initially on urban environments and cultures (Andrews 1985; Blaut and Stea 1971; Hill and Michelson 1981; Matthews 1984; Ward 1978; Winchester and Costello 1995). Rural geographies of childhood and youth in 'western' settings have only developed in breadth since the mid-1990s as wider debates concerning social exclusion, marginalisation, and otherness, have informed studies of children and young people as one group of marginalized or under-recognized rural dwellers (Matthews et al. 2000a; Philo 1992). Consequently, studies recording the lives and experiences of young people like 'Butthead' have sought to redress what has been reported as a countryside overwhelmingly recorded through adult eyes, and promoting adult interests (McCormack 2000; Valentine 1997a; Ward 1990).

This book celebrates the growth in rural studies of children and young people, and of childhood and youth. In this opening chapter we trace some of the history of these endeavours. But the genesis and motivation for this

book stems from our recognition that studies of rural young people can be
invigorated by cross-world dialogue. We heed Philo's (2000b: 253) call that:

> ... our scholarship must also look at the larger picture encompassing
> many different sets of children spread across different places, and must
> accept the challenge of tackling the macro-scale, structure-based geog-
> raphies of childhood as shaped by broad-brush political-economic and
> social-cultural transformations.

Consequently, this book demonstrates 'macro-scale' approaches to the
conceptualisation and analysis of young rural lives while also respecting
the value of in-depth, context-specific accounts of individual young people
in particular places. As a result, the following chapters include both individual research accounts and co-authored collaborations that seek to push
our understandings in more generic, conceptual directions.

While pursuing these goals we employ key definitions via a standard-
ized set of terminology; however, we also recognize that each term has
a diverse and rich history. First, in denoting the subjects of our research
we adopt both the terms *child/ren* and *young people*. We recognize the
critiques of linear, transition-oriented conceptualisations that situate
children, adolescents, and adults along a continuum of assumed increasing agency, competency, and rights (Punch 2002b; Valentine 1996; Wyn
and Dwyer 1999). In such cases, children are often uncritically considered
as pre-adults or 'human becomings' (Valentine 1996). Thus, we prefer to
employ the term *young person/people* as a way of acknowledging the integ-
rity of the person/people's lives and experiences in their own right, even
while registering that they belong to a particular 'young' age group.[2]

We concur with Wyn and White (1997: 10–11) who note that 'age is
socially constructed, institutionalized and controlled in historically and
culturally specific ways'. Consequently, the term *children* is included at
times when the institutional (e.g. school, legal system, government policy)
or historical and cultural particularity of a group of young people defines
them as children. For example, see O. Jones's (1997; 1999) discussion of
'children' as depicted in cultural constructions of childhood. The term
child or *children* is also included when culturally-specific acknowledgment
of immediate kinship to parent/s is relevant.

Second, the terms *childhood* and *youth* are adopted to convey the
socially and culturally constructed notions of particular stages of the lifecourse. While not pinpointing specific ages in years, the term *childhood*
identifies life periods associated with pre-adolescent contexts. In contrast
the term *youth* denotes life periods of older young people where cultural
and social constructions highlight contexts and expectations that constitute a separate and unique set of sub-cultures that are documented in some
cultural contexts after childhood and before adulthood (Skelton and Valentine 1998).

FINDING YOUNG PEOPLE IN RURAL SETTINGS:
A REVIEW OF EXISTING LITERATURE

In order to situate this account of global perspectives we first wish to explore how young rural lives have been identified, conceptually framed, and empirically recorded in the past. Reflecting the traditional separation of these works we first consider Majority world scholarship before noting the burgeoning Minority world studies. While disparate, we propose that these works provide a seedbed for the more challenging task of interconnecting and formulating cross-world approaches that are proposed in the following section.

Young people in Majority world rural contexts

Although in global terms the world is becoming more urbanized, in many parts of the Majority world most people still live in rural areas (Potter et al. 2004). Most young people in the Majority world live (and work) in rural areas yet most research is carried out with urban young people (Boyden et al. 1998; Johnson et al. 1995) since those in rural areas are less visible and accessible than their urban counterparts (Bequele and Myers 1995).[3] Compared with urban areas, rural areas tend to suffer from a greater lack of access to basic services (e.g. schools, safe drinking water, electricity, medical services, transport and communication networks—see Albornoz 1993; Ansell 2005; Punch 2004). Likewise young people's health and livelihoods are affected by higher rural rates of mortality and malnutrition (Potter et al. 2004; Wilkinson 2000).

Despite the predominantly urban focus there have been some significant rural studies of children's work in the Majority world. It has long been recognized that rural children are economically valuable to their parents for their work on peasant farms (Tienda 1979), both for their unpaid labour (Onyango 1988), and for security in old age (Nugent 1985), thereby reinforcing interdependent household relations. In these situations children are not subject to the same risk of exploitation as those working in labour-intensive industries or in an urban environment (Bequele and Myers 1995; Bonnet 1993), but children are not automatically protected when working with kin. Exploitation may be more concealed and difficult to accept in family enterprises but that does not render it non-existent (Boyden 1988).

In rural areas of the Majority world, young people are crucial in both productive and reproductive household tasks, and may contribute to their household maintenance in both paid and unpaid ways. However, frequently children's tasks are not recognized as work and thus can be compared to the invisibility and undervaluation of women's work (Nieuwenhuys 1994; Schildkrout 1981). It can also be disguised as 'training' or 'helping' (Goddard and White 1982; Punch 2001a). Partly this may be because such labour is often controlled by women (Reynolds 1991) and is intended to help or replace women's tasks; releasing them for more productive labour. However, care must be taken not to assume that all young people's work is within the stereotypical female sphere of domestic work and childcare. In addition, gender, age, and birth order can affect the division of labour (Punch 2001a; Robson 1996).

Since the 1990s an increasing number of studies have examined the nature of children's work in rural areas from children's own perspectives (Johnson et al. 1995; Katz 1991, 2004; Nieuwenhuys 1994; Reynolds 1991; Robson 1996), but only in the last decade has research begun to note a greater range of issues concerning rural childhoods and youth.[4] It is recognized that a more holistic view of rural childhoods and youth is necessary (Admassie 2003; Holloway and Valentine 2000d). Interconnections between various contexts should be considered since rural young people negotiate their everyday lives with a range of different people in different settings. For example, Katz (2004) shows that in rural Sudan the dividing line between work, play, and education becomes blurred, which enhances young people's local environmental knowledge. Thus, a more integrated approach, which encompasses multiple and overlapping arenas (such as work, play, school, and home), can lead to a more rounded and appropriate understanding of rural childhoods and youth (Punch 2003).

A further recurring issue in the Majority world involves the high levels of social change in the face of globalisation processes which impact to varying degrees on young rural lives (Kaufman and Rizzini 2002; Penn 2005). The global economy and global cultures are increasingly shaping rural childhoods and youth. Many rural communities in the Majority world are losing or adapting some of their traditional lifestyles and are incorporating more 'modern' behaviours (e.g. Taracena 2003). Whilst for young people this may open up new educational opportunities, it also leads to the formation of new identities which can be contradictory and difficult to negotiate (Hollos 2002).

In particular, changes in the role of education in rural areas of the Majority world have seen more young people participating for longer in schooling (Jeffrey and McDowell 2004). Education tends to be 'associated with the wider world, social mobility, urbanity and modernity' (Meinert 2003: 180). However, several studies have found that gaining a formal education does not necessarily lead to better employment opportunities and may just create unrealistic expectations (Ansell 2004; Jeffrey et al. 2004; Levinson and Holland 1996; Punch 2004). Others have argued that in rural subsistence economies child labour is common and often necessary for family survival, so that policies should be aimed at facilitating work and education, rather than attempting to eliminate child labour by introducing compulsory education (Admassie 2003).

Global economic restructuring has also impacted upon the lives of many young people living in rural areas of the Majority world (e.g. Chawla 2002; Katz 2004). For many, socio-economic transformations have resulted in increased levels of migration from rural to urban areas and across borders, such as from Mexico to the United States (Taracena 2003), Bolivia to Argentina (Punch 2002b), or Ecuador to the United States (Pribilsky 2001). Sometimes children themselves are involved in migration (Young and Ansell 2003), or use migration as a rite of passage to adulthood (Punch 2002b). Other times children are left behind in rural communities whilst their parents migrate, and the outcomes of migration can lead to increased inequalities and tensions between migrant and non-migrant households (Pribilsky 2001). Thus, processes of migration can affect rural young people's identities, their social relationships, and possible pathways to adulthood (Punch 2007).

In sum, research has highlighted many constraints surrounding children and young people's present and future lives in rural areas of the Majority world, including the relative physical isolation of some communities, limited education and employment opportunities, poor roads and transport services, lack of sanitation and medical services, and limited access to electricity and safe drinking water. Nevertheless, most rural young people actively participate in their household's livelihoods and find ways of coping with their precarious rural environment. One of the aims of this book is to compare and contrast the opportunities and constraints young people face in Majority world contexts with their counterparts in the Minority world.

Dis-/Re-covering young people in rural Minority world contexts

As noted previously, geographers' recognition of young people in Minority world settings was rare until the late 1990s. By their absence, young people appeared marginal to the adult-dominated agendas of rural geography and society. Rare exceptions included analysis of youth–adult relations in the division of labour and decision making on family farms (see Wallace et al. 1994). But since Philo's (1992) critique of Minority world rural studies, as peopled—and written by—white, middle-class, middle-aged, able-bodied, heterosexual Mr Averages, many researchers have responded to Philo's (1992: 201) call for attention to rural areas as 'fractured along numerous lines of difference constituted of overlapping and "multiple forms of otherness"'. Among them some scholars have sought to conceptualize and empirically record the positions and experiences of young people. Cumulatively, this literature has emerged as a discovery of young people in Minority world rural societies—complete with the energy and fervour often associated with discoveries.

The socio-cultural and rural nature of young people's lives is a common analytic theme across this literature. Cultural contexts are seen to shape both understandings of rural environments and childhoods. O. Jones (1997) and Valentine (1997a) have juxtaposed idealized constructions of free, adventurous, healthy, and safe rural childhoods with various adult power relations and constraints that young people (seen as children growing up through their childhood) must negotiate. These encounters include expectations about where 'children' can roam and play, what they can do, and what people they may or may not relate to. Critiques of adult constructions of (and fears about) rural childhood also highlight the 'child' as a vulnerable subject requiring protection and a range of guidance or services (Halliday 1997; Valentine 1997a; Valentine and Holloway 2001).

The sense of young people also requiring services and guidance is noted by McGrath (2001) and Shucksmith (2004) in UK and European settings. But the more common finding regarding these age groups is that adults can produce an environment of surveillance, marginalisation, and exclusions. Daily life in rural settings can be one of living in the 'village fish bowl' (Leyshorn 2002) where behaviour of young people and youth sub-culture are seen as problematic and unwanted. In such cases, constructions of 'youth' as a stage of the life course, and sub-culture, are also associated with adults' critical constructions of high spirits, risk-taking, idleness, mis-spent leisure, and even fear and prejudice regarding safety and crime (Kraack and Kenway 2002; Little et al. 2005; Matthews, Taylor et al. 2000a; Sibley 1997). Researchers have employed notions of social exclusion to explain the way young people are positioned socially and physically in rural spaces that create feelings of powerlessness and disenfranchisement (Davis and Ridge 1997; Matthews, Taylor et al. 2000). For instance, Kraack and Kenway's (2002: 151) Australian work notes 'large congregations of young people using public space are often seen as disruptive and threatening...[and] certain youth are understood as a form of "social pollution" (Urry 1995, p. 188) characterized by undesirable bodies and behaviour'. Similarly, in southern New Zealand some young people report experiences of exclusion from public spaces such as shopping areas, public monuments, and libraries (Panelli et al. 2002).

Minority world discourses of childhood and youth surround young people and combine with household, family, and institutional structures that affect the material and social shape of their lives. However, the growth in Minority world research has also been important for highlighting the capacity and agency of young people in the way they organize and complete their day-to-day activities. In productive and reproductive spheres (Robson 1996; 2004a), young people have been recorded as active participants on family farms, completing labour both that explicitly contributes to commodity production (McCormack 2002) and that which maintains and reproduces the culture of family farming (Leckie 1996). Alongside work activities, young people in Minority worlds have also been recorded as playful and creative in their pursuit of leisure and recreation. O. Jones (2000) and McCormack (2002) have noted British and New Zealand young people's ability to navigate polymorphic spaces, playing with temporary farm materials (e.g. hay bales and produce sacks) or using multi-function sites and equipment for pleasurable activities. And with older young people, Kraack and Kenway (2002) and Panelli et al. (2002) have recorded a range of pleasurable pursuits undertaken regularly, even in the face of adult disapproval and censure (e.g. surfing, swimming in rivers, skateboarding, parties, and minor pranks). These interactions indicate some of the negotiated power relations young people enter (as discussed below).

Minority world literature recovering the experiences of young rural lives focuses on settings dominated by agricultural, service, and consumption (including tourism-based) economies. Young people are noted as navigating wider economic and technological change (Laegran 2002; McGrath 2001; Smith et al. 2002; Valentine and Holloway 2001) as well as uneven cultural and power relations that differentiate young people's experiences. Besides the effect of notions of childhood and youth, noted above, these experiences are also recognized as reflective of axes of difference such as class, gender, and ethnicity (Haug 2002; O. Jones 2002; Kraack and Kenway 2002; Leckie 1996; Shucksmith 2004; Skelton 2000). The significance of unequal conditions and uneven power relations is implicit in many of these works and provides one component of the more integrating dialogue we propose in this book.

BEYOND SEPARATE WORLDS: INTEGRATING PERSPECTIVES ON RURAL CHILDHOOD AND YOUTH

The expanding literatures on young rural lives in both Majority and Minority worlds are exciting in their own right; however, this book aims to provide a cross-world dialogue. While not denying the differences and inequalities between Majority and Minority worlds, it is timely to invigorate our studies by thinking beyond separate worlds. In this respect we complement recent studies that have engaged in similar comparisons (Jeffrey and McDowell 2004; Katz 2004; Mayo 2001). While these other efforts primarily focus on urban situations, our book highlights both separate and common conditions for rural young people. In particular we acknowledge that connections, common interests, and structural similarities can be identified between Minority world and Majority world contexts, despite the cultural, political, and socio-economic differences of these two world areas.

It is our contention that many of the social relations and physical settings that rural young people negotiate in Majority and Minority worlds have more in common than frequently acknowledged. An early step towards a more multi-faceted perspective was provided when Panelli (2002) argued that there were key, recognisable dimensions and processes that shape all young people's lives everywhere. The case was made for synthesizing the contexts and negotiations that characterize young people's experiences (see also Punch 2000, 2003). Acknowledging that young people are neither passive, nor without competency, means that an increasing number of researchers are committed to recording their agency and, where possible,

conducting studies *with* young people, rather than *on* them (R
Johnson et al. 1998).

The specific case study chapters collected here provide a di·
tional collection. While some advancement is achieved by collating Majoɪ
ity and Minority world accounts, a more integrated consideration of young
rural lives can be achieved with increased focus on possibly generic concepts. Consequently this volume draws case studies and more theoretical
reflections together around three core themes which we believe can frame
and enhance future cross-world dialogue on young people's lives.

Theme 1: Contexts and identities

First we suggest that *contexts and identities* are a key entry-point in conceptualising the lives of rural children and young people. Consideration of
the contexts shaping young people's lives highlights the differences between
Majority and Minority worlds both in terms of material and socio-cultural conditions. For instance, Adamu must walk everyday with his father
to work on the land, whereas 'Butthead's' family have a number of farm
motor bikes and tractors that aid work efficiency and provide time and
opportunities for 'wheelstands' and fun being towed along on a sack. But
beyond immediate and particular material or other cultural differences, it
is possible to argue that the rural contexts in both Nigeria and New Zealand could be approached in a conceptual way that recognizes the dynamics of any specific rural setting and the way in which a young person is seen
or positioned within it. Table 1.1 summarizes some of the contextual lenses
that could be considered in this way. For simplicity different items have
been identified as separate contextual dimensions, however, it should be
noted that the interconnection between contexts is a complex and unique
dynamic in individual cases.

Part I of this volume engages with many of these issues and it is possible
that new research could fruitfully analyse how young people navigate a
range of simultaneously constraining and opportunistic contexts and identities. These types of complexities may be charted across both social terrain
and specific types of space. For contexts and identities are embedded in
contrasting spaces and epitomized and contested at key sites: for example,
the beach (Kraack and Kenway 2002); football pitch (Punch 2000); school
(Valentine and Holloway 2001); periodic markets (Robson 1996, 2004a);
and national borders (Dunkley 2004). In this fashion Chapters 2 and 4 consider the shifting contexts and multiple spaces that frame young migrants'
lives in both Africa and Central America. In contrast, Chapter 3 discusses
young people who are more settled in rural Norwegian contexts and shown
to establish specific gendered and techno-material identities around car-
based lifestyles. Then in Chapter 5, we are reminded that contexts and
cultures (and the identities available to young people) are also temporal
as a comparative historical case is made of young farming 'daughters' in

Table 1.1 Identities and contexts

Contextual dimensions	Examples of related identities	Analytic questions illustrating the dynamics of context and/or identity
Physical environment		
Distance from urban centres	Isolated child/young person	How do the physical
Access to water	Water carrier	environments and spatial
Access to land	Landless child/young person	contexts affect young
Quality of physical resources	Settled, itinerant, homeless,	people's day-to-day lives
Type of housing	refugee, displaced child/ young person	and/or institutional status?
Economy		
Food production	Farm worker, starving child	How does a young person's
Local land-uses	Unemployed youth	labour contribute to, or
Employment types	Domestic helper	sustain the household or
Levels of income	Unpaid worker, beggar, child prostitute	family or local economy?
Other economic exchange	Hawker, messenger, labourer	How are young people
External economic factors	Apprentice, dependent, beneficiary, street child	positioned and institutionalized as outsider (or marginal to) the formal economy and its key sites of production and consumption?
Socio-cultural setting		
Ethnicity and cultural identity	…various	How do cultural and social relations shape young
Values and religious beliefs	Observer, initiate	people's individual and
Adult–child relations	Child, minor	collective lives and
Gender relations	Girl, boy, young fe/male	identities?
Peer interaction and sub-culture	Friend and/or mate, gang member	What discourses and spaces
Systems of knowledge creation and transfer	Student, trainee, apprentice, dropout	constrain or enable young people in creating their own place-specific sub-cultures and lifestyles?
Political landscape		
Household and family structure	Child, foster child, orphan	How do expectations regarding authority and
Extended family network	Relative, grandchild, kin	respect affect young people's
Local community/village hierarchy	Community member Helper, messenger	opportunities to shape their own lives?
Wider institutional relations and systems (e.g. law, education, health, nation state: citizenship and political processes)	Minor, subordinate, youth, student, client, citizen, participant, child soldier	How do young people navigate institutional environments and discourses that usual place them in uneven and frequently inferior positions?

Australia, New Zealand, and the United States. Beyond the specificity of these cases, Chapter 6 reflects upon the generic challenges of conceptualising contexts and identities. But it also suggests that a stimulating advance will occur as future research explores the ways in which contexts and identities are mutually entwined in shifting patterns of opportunity or constraint for young people.

Theme 2: Agency and everyday actions

The second conceptual frame that might support a more integrated dialogue for studies of young rural lives involves a deeper recognition of young people's *agency and everyday actions*. Children like Adamu (and to a lesser extent also Butthead) do useful work for their family farms contributing to their household economy. The possibility, of thinking, knowledge-constructing actors highlights young people's capacity to participate and make meanings, lives and futures. Part II of this volume illustrates these possibilities in some detail by considering the limited agency of domestic child workers in Tanzania in Chapter 7 to remind us that even severely exploited and disempowered young people exercise some agency. Chapter 8 examines the way limited access to transport curtails the 'doing' of teenagers in rural Britain; while the young people in Indonesia portrayed in Chapter 9 respond in several active ways to secure livelihoods in the absence of out-migrated parents. Similarly Chapter 10 shows how secondary school students in the former East Germany take control of determining their future careers. Chapter 11 examines the notions of agency and action in more depth, considering the implications of a range of theoretical approaches adopted by scholars working within different traditions.

Theme 3: Power relations and processes

The third conceptual frame that may support further synthesis or cross-world dialogue about young rural lives involves concepts of power and the relations and processes by which young people negotiate the politics of the rural societies in which they live. To date many researchers have pointed to the intergenerational and institutional power relations that contextualize young people's lives—noting the importance of parents and other adults and adult-systems in determining the behaviours, requirements, and rules expected of young people (e.g. in families, schools and public spaces). Adult family members clearly shape the material realities of young rural lives in terms of household interaction, work expectations, spatial range, and activities (Katz 1991, 1993; Punch 2000; Valentine 1997a). These and other influential adults also have a powerful influence over their access to, and production of knowledge (Haug 2002; McCormack 2002).

The analytic perspectives on power that are adopted by researchers may vary as greatly as those addressing agency and it is true that few scholars have exclusively focussed on notions of power in rural youth studies. Instead, they have preferred to consider the products and outcomes of power relations (e.g. young people's opportunities to access rural space, or young people's experiences of uneven power relations or exclusion; see Matthews, Taylor et al. 2000; Valentine 1997a). While we recognize the significance of work that considers the products or outcomes of power relations shaping young people's lives, it is also worthwhile to more directly and explicitly consider power relations and 'entanglements' of power and resistance that texture their social worlds (Sharp et al. 2000). Approaching power as a composite dynamic enables young people to be seen simultaneously as both subjected to and articulating power. This includes the daily ways young people navigate their responsibilities and interest in play and social connection (Robson 2004a; Punch 2000) as well as more intermittent expressions of insistence or resistance that enable young people to socialize and claim space for themselves at irregular intervals (Kraack and Kenway 2002; Panelli et al. 2002). Finally, it is also important to recognize a more nuanced understanding of power relations operating between young people themselves, including unequal power relations in institutional settings (e.g. Valentine 2000).

The third part of this volume begins to unpack some of these issues in more detail. Chapters 12 and 14 explore the ways in which young people accept, negotiate and resist both inter- and intra-generational power relations in a variety of rural settings in Bolivia and Uganda respectively. Similarly, in Vermont in the United States, young people experience spatial and generational exercises of power and Chapter 13 considers how their clique identities are played out amongst their peers. Chapter 15 argues that the powerful adult discourse of the country childhood idyll can allow some children in Britain the space and freedom to express themselves as 'other', thereby building their own worlds. These chapters use contrasting approaches to power which are discussed in Chapter 16 and include material, discursive, relational, and spatial aspects of power.

To close, our last chapter reviews the contents and also looks beyond the major themes of Majority–Minority world binaries and the analytical concepts of identity, agency, and power cutting across the everyday lives of young rural dwellers. We finish by highlighting the possibilities opened up by taking a global perspective on studies of rural children and young people. Thus, Chapter 17 concludes with some recommendations for future directions by which readers might continue dialogue and extend their explorations connecting with wider contemporary debates in geography, sociology, rural, youth, and childhood studies to further enhance the dynamic research agendas on young rural lives.

NOTES

1. The terms *Majority* and *Minority* worlds are used in this book, in support of Punch's (2000, 2003) argument that we need to shift the balance of our world views that frequently privilege 'western' and 'northern' populations and issues. Throughout this book we adopt the terms *Majority* world (for the 'Third World') and *Minority* world (for the 'First World') to acknowledge the 'majority' of population, poverty, land mass, and lifestyles in the former (see also Penn 1999).
2. For the purposes of this work, although we mostly consider young people under the age of 18, we do not strictly adopt what is a widely used legal age-based definition because this is problematic to apply universally. However, we recognize that many issues specific to young adults over 18 are extremely diverse and beyond the scope of this book.
3. This may be partly due to 'tarmac bias' (Chambers 1990) where researchers only venture as far as is easily accessible by road, so are less likely to head into remote rural areas.
4. Including young carers (Robson 2004b), child refugees (Jabry 2002), Africa's orphan crisis (Guest 2001; Urassa et al. 1997), child migration (Young and Ansell 2003; Pribilsky 2001), youth transitions (Ansell 2004; Punch 2002b), young people and war (Boyden and de Berry 2004), and education (Jeffrey et al. 2004; Punch 2004).

Part I

Contexts and identities

2 Doing and belonging
Toward a more-than-representational account of young migrant identities in Lesotho and Malawi

Nicola Ansell and Lorraine van Blerk

The notion that identities are contextually constructed, and that the dynamism of identity in part reflects movement between places, is now commonplace in geography. Southern African societies have long been characterized by high levels of mobility, but in the context of the HIV/AIDS pandemic migration patterns are changing and young people in particular increasingly engage in forms of voluntary and involuntary migration. This chapter draws on stories told by young migrants in Lesotho and Malawi about their migration experiences. From the young people's accounts we uncover how their migration impacted on their relationships to rural contexts. In doing so, we find the conventional notion of 'narrative identity' to be an inadequate expression of how young people come to 'belong' in rural settings. Instead, we focus on three components of belonging: (in)activity, relationality, and familiarity.

THE CONTEXTS: MIGRANCY AND RURALITY IN SOUTHERN AFRICA

Contexts surrounding the lives of young people in southern Africa are characterized by remarkably high levels of migrancy and complex experiences of rurality. Historically, most of Lesotho's adult men worked as miners in South Africa. Although many miners have been retrenched, both temporary and permanent migration to South Africa continues (Sechaba Consultants 2002). Recently, many women, some with young children, have migrated to Lesotho's urban-based garment industry (Kingdom of Lesotho 2003). Malawi, too, sent miners to South Africa, but this declined following independence in 1964, and ended in 1989 when South Africa banned Malawian mineworkers due to fear of AIDS (Englund 1999). Internal migration, however, continued, populating tea, coffee, and tobacco plantations and the expanding cities of Blantyre and Lilongwe (Englund 2002b). Thus, contrary to the popular view that African societies have only recently been disrupted by globalisation, 'loss of place' is a long-standing identity-shaping experience for people in southern Africa (Usher 2002: 44).

Prevalent migrancy has long impacted on young people: traditional childcare patterns (for instance, fostering by grandparents) have entailed migration over considerable distances between extended family households. With the alarming spread of HIV/AIDS across southern Africa, young people's migration is increasing (Ansell and van Blerk 2004; Young and Ansell 2003). When parents die, orphans are distributed among often spatially dispersed relatives. Even before parental death, AIDS has economic and other impacts that may require movement of entire households, or reduction in household size achieved by sending some members elsewhere. Moreover, young people can be valuable workers in AIDS-affected societies where many individuals are unable to work through sickness, and may also need care. Thus young people migrate to undertake paid, domestic or caring work (Ansell and van Blerk 2004; Robson 2000).

A further characteristic of southern African rural contexts is their interweaving with the urban. Migrancy binds urban and rural more closely through ongoing movements of people and links of experience or expectation. The terms *urban* and *rural* in themselves seldom arouse a strong sense of belonging among Africans (Silvey and Lawson 1999), although most urban dwellers in Malawi and Lesotho identify strongly with the village of their birth or marriage. Migration, even from rural to urban areas, is seldom considered permanent. Hence, Englund (2002a; 2002b) argues, Malawian migration is a simultaneously urban and rural experience, a migrant's urban life being intricately related to their aspirations to improve their village life. Rural southern African youth thus inhabit contexts where place connection is fractured but, as we will show, emotional, cultural, and imaginative ties to place continue, and contribute to identity production.

IDENTITY, PLACE, AND SPACE

Recent research with young people has focused heavily on identity. This in part reflects traditional assumptions that identity construction is young people's key developmental task (Bagnoli 2003). Its prominence in the 1990s also reflects two epistemological trends: first the 'new' social studies of childhood, which have conceptualized children as social actors, engaged in making their own lives (James et al. 1998); and second, the arguments of Beck (1994) and Giddens (1991) that in Western 'risk society' individuals increasingly write their own biographies, drawing on a selection of available scripts, rather than following socio-culturally predetermined pathways.

Geographers studying identity have focused on categories of gender, sexuality, class, 'race', ethnicity, (dis)ability, and age (Vanderbeck and Dunkley 2003). Young people's identities are, however, multiple—they draw on a number of categories to define themselves, and these categories intersect (rather than add together) in complex ways (Skelton and Valentine 2003), and are further destabilised by time, space, and dimensionality (Somers

1994). Of particular interest to geographers is the situatedness of identity construction (Pile and Thrift 1995a; Pratt 2000). Young people are seen to employ experiences and images of place in constructing identities through both similarity and difference (Desforges 1998; Hall et al. 1999; Hengst 1997; Holloway and Valentine 2000c).

Relationships between identity and place are not isomorphic. Spatiality is important, and identity construction has been a key theme of migration research (McHugh 2000; Silvey and Lawson 1999). Individuals may construct identities disconnected from their places of origin (Giddens 1991), and migration also increasingly disrupts notions of bounded communities sharing symbolic meanings (Silvey and Lawson 1999). Rather, as Liechty (1995: 167) suggests: 'identity formations are always "in the making" as subjects move through time and space'. While migration research has largely neglected young people (McKendrick 2001), Vanderbeck and Dunkley (2003: 241) have examined 'the significance of narratives of rural-urban difference for young people's identities', and van Blerk and Ansell (2006) discuss the roles played by young people's images of migration. The research presented below further explores the significance of migration and rurality in young people's identity construction.

FROM NARRATIVE TO EMBODIED AND NON-REPRESENTATIONAL NOTIONS OF IDENTITY

One way of understanding identity is as a form of narrative construction. Somers (1994: 606) explains that 'all of us come to *be* who we *are* (however ephemeral, multiple and changing) by being located or locating ourselves (usually unconsciously) in social narratives *rarely of our own making*'. This conceptual framework has been adopted by geographers in relation to migration (Gutting 1996). It has also been used to make sense of how young people draw on a combination of public discourses and lived experience in interpreting their own lives and constructing ideas about place (McCormack 2002; Valentine 2000; Vanderbeck and Dunkley 2003).

Geographical research on young people and identity has largely focused on Minority world settings, yet Western narratives of childhood and youth have been exported to the Majority world (Boyden 1990), where they impinge on identity construction. In Kathmandu, for instance, many urban young people see themselves through a globalising western narrative of 'teenage' identity (Liechty 1995), while affluent young people in Bangalore self-consciously assert a 'global' identity through consumption practices (Saldanha 2002). The latter study echoes Giddens's (1991) notion of life as an increasingly individualized 'biographical project', wherein young people construct their own identities (Hall et al. 1999; Jones and Wallace 1992).

Giddens (1991) applies his ideas to a globalising world in which social relations are becoming disembedded from local contexts, and restructured across space. Scholars of migration have explored the notion that identities are no longer stable products of bounded places: 'Migrant identities are…constructed through the process of mobility itself in ways that incorporate and blend experiences of multiple places simultaneously' (Silvey and Lawson 1999: 125).

The idea that young people self-consciously construct identities for themselves, choosing elements from contrasting public narratives as they move from place to place is, however, contentious. For many, the choices are clearly limited, and the illusion of choice can itself be problematic (Liechty 1995). The limits to reflexivity (Rose 1997) must also be recognized. The idea that 'a process of representation is central to identity formation' (Ackroyd and Pilkington 1999: 447) and that '"experience" is constituted through narratives' (Somers 1994: 614) seemingly acquired the status of axiomatic truth in the 1990s. However, the constructivist view of identity has been critiqued by those who consider identity to be more fixed and less easily adaptable to changing conditions (Bendle 2002). Perhaps more significantly, the primary place of discourse has been questioned by research that recognizes the importance of embodiment. For Angela Martin (1997: 108), 'the practice of identity [is] a process in which subjectivity and identity of place are mutually constituted via bodily practice in culturally defined spaces'. Narrative identity is also challenged by research that attends to the senses and emotions. This can be particularly significant in relation to the young, since: 'In childhood, sensations are particularly acute, but they are often unarticulated' (Sibley 1995a: 136).

There is, therefore, a need for an alternative epistemological position from which to examine young people's identities that takes seriously embodied and non-reflexive aspects of being. A potential, though somewhat problematic, tool is non-representational (or 'more-than-representational' [Lorimer 2005]) theory. This is concerned with 'how life takes shape and gains expression in shared experiences, everyday routines, fleeting encounters, embodied movements' (Lorimer 2005: 84), or alternatively 'the empiricism of life in its *doing*' (Dewsbury 2000: 473). Non-representational theory has underpinned research focusing on the unremarkable (e.g. gardening). Rather than examining how young people incorporate discourses of place into their personal identity narratives, non-representational theory would be concerned with 'how belonging *happens*' (Lorimer 2005: 86), through everyday and embodied activity. The emphasis is on the non-reflexive, non-cognitive present, although recognising the significance of repetition and the sedimentation of experiences. While little examined in relation to children's geographies (Horton and Kraftl 2005), it is a body of theory that might have particular application to making sense of the experiences of the young. Thrift (2003: 2020), for instance, draws attention to 'the way that our bodies are fired up by body disciplines often learnt in childhood and which push us in particular ways even before cognition has had its say'. In the discussion that follows, we apply aspects of non-representational theory to an examination of the contexts and identities of selected young people in Lesotho and Malawi.

RESEARCH OUTLINE AND SETTINGS

The research reported here was undertaken in urban and rural Lesotho and Malawi with young people who had engaged in HIV/AIDS-related migration. The chapter draws on storyboards produced by young people who had moved home or (in a few cases) had had other young people move to their homes associated with the sickness or death of a family member. Participants were given paper and drawing materials and invited to draw a sequence of six pictures illustrating their migration stories. They were then interviewed individually, with the help of an interpreter, to elicit accounts of their experiences and feelings. The narratives discussed in this paper are from young people who had experience of rural life, having moved between rural areas or between urban and rural areas.

The purpose of the research was to explore young people's experiences of migration. We did not set out to investigate questions of identity, or to explore the relevance of non-representational theory. We did not elicit reflexive accounts of 'who I am', but have subsequently interrogated lengthy transcripts for insight into young people's identities, and their association with migration and rurality. That we have subjected these narrative accounts to a (partly) 'non-representational' reading may appear incongruous. However, it reflects a realisation that to read the young migrants' accounts simply as narratives shaped by wider discourses would require us to leave aside much of what they were telling us about 'belonging'. As Lorimer (2005: 86) points out, 'there is no 'one-size-fits-all' policy for accessing embodied knowledge and emotional response'. Instead these stories point to active and relational experiences of belonging that link specific contexts and identities.

The rural settings of the research were Ha Tlali, Lesotho, and Mpando, Malawi (Figure 2.1). Ha Tlali is a village in the foothills of Lesotho's Maluti Mountains, about two hours drive from the capital city, Maseru. Here people undertake subsistence cultivation and livestock rearing, supported by the remittances of household members employed elsewhere, usually in town or in South Africa. Mpando is located in the tea-growing Thyolo District in southern Malawi, about two hours drive from Malawi's largest city, Blantyre. While households generally have fields to cultivate, many depend also on employment on commercial tea estates, and have been drawn to the area by the prospect of such employment. The urban settings of the research were the eastern edge of central Maseru, and Ndirande, a low-income neighbourhood of Blantyre. The young people were predominantly aged 12 to 15. Most were attending primary school (some in Lesotho were

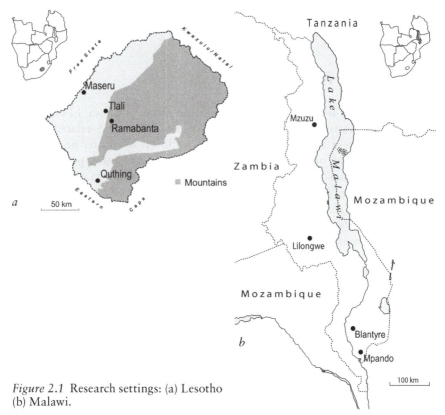

Figure 2.1 Research settings: (a) Lesotho (b) Malawi.

in the first class of secondary school), but storyboards were also drawn by young people who were not attending school, including street children.

YOUNG MIGRANTS' VIEWS ON LIFE AND BELONGING IN RURAL AREAS

Many young people participating in the research had experienced migration between urban and rural environments. To gauge the significance of rurality to their lives, we begin by examining the direct comparisons that a minority of young migrants drew between the urban and rural places in which they had lived. Bontle[1] (Tlali boy) for instance, complained that he had more fun when he lived in Johannesburg: there was more to do, like going to the stadium to watch football, learning to ride a bike, and learning different subjects in school. Likewise, Limakatso (Tlali girl) resented returning to the village from Maseru, because they spoke Sesotho rather than English in school and she had to get up at 5 am to get to school on time. On the other hand, Victor (Blantyre boy) preferred rural life, as there was less need for money.

To some extent the young migrants are drawing on public discourses in interpreting their experiences. Limakatso's attitude to the language spoken in school may well reflect a discourse that represents English as a more valued language. Even the sense that there was 'more to do' in Johannesburg may relate more to discursive constructions of urban life than to any objective 'reality', and Victor's economism probably reflects his parents' articulated concerns. However, these are not simply accounts of rural life as interpreted by reference to public narratives; for example, the objection to rising at 5 am points to embodied experience. 'Rural' thus has both representational and extra-representational meanings for these young people.

Reflexivity, identity, and belonging

The young migrants were not wholly unreflective about their identity positions. Some commented on the positions in which they believed they were placed by others. Several remarked on their identities as newcomers, and the impact this had upon how they were treated. Jimms (Mpando boy) explained: 'As I was the new boy, I had to suffer a lot'. Likewise Theke (Mpando girl) revealed: 'It was difficult to make friends as I was a visitor'. In contrast, Maleshoane (Maseru girl) was happy with her new home as she was treated as a 'member of the family'. These young people thus interpreted their experiences by reference to wider discourses of 'newcomer', 'visitor' or 'family member'.

Some young people also reflected on the emotional impacts of migration. Whereas Agnes (Mpando girl) declared, 'I was happy doing these things', Tumelo (Tlali boy) complained: 'All this movement is making my life very unstable'. For some young people, their identities reflected their spatial mobility in more embodied ways: Agnes (Mpando girl) told us: 'My body got fat in Blantyre, but in Mpando I was thin'. While notions of reflexive identity help us to interpret some aspects of the young people's identities, however, much of what they had to say about belonging cannot be analysed in these terms.

Identity as belonging; belonging as performance

Reflective accounts of identity were rare in young people's narratives of their migration histories. Much more common were descriptions of how they 'got used to' new places. We include here a lightly edited version of one migration story, to illustrate the everyday embodied experience of coming to belong to new places that characterized many young people's accounts (see Figure 2.2).

Lebohang was a 14-year-old boy attending primary school in Ha Tlali. His story is reproduced, not because it is 'typical' or contains individual noteworthy elements, but because overall it demonstrates the process of 'getting used to' a new place. Although never explicit, the story suggests

1. This is my house in Ha Ramabanta. My father worked in the mines, but came home because he was sick. I moved from here to Ha Tlali because my father had passed away. Before then it was very pleasant. I used to play with my friends and sometimes we used to play in the [country]. I attended school there also. School was good. We were allowed to play and given time to do our work. It was fun living there. [...]

2. This is a truck going to Maseru. We went there because we were building a house in Ha Tlali. [...] My mother decided we wanted to live in Ha Tlali, but I don't know why. My sister was in Maseru working. Mum said she didn't see how we could survive in Ramabanta without my father. My mother worked in Johannesburg while Dad was alive, but now there was no one to look after me, so Mum left Johannesburg and we came to Ha Tlali so she could look after me. Dad died in 1998, so it is still painful to think of this now. [...] We only stayed two months in a rented place [in Maseru]. Living there was okay as my sister was working, so we weren't needy. My mother moved to town with me, but she went to her home village and left me there with my sister, so I had to fetch water from the well and cook for my sister so she had food when she came back from work. It was hard to be without both my parents at this time, and I missed my mother when I was there. Living with my sister was fun, as we used to talk and as my sister worked we had food and clothes always.

3. Offloading the luggage in town with my mother before she left.

4. The rented house in town where I lived with my sister. Making friends in town was easy as there were a lot of children and we made friends very quickly. The friends I made, however, weren't so good as we only played football, and in Ramabanta it was more fun – we played football and with clay building things, and hide and seek, but that wasn't often. Comparing my friends in all these places, the ones in Ramabanta were the best, but when I compare town and Tlali, Tlali is better than town. Moving from town was difficult as I wasn't used to this place and I had to get used to another new place. Leaving my sister was difficult and painful as I had got used to being with her, but now I was happy as I was going to live with my mother, but I still missed my sister.

5. [This is us moving to Ha Tlali ...] Adjusting to the new place was difficult as I always thought about the old place [Ramabanta]. There wasn't any difference in the places, but when I was at school here, playing football reminded me of the place and my friends there, and that made it difficult to adjust. When I'm here now I have to fetch water, cook and work in the garden, but in Ramabanta, my sister did all these chores. Now it's just me and my mother, and she doesn't work. Sometimes she gets small jobs to do like washing clothes, but mostly my sister pays as she works in town. At first it was difficult but now I'm used to this place and we still manage to get food to eat.

6. This is the school in Tlali. This was my final destination, coming to school in Tlali. It's fun here, but not as fun as Ramabanta. I still miss that place and my friends there. We don't have football matches here and when we do play football it's not a real ball, it's only rags, and when we go for celebration in March, now we only go to Roma, but in Ramabanta we went to lots of schools.

Figure 2.2 Lebohang's migration story.

much about Lebohang's sense of belonging—about where he feels at home. Rather than drawing on 'public narratives', the account is descriptive of day-to-day activities. It focuses on incidental, banal, and everyday elements of the process of accommodating to a new place. It reveals the importance of activities (both work and play); changing emotions; relationships with family and friends; the significance of material well-being (access to adequate food); and perhaps above all the ambivalence of his feelings. 'Places' in the sense of physical environments do not figure highly in his conscious account, but the people who occupy the different spaces of his life are of great importance. Contexts are not only locational but highly textured by social relations and emotions. Instead of narrating a biography in which he is the key actor, taking charge of his life and shaping it to build an identity, he describes what has happened to him, how it made him feel, and how he gradually came to belong. We have identified three components to Lebohang's story and those of the other young migrants: (in)activity, familiarity, and relationality.

'Doing' rural lives: The role of (in)activity

Most young migrants, like Lebohang, eagerly described their daily activities, particularly as these changed when they moved. Those moving from urban to rural areas, in particular, learned new tasks; those who moved away sometimes missed those tasks. Changing work activities reflected differences in household composition as well place-related factors. For many young people, performance of day-to-day activities amounted to a daily performance of identity, and contributed to a growing sense of belonging.

Several Tlali boys depicted themselves herding. Becoming accustomed to herding was the key to belonging in the village, and some talked about their initial difficult experiences. Thabo (Tlali boy) told of the first time he went herding, having moved to the village: 'This is my uncle beating me because I had been looking after the cattle and sheep and they had eaten the crops belonging to someone else.... This was the first time I had been herding so I didn't know that was wrong, but now I know how to do it'. Most claimed they had come to like herding.

Other tasks, too, needed getting used to. Junior (Mpando boy) explained: 'I had to water in the garden. At first it was difficult, but now I am used to it'. Young people generally gave positive accounts of their work. Matlo (Tlali girl) revealed 'my job was to collect water from the well. I also used to collect wood. I liked doing both jobs'. Amosi (Blantyre boy) said that when living in the village 'I was happy because I was learning to work. It wasn't hard work'. But even hard work was acceptable if there was a good reason for it. Limakatso (Tlali girl) explained: 'I did everything—fetched water, wood, cooked, washed up, everything. But I wasn't working too hard because grandma was sick'. On the other hand, for urban young people, the prospect of having to become accustomed to rural life was unappealing. Mamateleka (Maseru girl) was not looking forward to moving to the village because 'There will be a lot of work'.

It is not only work activities that define young people's lives differently in different places. Play, too, is a significant marker of place identity as Lebohang's story of football, clay building, and hide and seek illustrates. Young migrants also reflected on other banal and everyday activities. Agnes

(Mpando girl) told us: 'I used to drink tea when going to school in town'. Others talked about doing nothing. Here, rural landscape features held emotional significance. Maleshoane (Maseru girl) told us how, when living in a village, she would sit under a tree when she was sad. Anicia (Maseru girl) also depicted herself sitting under a tree, enjoying the shade, when she lived in Quthing.

Familiarity and relationality

For most of the young migrants, familiarity of place was important. This was something that was either established through birth: 'this was my place of origin' (Junior Mpando boy); or acquired over time. For instance Anicia (Maseru girl) told how it was 'difficult to move as I was used to Quthing'. These accounts and Lebohang's story show that getting 'used to' a place was an embodied, repetitive process, requiring physical exertion, which generated a sense of belonging. As important as this individual process was, however, relationships with people were necessary for a young migrant to cement their identification with a place. In relation to everyday activities, relationships with people were often important, a number of young people reporting activities that they undertook collectively with people who mattered to them. Marko (Blantyre boy) described his picture: 'this is me sweeping every day outside. The men in our house do the sweeping'. Similarly, Chisomo (Mpando boy) explained: 'this is our field in Mpando. I work there. I like working there doing the digging. Everyone works in the field with me, the whole family'. Lebohang's story was replete with references to both family and friends, whenever he expressed an opinion about the places he had stayed. Similarly, Amosi (Blantyre boy) told us: 'In town it's beautiful—but I would prefer to live in the village with my brothers'. For Njakhotla (Tlali boy) the village had been very pleasant, but was no longer nice since his mother passed away. Doreen (Blantyre girl) explained that she now preferred to live in Blantyre as she had no relatives left in the village. Some young people chose to depict houses where they had not lived, as they held emotional significance as the homes of relatives who were no longer alive.

CONCLUSIONS

All of the young people's stories cited here describe specific relationships to rural places, but none expressed a strong sense of rural identity, and trying to reduce their identities to a single dimension of place is not helpful. Nonetheless, it was important to many that they *belonged* to (rural) places: where they lived, who they lived among, and what they did there were clearly important to them.

Belonging to place has received relatively little attention from those concerned with identity. Dodman (2004: 192) explains in relation to his research with young people in Jamaica: 'A sense of belonging is ephemeral, and difficult to measure directly, yet the feelings towards a particular place are indicative of the ways in which it is imagined and constructed.' This sense of belonging differs from the biographical identity upon which so much research has focused. Gill Jones (1999: 2–3) contrasts the young rural Scots who are 'involved in a personal project' (and thus inclined to migrate in order to perform particular identities) from those who 'derive immediate comfort and identity from their communities'. Belonging to a place is about what one does there (whether active or passive)—about the banal and familiar. Furthermore, 'feelings of belonging [can be understood] as both sited and mobile' (Lorimer 2005: 87): migration makes a difference, and belonging generally becomes established over time. In a similar way to that in which young ethnically Chinese people in Canada feel they become more Canadian over time (Tsang et al. 2003), Lebohang tells us: 'I had to get used to another place'.

Migration, then, is not simply a case of moving from place to place, or of uprooting contexts and identity. Rather, it involves becoming part of a place. It involves not just settling, but settling in, where place and identity interact in daily activities and social relations. Our young research participants had no desire to retain an identity as migrants—indeed, a migrant identity was quite negative,[2] particularly in Malawi (van Blerk and Ansell 2006). In contrast, through performing daily activities of work and play, migrants gradually come to belong. This is not, however, 'identity work' as Beck would envisage it. Getting used to work is an embodied experience, involving physical effort, but not necessarily directed or purposeful, neither a wholly positive or negative experience. As Lorimer (2005: 86) suggests: 'the experience of physical effort does not fall neatly into opposing registers of pleasure *or* pain'. The young migrants' accounts thus reveal performative and emotional aspects of identity—'what I do and how it makes me feel'.

Beyond 'doing', though, identity and belonging were associated with evolving relationships with people. Some young people were very clear about a collective identity—about becoming part of a household or community. In earlier research in Mpando, many young people were insistent that, rather than being migrants, 'we are the citizens of this village'. Bagnoli's (2003) relational model of identity construction, that sees young people construct identities in relation to others, rather than through differentiating themselves from others, is appropriate here. The young people were not self-consciously reporting on how they identified with or against groups of peers, but how they 'got used to' the people in their household or community—or how they failed to do so.

Non-representational theory, as a reaction against a focus on categorical identities, has proved useful in exploring young migrants' identities, offering a lens onto the more transient and non-discursive aspects of living (Lorimer 2005). We cannot, however, pretend to have taken onboard non-representational theory in the design of our research. Since our argument draws almost exclusively on narratives, provided in relation to a visual task and elicited in response to the questions of an interviewer, our material remains as text and we acknowledge the key role of representation. Language, in any situation, has limitations, and no written (or drawn) account is unmediated. We do, however, feel that the storyboard exercise uncovered aspects of young migrants' experiences and relationships to rural places that were very real and significant to them and that, while not unmediated, drew more on their repeated day-to-day embodied lives than on public narratives of migration or rurality. This would appear to provide evidence that non-representational approaches to research can be usefully drawn upon within a 'mixed' research framework, and permit a renewed focus on (in)activity, familiarity, and relationality as significant components of identity.

Acknowledgements

This research was funded by the UK Department for International Development but the views and opinions expressed are those of the authors alone. We gratefully acknowledge also the institutional support of the Institute of Southern African Studies, National University of Lesotho and the Department of Geography, Chancellor College, University of Malawi, and thank Motsilisi Motsieloa, Lloyd Chitera, and Lumbani Pete for their work as research assistants on the project.

NOTES

1. Pseudonyms are used to preserve anonymity.
2. This contrasts with the more positive identity of migrants in Bolivia reported by Punch (this volume).

3 Exploring masculinity, technology, and identity in rural Norway

Anne Sofie Laegran

Geographic research on youth has shown how public space is produced mainly as adult space (Skelton and Valentine 1998). But the street or similar 'third spaces' (Matthews, Limb, and Taylor 2000) provide spaces for youth to claim as their own, often in resistance to adults who see young people gathering in public places as problematic. In rural areas in Norway the petrol station is such a space, adopted by young men popularly known as the 'råners.'[1] The råners, known for 'hanging out' at the petrol station and driving up and down the main road, constitute a minority of young men in the countryside, yet the image of the group is significant in popular constructions of rural youth (Bjaarstad 2001). The råners are associated with rural areas that are understood as backward and boring, and as a dull rather than idyllic space for young people. As a group the råners often feel stigmatized and excluded in the local communities. However, by adopting the petrol station as a meeting place and cruising around the main roads, they work within their rural contexts to make space for their own identity.

This chapter introduces a village in mid-Norway and explores how technologies such as the car and the Internet, as well local spaces such as the petrol station and the Internet café are integrated or rejected in the rural and masculine identity work of the råners. The aim is to show how råners reproduce a particular masculine culture, whilst adapting to new times. The following sections outline a theoretical framework, describe the study context and methodology, and present and analyse the råner's encounters with familiar and new technologies and spaces.

MASCULINITIES, TECHNOLOGIES, IDENTITIES

Since the mid-1990s, there has been an increased focus on the lives of young people in rural areas, but few studies have looked specifically at constructions of masculinities (but see Bye 2003; Kraack and Kenway 2002; Skelton 2000). Campbell and Bell (2000) question whether it is possible to identify a rural masculinity and, to avoid essentialist conceptualisations of rurality as well as gender, they advocate a focus on how the rural and the masculine intersect on a symbolic level. They distinguish between 'the masculine in the rural' as an expression of how masculinity is constructed in rural spaces, and 'the rural in the masculine' as an expression of how rural themes are used in notions of masculinity, irrespective of being performed in a rural or urban setting. This distinction enables multiple understanding of masculinity where urban and rural elements may be included in various ways.

The young men in this study were between 17 and 23 years old at the time, and identified themselves as youth rather than adult or grown up. This is in accordance with social and cultural constructs of youth as a liminal stage in the life course rather than a fixed age category. It is a period between child- and adulthood signified by freedom and independence to explore activities and identities before settling down. Research on young people in rural areas in Norway identifies a distinction between those who want to 'reach out' and those who want to 'stay at home' (Fauske 1993; Fosso 1997; Jørgensen 1994; Paulgaard 2001). This distinction is largely class based, and becomes particularly visible when choosing secondary education at the age of 15 to 16; some prepare for university elsewhere, while others aim for locally-based apprenticeships. It is also reflected in use of leisure time; the former are overrepresented in organized activities such as music and sports. The petrol station often becomes the only alternative for the 'unorganized' groups, including the råners.

In the minority world, the formation of particular groups and subcultures are characteristic of youth (Epstein 1998; Skelton and Valentine 1998). The råners constitute a group or youth culture, sharing a strong interest in cars, as well as an orientation towards vocational training rather than academic education. While youth cultures are spatial as well as social constructs, Massey (1998) stresses the importance of overcoming the distinction of geographic scales in studies of culture. Youth cultures do not develop in isolation, in urban nor in rural areas, but through negotiations between existing elements and new impulses transmitted from elsewhere. Research from other countries (Bjurström 1990, Kraack and Kenway 2002, Vaaranen and Wieloch 2002) describe similar car-oriented, classbased cultures to the råners, which shows that this is not an entirely local phenomenon, but rather a hybrid culture with some similarities yet with local distinctions (cf. Massey 1998). The råners also have similarities with 'lad' identities commonly associated with urban areas (McDowell 2002, Willis 1977), who, in their experience of subordination within the school as well as labour system, may express what Connell (1995) talks of as 'protest' masculinity.

Hebdidge (1979) has emphasized the role of artefacts in constructing youth identity. In line with what we may see as a re-materialisation of social and cultural geography (Anderson and Tolia-Kelly 2004; Jackson 2000; Philo 2000a), this chapter highlights the significance of technologies as material objects in the practice of identity. Technologies and material objects are, according to Latour (1992) the 'missing masses' knocking on the door to be included in social analyses. Understanding identity as prac-tised, enables technology to be seen both as tools that enable particular practices and as symbols in distinguishing identity boundaries surrounding 'us' and 'them'. Identities of individuals and groups, but also particular interpretations of technologies, are constructed in this process. This illus-trates the seamlessness of technology and the social context, for technol-ogy and the social are not discrete entities having impact in one way or the other. Rather, technology materialises as diverse technosocial practices (Bingham 1999, Escobar 1996, Laegran 2003a), which may have just as many everyday translations as the contexts in which they are used.

Feminist studies of technology have emphasized how technical artefacts are gendered; for example, through the way they are integrated in sexual division of labour, by the symbolic connotations they entail, or by the way gender has been inscribed in the design of the technology (Faulkner 2001; Oudshoorn et al. 2002). This does not mean that technologies are essen-tially masculine or feminine, but that gender and technology are mutually shaped in a process of negotiation and practice. Regarding technology as 'masculine culture,' Wajcman (1991) highlights the durable association of technology with masculinity. However, as she points out, just as there are different technologies, there are also different masculinities associated with them. One dichotomous distinction is between technologies such as the car, demanding mechanical skills associated with physical toughness, and computers, which demand other kinds of technical skills signified by the professional calculative rationality of the technical specialist.

Drawing upon these various theoretical insights, this chapter develops the understanding that technology, space, and gender are co-constructed in the 'doing' of identity. The contexts of the research presented in this chapter are now outlined.

CONTEXT AND STUDY DESIGN

This study focuses on the village of Fjordvik,[2] idyllically situated by a fiord in mid-Norway, an area of the country which has traditionally been based on agriculture, manufacturing mainly being restricted to agricul-ture-related processing industries. The region has been marked by cen-tralisation internally as well as migration to other more central regions in the last decades. In recent years, governmental institutions and local enterprises have focused on developing innovation and entrepreneurship in response to increased insecurity within agriculture, as well as rationalisa-tion in government related industries. Regional policies have also focused on 'place development' as a strategy to increase the attractiveness of rural areas and small towns, particularly for women and young people (Depart-ment of Local Government and Regional Development 2001). One of the measures involves provision of informal meeting places for young people as alternatives to the petrol station. Thus Internet cafés have been opened in several rural communities since the turn of the century. The Internet café was seen as a novelty, opening up the cultural and social repertoire locally as well as providing possibilities for accessing the virtual translocal sphere (Laegran 2002). The research that informs this chapter was conducted about a year after an Internet café was opened in Fjordvik.

Fjordvik is the centre of a municipality of 6,000 inhabitants, containing a fertile agricultural landscape, but also serving as a 'dormitory' for commuters working in neighbouring towns. It is well known for what might be termed 'high' culture, including a modern art gallery, a comprehensive cultural center, a jazz club, and professional musicians working from the area. While this attracts new residents as well as tourists to the municipality, the cultural profile is not appreciated by all the inhabitants. Some, including the råners, see this artistic orientation as a rather exclusionary middle-class phenomenon.

This chapter draws on fieldwork in and around the Internet café and petrol station during repeated visits (1999 and 2000). Fieldwork comprised observations, informal chats and interviews with young people individually and in groups, and key informant interviews with relevant adults. This chapter concentrates on the young men at the petrol station, but interviews with girls at the petrol station as well as the clientele at the Internet café have also informed the analysis.

CARS AS A KEY TECHNOLOGY FOR RÅNE IDENTITY

The petrol station in Fjordvik is popularly named 'Auto'n', and appropriated as a 'home away from home' for the car-enthusiast young men and their female friends.[3] The cars constitute the furniture. Parked side by side, or 'nose' to 'nose', the cars are used to sit in and lean on in fine weather. Some prefer to sit inside, keeping their windows open to participate in the social activities. The inside of the car provides a more private space. The owner may allow the car to be a party venue, or limit access to closer friends or his girl friend. Girls are normally seated in the back seat, but may be promoted to the front according to the driver's wishes. Controlling the micro-geographies of gender relations in this way is a key feature of the masculine råne identity. Many of the råners spend most of their spare time in the car, eating, listening to music, and socialising. As most of the råners live with their parents, this becomes their 'bedsit on wheels' where they can do what they want without parental control (Lundbye 2005).

With limited public transport systems, an active young life in rural Norway almost requires access to a car. For the råners, however, the driving is not limited to transport, but is a leisure activity in itself. During the week it is mostly restricted to the village, driving up and down the main street playing loud music and looking for 'life'. At weekends the car becomes a mobile party venue as råners constantly drive between petrol stations and squares in several towns within the region. On these occasions, speed limits are not always followed:

ASL: Do you drive fast?
Young Man 20: Yes, I have to.
ASL: Have to?
Y.M. 20: Yes, there is no point in driving otherwise! I do not need a car really, it is just a toy.

Driving is one way of achieving the excitement and taking the risks often associated with exploring young masculinities (Kraack and Kenway 2002; Vaaranen and Wieloch 2002). Driving fast is seen as a sign of courage and gives status. Most of the young men do not use safety belts, it is considered unnecessary as well as cowardly. However, they claim they never drive dangerously; the ability to drive fast demands excellent skills and good drivers 'do not crash'.

The car is a key identification object. Owners are recognized and referred to by their cars (as much as their personal) names, illustrating seamlessness between people and cars. The brands differ according to financial means as well as local preferences, but in Fjordvik Volvos are most popular. The cars are not seen as 'ready made' (i.e. as standard factory issue). On the contrary, owners decorate and refurbish their cars according to their preferences, for example:

ASL: What kinds of cars do you find attractive?
Y.M. 21: Well, you have to spend some on cosmetics.
Y.M. 19: Yeah, rims and lowering and things like that.
Y.M. 21: That's half the car. If you put on the original rims, it is suddenly not that attractive anymore.

Interestingly the notion of 'cosmetics' is used to describe the modifcation; this is not just about technical mechanics, but also affectionate caring to make the car look beautiful. According to the respondents, a råne car should be slightly lowered and have specialized wheel-rims, dark-shaded windows, white flashlights, spoilers, and various pieces of extra equipment. If the owner has the means, the engine and the gearbox are changed to achieve more horsepower. A good sound system is also important, and this together with the enhanced engine capacity ensures the car is not only seen, but heard.

Most of the young men do the mechanical work, modifying the cars themselves with help from their peers. The tinkering is part of practice of the råne identity, and the car constitutes an arena for performing it. Garages at some of the parent's homes around the village provide additional meeting places where the work is being done. This creates a community where masculine identity is practised, and where learning takes place

(Mellström 1995). While the majority of respondents were in apprentice-ships to become car mechanics, they had actually been learning the trade informally from a very early age:

> You just look at the others, and learn gradually. But a lot of it is obvi-ous though, just logical, if you have some technical insight. (Y.M. 19)

Råners learn not just from peers, but also from elder brothers and their friends. Constructions of this knowledge as 'just logistics' suggests the tech-nological skills are tacit knowledge that has been internalized and embod-ied over a long period.

This section has highlighted how symbols as well as practices involving a particular technology are linked with a particular form of masculinity, in sum constituting the rural-oriented råne culture. Having the car as an icon for their culture the råners signal a collective identity when driving through the landscape. In this way the car is a transport medium for a lifestyle as much as for persons and goods (Lamvik 1996). And it is this lifestyle, which according to some adults as well as young people, is creating a nega-tive construction of rural life. An attempt to combat this was to open an Internet café in the village.

CONTRASTING IDENTITIES AND CONTEXTS: RÅNERS' RESPONSE TO THE INTERNET CAFÉ

In contrast to the car-related identity of the råners, recent regional policy contexts (noted above) have resulted in new meeting places in rural areas, most notably Internet cafés targeted at young people in particular. This has resulted in contrasting public spaces and identities being present in Fjord-vik, a development that the råners have encountered with some ambiva-lence. The Fjordvik Internet café was initiated (in late 1998) by youth and adult volunteers, with support from local enterprises and the municipality. According to the guidelines developed by the initiators, the café targets 'youth between 0 and 100' years old, with the aim of creating a sound youth environment, free of drugs, drinking, and prejudices. In the café, young people as well as adults can meet for a cup of cappuccino, and access the rest of the world via the Internet. In this way, young people have a safe indoor place to meet, with adults present, but without the surveillance and control associated with 'youth workers'. The Internet, in the guide-lines, is presented as a symbol of openness, knowledge, and curiosity about the world. Alternative media interpretations portraying the Internet as an unsafe place and passive toy are not mentioned.

In principle, the café is open to everyone; however, some groups tend to dominate the space. Students at the performing arts branch of the second-ary school were among the initiators of the place. They took part in refurbishing and running the venue, and adopted it as 'their place'. The 'trendy' café atmosphere resonates with elements of their own identity, as well as with the cultural profile of the village as a whole. In contrast, the råners, although approached and officially invited, did not feel this was their kind of place. Instead, they saw it as promoting artistic oriented youth who (in their eyes) already had enough activities as well as were receiving too much positive attention. That this more fortunate group of youth 'got' a place like the café, was seen as unfair by the råners in comparison with themselves who, as one of the young men (aged 19) expressed it, 'get nothing but bad stories in the newspapers' every so often. It contributed to the feeling of subordination, and did not decrease their noisy driving on the street where the café is located.

The Internet provides information, discussion groups, and social networks linked to almost any interest group or topic, including cars. At the time of the fieldwork, it was possible to download pictures of cars, including råne cars, and spare parts could be ordered through any of the car demolition businesses in Scandinavian countries. But the råners in Fjordvik did not use the Internet. Having been introduced to it at school, and knowing that there were possible useful resources online, råners resisted integrating the Internet into their everyday practice. In the Norwegian context, where Internet adoption has been relatively rapid, råners were perceived as 'laggards' according to the innovation and diffusion model of Rogers (1995). However, as Wyatt (2003) shows, it is important not to look upon non-users of technologies as 'have-nots' or 'drop-outs' but to understand why people do not take up innovations like the Internet. For instance, Holloway et al. (2000) found in their study of school students, that the 'lads' tended to stereotype 'techno-boys' as being 'wimps' who were not fulfilling masculine ideals. The rejection of the Internet among the råners may be understood in a similar vein—Internet use is not currently understood as compatible with the råne masculinity. But what lies behind this rejection?

RESISTING THE INTERNET WHILE 'DOING IDENTITY'

There are symbolic constructions at play in the way the råners resist Internet use. Whereas the 'lads' in the Holloway et al. (2000) study rejected those they identified as computer enthusiasts, the råners' response is more profound. Their rejection of the Internet and associated youth identities stems from both anti-urban sentiments (regarding cafés and the culture of the performance art students) and certain ideals of active masculinity. For instance, the image of the 'pear shaped computer nerd' was noted by several of the interviewees and rejected as not representing a masculine ideal. By 'doing identity', råners actively perform their masculine identity via a diversity of activities related to their cars, described earlier. Several informants talked further about being restless, wanting to be doing something, preferably with the car, or on the move within the car. In contrast, the Internet, while giving access to almost any place in the world, was a rather stationary devise.[4] When asked if the computers at the Internet café would be useful for ordering spare parts for their (sometimes old and rare) cars, one informant said:

> When I realise I need a spare part it is most likely I am actually under the car working on it. And then you can't just go onto a computer anyway can you? I'd rather use the mobile. (Y.M. 20)

While Internet communications involved a technology not appreciated by the Fjordvik råners, mobile phones provide an interesting contrast that shows quite differentiated relations between identities and technologies. Mobile phones were taken up relatively early by Fjordvik råners. They all had one when the fieldwork was conducted and the technology was used frequently for communication within the group, including distributing jokes through text messages. This shows that there is not a general reticence towards new technology, but it must fit into the symbolic image and practices associated with the råne identity.

Linked to the practise of identity, is knowledge. When talking about why he was not interested in computers and the Internet, one råner explained:

Y.M.18: No, I have never been good at computers. I have never been interested in just sitting down doing things.... I can't sit still more than half an hour.
ASL: But some people unscrew and rebuild computers too—have you never been interested in that?
Y.M. 18: You don't get dirty hands then!

This illustrates the embodied knowledge of car mechanics in another form than with the tacit knowledge mentioned earlier. It emphasizes the 'hands-on' experience and the working class association between 'dirty hands' and 'real work' (cf. Willis 1977). It is also worth noting how he claims that he has 'never been good with computers.' Interestingly he does not see this as a matter of learning in the same way as he has learned car mechanics. Instead, as another interviewee phrased it: 'You can't mend a computer! Then you really have to know what you are doing' (Y.M. 20). Whereas mechanics was interpreted as 'just logical' (quoted earlier), repairing computers requires a different form of knowledge, which is currently not part of the repertoire of the råne identity.

In discussing what the Internet has to offer, one of the råners stated:

> Yes—you can find out what the weather is like at Svalbard—but honestly, that does not really interest me. (Y.M. 19)

As noted above, the Internet café portrayed the Internet as a source of knowledge and a means to trigger curiosity. Although the example of Svalbard's weather is trivial, the quote signals that 'curiosity about the world' is not necessarily valued by all Fjorvik youth. This reflects the distinction between academic and practical knowledge—where the focus for the råners is on improving skills related to the car rather than acquiring knowledge for its own sake.

Wajcman's (1991) distinction between an academic masculinity associated with computers versus a more physically oriented masculinity associated with mechanics and cars seems to be at play in the råner's interaction with technologies. Though recognising this distinction as being class-based, this chapter has focused on the active relationship between the young men and their technical artefacts, rather than structural forces in the formation of identity. This is not to say that structural factors are not important, rather, it is to stress that it is also important to understand how technology is integrated or rejected in the practice of gendered identity. For these young men, the Internet with its symbolic connotations, practical use, and particular forms of knowledge, did not complement their (gendered) everyday practices. Instead, they chose other alternatives like the car and the mobile phone as more appropriate for a mobile (albeit locally-oriented) lifestyle.

CONCLUSION

This chapter has shown how technology, in this case cars and the Internet, may play an important part in identity practice. The material, the symbolic meaning, as well as the knowledges the technologies provide and require, are all features that may be interpreted differently and thus be embraced or rejected as part of 'doing identity'. Whereas the car, and especially manual mechanics, is technologically affiliated with the industrial society and the past, the Internet is said to be the technology for the future. In this respect the råne culture, by rejecting the use of the Internet, may be understood as a culture not adapting to but rather falling behind in modern society. The competence gained within the råne culture is not necessarily compatible with other contexts. However, the råners are not interested in moving to other places; the village is their home. They do not want to affiliate with an urban and global culture. The råners' reticence regarding the Internet becomes part of reproducing a culture that is not just signified by its interest in cars, but associated with a particular masculinity anchored to the local.

The particular construction of the Internet we have seen among the Fjordvik råners must, however, be understood as a time- and place-specific phenomenon. For instance, during the fieldwork some younger boys were identified who dreamed of cars with rims and dark-shaded windows, at the same time as being computer enthusiasts (Laegran 2003b). For them, being in the generation that 'grew up digital' (Tapscott 1998), the knowledge linked to the Internet was not in conflict with tinkering with cars. Local media reports and websites suggest that råners are now utilising the car as well as the Internet in their struggles for visibility and appreciation in the community, which calls for updated fieldwork and research in this field.

By 2006 several råne groups around the country have established their own web pages, where they present themselves as well as discuss relevant topics.[5] In spring 2005, a town in the region banned driving through the centre on weekend nights, an action that the råners saw as a provocation and attack on their lifestyle. As a direct protest action, the Internet, as well as mobile phones, was used to organize more than 100 cars from the whole region to drive into the residential area where the mayor lived. Some youth threw stones at the mayor's window, only to realise they had attacked the house of a neighbour. The incident was reported widely in regional and national media,[6] subsequently discussed on the Internet, with leading individuals as well as organisations condemning the stone throwing. The group was invited for a meeting with the mayor, discussing alternative places where the car enthusiasts could meet without disturbing the public. This event shows that the råne culture is not static or fixed in the past, unable to adapt to new technologies. Instead, 'doing' råne identity will continue to involve actions and changes in an active and dynamic masculinity.

This chapter has shown how the råne identity articulates a particular form of masculinity in rural Norway by identifying with (and against) 'urban' as well as 'rural' elements. They integrate new technologies, but in a way and at a time that makes sense for them. It seems in a Norwegian context, that the råners constitute a durable form of masculinity that is reproduced as a part of the social life in rural areas, no matter how problematic others in the community may find it. While strategies for improving the image of rural area and for making communities inclusive of social diversity can be supported, it is nevertheless important not to stigmatize and exclude, but recognise the råners as one group, and one identity, within a more diverse and multicultural rural Norway.

NOTES

1. The word Råne means boar, but the word has developed in youth slang as a verb for driving up and down the street, and 'råner' is used as the noun for the young men who do so. The label is used widely, also among the young men themselves, although some prefer to be called car enthusiasts. As this chapter is focused on this particular culture, I use the label, though in a non-patronising way.
2. The name of the village has been changed to preserve its anonymity.
3. Matthews et al. (2000) highlight the importance of not overlooking the agency of girls in the use of public meeting places. Although girls are present, it is fair to say that the petrol station and the råne culture are dominated by young men. The girls participate in partying, but do not own cars (some are under 18, the driver's licence age limit). According to the girls interviewed

they are not interested in talking about or tinkering with cars, and actually find the young men's obsession with cars rather annoying. Although confirming a masculine culture, Lundbye (2005) finds a more varied picture in her study from another part of Norway, so it is likely that girls' participation in this sub-culture varies.

4. At least this was the case during the period of fieldwork, although developments combining Internet and mobile phone technology provide an interesting new development that may alter the experiences and activities of råners in future.
5. See for instance the homepages of two organised clubs: http://www.westside-racing.net/, http://www.volvoklubbentrondelag.no/ and the 'råne' festival first arranged in 2005. All links accessed 16 January 2006.
6. See for instance: Dagbladet: '50 rånere steinet huset til ordførernabo.' 18 April 2005. http://www.dagbladet.no/nyheter/2005/04/18/429191.html. Accessed 16 January 2006. Trønderavisa: 'Bilaksjon mot nattestengt gate.' 16 April 2005; 'Råner fikk møte ordfører.' 20 April 2005, 'Råneraksjon i natt.' 23 April 2005. Accessed 16 January 2006 through http://www.tronderavisa. no/.

4 'Our lives are like a sock inside-out'

Children's work and youth identity in neoliberal rural Mexico

Fina Carpena-Méndez

Experiments in economic development, contingent to flows of transnational investment and disinvestment, set up the particular contexts for different ways of traveling in history. A focus on the everyday experiences of children and youth offers a critical site for theorising the links between past, present, and future and for discerning the unexpected, contradictory, messy yet inventive ways in which communities navigate political and economic agendas. This chapter explores the experiences of children and youth in a Mexican peasant community that has been recently incorporated into transnational circuits of undocumented labor migration to the United States. It is concerned with the ways in which Mexican rural youth are being uprooted from subsistence activities in their local communities and incorporated into transnational spaces and global consumer practices and identities. In doing so, it also uncovers how youth negotiate the incorporation of new material social practices while struggling to forge new forms of belonging to rural spaces and social life.

THE CONTEXTS: ECONOMIC RESTRUCTURING AND NEW MIGRANT-SENDING COMMUNITIES

In 1994 a challenging decade began for Mexican people when Canada, the United States, and Mexico formed the North American Free Trade Agreement (NAFTA), the world's largest free trade area. The new rules of trade liberalisation included the reform of the Mexican constitution, offering a new legal framework for the progressive privatisation of *ejido* lands,[1] and the restructuring of agriculture.[2] Consequently, in the last decade many Mexican peasants have noticed that the income from their agricultural produce has been drastically reduced. In many cases, communities strive for developing alternative crops to corn and beans that might have a better price in the market, finding other ways to to keep their lands productive. Yet the abandonment of cultivated land has intensified in states where subsistence agriculture predominates. Neoliberal reforms have resulted in increased levels of migration from rural to urban areas and across borders. Thus during the 1990s, international migration has spread like wildfire through rural communities without previous experience in U.S. migration.

In rural Puebla, central Mexico, the rapid dismantling of local subsistence economies, widening social inequalities, and emerging new migration processes to urban areas of the United States have come to mediate everyday lives in peasant and indigenous communities. This chapter explores the transformations of children's spaces and practices and youth identity formation in the context of rapid and broad-scale changes in everyday life in new migrant-sending, rural communities. It focuses on the experiences of young people in the village I call San Matías[3] (see Figure 4.1), a Nahua mountain community in the state of Puebla engaged in seasonal corn and bean farming. Traditional forms of everyday life in the community have been disrupted recently by a rapid process of youth out-migration to the United States, after the implementation of NAFTA. Research reported in this chapter is based on one year of intensive fieldwork in San Matías, following young people's everyday interactions across social domains, within households, school, community, agriculture, and other informal jobs (Carpena-Méndez 2006). I focus on the experiences and practices of both children growing up in the village and young migrant returnees.

San Matías resembles many other indigenous communities in Mexico. It is an extremely endogamous community where people have lived in isolation. The first dirt road to this mountain community was constructed in the mid-1980s and was only recently paved. Villagers have practiced barter through a web of tracks traced for centuries with neighboring villages with which they have woven ties of ritual kinship and reciprocity. The concepts

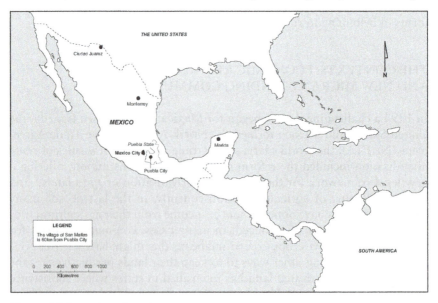

Figure 4.1 Location of study area.

of 'close corporate community' (Wolf 1957) and 'region of refuge' (Aguirre Beltran 1979) have been used to describe the historic circumstances in which indigenous communities were insulated in inhospitable terrains while at the same time incorporated into regional socio-economic and administrative systems from colonial times to the development of the modernising Mexican state.

Villagers perceive themselves as part of a sleepy, closed community that is suddenly awakening via a process of 'development', thanks to the remittances of the youth who have migrated to the north.[4] Adults often told me:

> In this village we have been sleeping for a long time...because the ones who do not know are like blind, they cannot see....We have been stuck like a rock, without changing, repeating the same over and over again....Just now the village is progressing; we were like asleep. (Pedro, middle-age man)

The sudden burgeoning of small shops, construction of block houses, and the increasingly ostentatious *mayordomía*[5] celebrations in this mountain village is financed by young migrants in U.S. cities. High-tech goods like TVs, VCRs, camcorders, digital cameras, and CDs are brought to the village by young migrant returnees or bought with remittances from the United States. These external goods and the practices associated with them coexist inside the domestic spaces with clay *comales* [griddles], *metates* [grinding stones], *petates* [woven reed mats used for sleeping], and windowless, smoky *jacalitos* [dirt-floored, wood plank kitchens].

This experience of 'development', with its connotations of improved well-being, paradoxically has emerged not by way of investment in new production but via cash remittances that are spent in construction and consumption. Previously, the main form of social differentiation in the village was between the *caciques* [local political strongmen] and local elites with more land, and the families without enough land for their maintenance. Nowadays, a new form of social differentiation occurs between the families receiving cash remittances from the United States and those who do not. For instance, families receiving cash remittances not only have access to consumption but also are hiring other families at peak moments of the harvest and sowing, thus commodifying the production of subsistence corn.

Yet, despite the community's emerging sense of 'development' and 'modernity', many families strive to find alternative ways of keeping their lands productive, for instance with the introduction of cattle that roam free on their mountain plots. One of the most striking experiences during fieldwork was the sense of desperation of many families trying to gain knowledge of how to develop possible cash crops in inhospitable terrains that cannot be irrigated or farmed using machinery. Related to this search for alternative ways of production there is another important dimension of adults' anxiety: the lack of labor due to youth migration to the United States and the future of the *ejido* land.

Within this world of rapid transformations, work practices continue to be essential to village social life, sense of belonging and identity, but are not without contradictions. Work is lent in the form of mutual aid and circulates within networks of kinship, neighbors, and *compadrazgo* [co-godparenthood]. Reciprocal arrangements in the form of help with days of agricultural work that will be returned in the future, as a moral obligation, in the form of gifts and services, lie at the core of social life. In the context of labor migration, villagers conceptualise 'going to the cornfields' and 'working' for a wage as belonging to different orders of experience. The nature of work done in the fields is understood as constituting social relations and is central to the maintenance of the household, while *trabajar* ('working') entails by definition commuting, weekly, biweekly, seasonal, or circular international labor migration, and is associated with the possibility of consumption.

Everyday forms and sense of work are mediated by bodily experiences. Adults often complain that in the fields their bodies are being 'finished off', soon wasted away, and they associate the very idea of 'modernity' with other forms of work that involve different perceptions of body formations and forms of aging. In this new neoliberal era therefore, youth pursue the experience of consuming 'things' instead of 'consuming' their bodies, in a context in which notions of what a good life means are being profoundly altered.

Work, understood as physical labor in the cornfields, has been central to the Nahua way of life, sense of identity, and notions of local citizenship. In this gerontocratic society, the control of youth labor empowered adults in the past. Thus, labor migration to the United States runs the risk of severing young people from networks of exchange and reciprocity, therefore expelling them from a broader social life and life course expectations. Since the mid-1990s, there has been a floating population of 500 youth (in a village of 2,700 inhabitants) between the ages of 12 and 24 in and out of the village in labor migration cycles to the United States lasting two or three years.[6] When returning to the village some migrant youth tend to spend their time '*paseando en la calle*' (hanging out in the street) until they exhaust their savings and decide to go again to the north, thus initiating another cycle. Elders often accuse youth of being 'lazy', not willing to work in the fields. Yet some parents are making practical efforts to develop alternative, productive projects that might prevent the migration of youth to the north. For instance, Don Pancho has experimented with a self-made mushroom nursery and Doña Maria grows vegetables in an experimental greenhouse. Both produce sufficient quantities for local markets and they hope that their children will work with them and will not migrate. Despite Doña Maria's efforts, her daughter, who was 19, left one night to go the north with a group of friends and a *coyote* [people smuggler operating across the Mexican-U.S. border], without informing her family until she was already on the other side of the border.

EMERGING YOUTH IDENTITIES AND THE TRANSNATIONALISATION OF *PANDILLERISMO*

Unlike other Mexican regions with a long history of migratory experience, this mountain region in the state of Puebla had no international migratory tradition until the mid-1990s. In 1995 a village census found out that only 4 per cent of the total population was working outside of the community. But, after the implementation of NAFTA, an accelerated migration to the United States began to take place. This migration has involved a rapid out-flow of migrants over a short period of time without previous transnational networks constructed gradually over several generations to provide knowledge and sustain the process. Boys and girls between 12 and 18 years old are taking the lead in emerging patterns of migration by using gang membership and practices as social capital to construct support networks in their passages to the north.

Despite much literature on the local effects of globalisation and transnational practices, the experiences of children and youth are frequently overlooked, on the assumption that children are 'passive dependents' and that the decision to cross national borders is always taken by adult members of the family (Orellana et al. 2001). Moreover, unlike the media and research attention given to the experiences of so-called urban street children, the invisibility of rural conditions in the public sphere has rendered young people's contributions to the remaking of rural communities and the workings of transnational fields as marginal or understudied.

As in other countries (see Punch, this volume), Mexico has a long tradition of rural–urban migrations. However, scant attention has been paid to how the production of rural spaces and the reformulation of youth identities are mutually constituted. San Matías has two different historical experiences of labor migration: an earlier migration to Mexico City that began in the 1970s and later, an accelerated process of transnational migration in the mid-1990s. I am concerned here with two interrelated questions. First, how the earlier historical experience of youth migration to Mexico City set up the context for the emergence of youth gangs in rural areas, which later became a social resource available to the youth for taking the lead in transnational migration. And second, I am concerned with how young migrant returnees are introducing and negotiating changes in material social practices in the community.

Ethnographers visiting the village in 1959 (Nutini and Isaac 1974) reported that, despite the meager subsistence that the available land provided and the lack of any other commercial activity, there was no out-migration and the community was basically monolingual in Nahuatl. During the late 1960s and 1970s, Mexico's import substitution policies and growing centralised bureaucracy drew Nahua peasants of central Mexico to the capital's nascent labor market. Youth at that time went to Mexico City in search of temporary construction and factory jobs, and also worked as street sellers and maids. Labor migration to Mexico City has been a central dimension in the experience of being young in this community for the last three decades, albeit the majority ended up returning to the village to work in the cornfields. This practice occurred as part of the marriage process, a means to make some cash for the bridal petition, and to build up an independent house for a new nuclear family. The ones who remained living in the fast growing shantytowns in the periphery of the capital have been returning to the village for the fiestas,[7] times in which they reinforce their sense of belonging by constructing *compadrazgo* [co-godparenthood] relationships, resolving a possible *apadrinamiento* [to sponsor a child as godfather], or formalising a bridal petition.

The life course became spatially marked in the movement from the village to Mexico City while the experience of labor migration became a sort of rite of passage from childhood to adulthood. Throughout the networks of kinship relationships and economic cooperation extended between the peasant village and the shantytowns in the capital's fringes, children and youth imitated and experimented with new practices or forms of 'being young' in urban marginal areas. *Pandillerismo* or 'being *banda*' (youth gang practices) emerged in the late 1980s in the rural landscape of central Mexico introduced by the back and forth processes of youth labor migration. Over time, gang practices became a bridge for youth from the village to the city, and a way to adjust to—or cope with—the conditions of life in the shantytowns. *Pandillerismo* was the particular form that rural youth practices took under their increasing dependency on, and time spent with, peer groups in the streets. The existence of youth *bandas* or *pandillas* in Mexico City is not a recent phenomenon and was already depicted in the early 1940s by Buñuel in the film *Los Olvidados*. The majority of youth bandas in Mexico City shantytowns are migrants from villages in the countryside (Magazine 2003). Following a migration pattern found in many Mesoamerican villages, young people leave home between the ages of 9 and 20 to search for work and adventure in cities. Rural children migrate in search of labor but also to see the world outside of their village.

Young migrant returnees from Mexico City are seen by the children growing up in San Matías as 'streetwise', introducing new exotic practices and glamorous styles. Thus graffiti, *sonidero* music, and the use of cheap drugs like glue and marijuana are part of the contemporary experiences of growing up in indigenous peasant communities. Children and youth in San Matías are creating new times (the night) and spaces (the street) by and for themselves. In this way they incorporate external and urban youth practices into a rural landscape, while usually also fulfilling daytime responsibilities as 'workers' in their households. For instance, David, from the banda of *The Uncorrectables,* asserted:

> The banda is just a group, a group of youth for diversion during the night…but most of us…we fulfill our duties in our homes, we are responsible.…We [also] gather in the street corners for hanging out and listening to music, because the house is not appropriate for diversion, there we have to work and respect our parents.…Playing in the house is not respectful to our parents.

Youth gangs have been absorbed and integrated into the social organisation of the community, for gangs in this rural area are territorialised by village *barrios* and affiliations to preexisting village divisions. These divisions find their original forms in kinship and *compadrazgo* networks as well as fusion and separation of political factional groups. Other authors have explained how social conflicts in rural Mesoamerica are often tied to a community's geographical divisions into *barrios*[8] (Hunt and Nash 1967). But at the same time the barrio not only demarcates social and political alliances, it also manages and organises work groups and ritual celebrations (Brandes 1988; Cohen 1999). With the arrival of remittances, many families are transforming their single room wood plank *jacales* into the divided spaces of the block house. Walling off domestic spaces in this mountain village has provided the youth with a public space in which to socialise and symbolically territorialise through the use of graffiti on the village walls (see Figure 4.2). Thus, the experience of childhood and youth is a space of constant negotiation and conflict between children's cultural

Figure 4.2a Spray-painted gang markings in San Matías. Girls' gang: Chicas Divanni, Las Creizzis—[Divanni Girls, The Crazy Ones].

Figure 4.2b Spray-painted gang markings in San Matías. Boys' gang: Niños sin Amor—[Children without Love].

legacies (based on work and respect) and the creation of new identities. The production (and tagging) of new spaces in the rural landscape of central Mexico and the emergence of new youth identities are mutually constituted as rural youth blur the boundaries between rurality and urban marginality.

CHILDREN'S WORK AND IDENTITIES GROWING UP IN A TRANSITIONAL SOCIETY

Despite grim agrarian prospects and increasing dependence on cash remittances, children continue to engage in household and agricultural work in the region. They are currently assuming greater workloads and responsibilities at a younger age, given the migration of older siblings and parents. Local forms of work, and the introduction of new youth practices and imaginaries, are contradictory and complex forces shaping children's everyday experiences and identities. The stories of Miguel, Regino, and Rosa may help to illustrate this point.

Miguel is 8 years old and a first grader in the primary school. He still cannot read and has difficulties writing his name, and his teacher complains that he often misses class. Miguel lives with his grandparents, mother, and siblings and he knows how to do many things. Everyday after school he takes his sheep to the fields, either alone, or with his school friends who also take their own animals. Coming back home he gathers wood for the *comal* [griddle]. He often goes with his grandparents and mother to the cornfields to help them with the sowing, land preparation, and harvest. On those days Miguel misses school. Other times he goes with his cousins to Ciudad Neza (in Mexico City)[9] to help them as a garbage collector. Sometimes Miguel also helps his uncles to sell tamales and *mixiotes* in the regional market. There are also times in which Miguel also misses school '*de pura flojera*' [from pure laziness], because he falls asleep in the morning after staying in the street part of the night with older gang friends. They spend the night at the street corners, listening to music, playing soccer, and smoking marihuana or sniffing glue, dressed in their black T-shirts and with spiky hair.

Miguel's older brother, who is 18, went to the north three years ago and still cannot come back; he says he is hardly making enough money to pay the *coyote*. Sometimes he works in restaurants as a waiter, sometimes he works in factories, and at other times he is unemployed. Miguel goes to the cornfields to help his grandparents more frequently since his brother migrated to the north. His sister Ana is 14 years old; she dropped out of school and went to the city with one of the teachers to help care for the teacher's baby. She also sells clothes in the market on weekends in the stand owned by her teacher. Anna asserts that she is happy with the teacher and whenever she comes to visit her grandparents she looks very pretty with her new clothes. However, because of his sister's migration, Miguel has to light the *comal* by himself and prepare the tortillas when he comes back home from school. Some mornings Miguel lingers playing with the arcade videogames. There are many amusement arcades in the dusty streets of the village since numerous migrating youth send back remittances to their families and others receive money from the welfare program '*Oportunidades*'.[10] Then, the teacher has to go out in search of Miguel and bring him back to school.

Despite his irregular attendance, Miguel likes going to school. He likes playing with his friends and learning songs. He likes to prepare the dances for Spring Festival, which commemorates of Benito Juarez. Maybe this year he will dance if his sister Ana or his brother in the north sends some money for the outfit. Like many other youth from the gang, Miguel wants to go north as soon as he finishes primary school, but he hopes his brother will take him. He contends that later he will come back to the village, buy a big TV, a VCR, and a camcorder to record how the village is changing. Eventually, he hopes to construct his own block house in order to get married without having to live with his parents.

The case of Miguel illustrates the tensions and contradictions between expectations of living as a modern, consumer-oriented youth, and patterns of necessity, practice, and belief that underpin other ways of organising children's lives in rural Mexico. In his everyday practices and sense of self Miguel negotiates and navigates family commitments, work expectations, consumer and migrant dreams, and the identity provided by belonging to his barrio's *banda*.

Children's work is delineated and controlled by, but at the same time plays a central role in, the kinship and *compadrazgo* networks that are the base of social support systems in rural Mexico. Children have an active role in the negotiation of their own relations with family and godparents. They fulfill their obligations and responsibilities as workers while at the same time negotiating their own trajectories and destinies. The case of Regino, an 11-year-old boy, illustrates how children maneuver in these networks of obligation to meet their own ends. I found Regino one Monday morning at a neighboring village's celebration. He was with his grandfather and other men in the Aztec music band playing the *teponaztle* [traditional drum]. Regino explained he could not go to school that day because he needed to work in the band to make money for his mother to pay the school contributions, for that year she had a *cargo*[11] in the school committee. Later, Regino decided to move out of his parents' home and live with his godfather due to domestic discord. He is supporting his schooling and sometimes his siblings by working in the Aztec music band. Children often have to rely on their own resources and seek ties with others wherever they can. They maneuver in a plurality of social networks (kinship, *compadrazgo*, and youth gangs), becoming subjects of their own life trajectories in reciprocating determining relations. Thus children like Regino are increasingly active agents in the course of their own lives, which in turn affect the experiences of those close to them.

Rosa is 12 years old and lives with her three younger siblings. She has been the head of the household since her parents migrated north four years ago and later got divorced there. Her mother plans to take her children one by one to the United States to live with her, as she can afford to maintain them there. Thus, Rosa is burdened with the responsibility of raising her siblings while her mother gradually takes them to the north as Rosa expects to be the last one to leave. Rosa manages the remittances that her mother sends her regularly, and takes care of buying food, clothes, and other household items. Going to neighboring towns to purchase food and clothes that cannot be found in San Matias has allowed Rosa to develop cash management and purchasing skills, an activity that she carries on several times a week and the one she enjoys most. Unlike other families in the community, Rosa can afford to eat meat on a regular basis and cook using electric food processors. Although Rosa has never lived outside her mountain village, other children perceive her as streetwise. She has also set up a small business selling materials for learning English, such as books, VCRs, and CDs, sent regularly by her mother from the United States.

Rosa, however, is not alone in raising her siblings. She is supervised and at the same time taken care of by her grandmother and a network of family members living close by. Her grandmother regularly visits Rosa's house to cook tortillas in the *comal* in the smoky *jacalito* kitchen and to help her with the children. Her grandmother would like to move permanently to her house, a proposal that Rosa has strongly opposed since her grandmother has recently remarried a much older man in the community, following traditional marriage rules for a widow. Rosa rejects these traditional rules and she does not wish to recognise this man as a grandfather. The power that Rosa has in her household (e.g. communicating with her mother in the north by phone and managing remittances) has greatly diminished her grandmother's authority over her and her siblings.

As a consequence of the massive migration of young women and men between 14 and 35 to the United States, in the Mexican countryside it is common to find households composed of women, and children taken care of by their grandparents, who lack the authority, energy, and communication abilities to control children and youth. This difficult family life is often satisfied by youth joining gangs. Rosa is very fond of renting and purchasing youth gang movies—mostly American but also Mexican—that she watches repeatedly. Rosa asserted:

> I feel very attracted to movies about bandas....I do not like any other type of movie. I like them because young people are respected...and because you learn friendship and to excel yourself. I really admire the youth in the stories, because they grow up without the love of their parents but they learn to overcome their shyness....

Even for children like Rosa, who have never migrated, imageries of powerful gang youth have captured their imagination about possible future identities or ideas of who they want to be. These films project a specific model for transnational migration and the life of Mexican, migrant youth in New York and Philadelphia. Imagination overflows experience in a context in which experience is deprived of hope. Rosa is one of many teens left behind by migrant parents, navigating the contradictions of being burdened by responsibility at an early age, feeling abandoned even though she is supervised by an extensive (though varyingly effective) kinship network of care, dependent on remittances, with disposable income, and increased social status, while also dreaming of other identities.

CONCLUSIONS: CONTEXTS, DAILY PRACTICES, AND IDENTITIES

As other authors have noticed for other regions of the world (Katz 2004), and these rural Mexican cases illustrate, children's everyday practices are being reorganised and relocated under the effects of transnational capitalism. Under the globalising process taking place in rural Mexico, the experiences and life trajectories of children and youth are articulated to economic processes, material social worlds, and the flow of images and information that penetrate local communities, differing to a great extent from the conditions of life, work, and knowledge of their elders.

The experiences of Miguel, Regino, and Rosa show how their everyday practices incorporate socio-historical forces of transformation while combining them, in unexpected and arbitrary ways, with local traditional forms of organizing children's lives that are based on work for the household and respect for elders. In their everyday experiences, these children blur the boundaries between urban and rural identity, traditional age identities based on generational hierarchies of power, and identities as workers and global consumers, combining them in fluid and shifting ways.

Anthropological debates on identity have moved away from essentialised conceptions to include dynamic, shifting, fluid processes, clearing a space for the strategic handling of multiple senses of belonging in the different social fields and contexts in which people navigate (de Certeau 1984; Liu 2002). Therefore, certain mechanisms of transmission and acquisition of stable cultural worlds between generations can no longer be assumed, since 'culture' and 'identity' have become politically contested terms and understood as the changing outcome of practices in a globalized world (Stephens 1995).

There is no such essential identity as a 'peasant Mexican child' or a 'Nahua boy or girl', perfectly shaped and representable. Indeed, as this chapter has demonstrated, there are no identities whose boundaries are not blurred and constantly modified. The social contexts in which children grow up shift as do their identities of emerging subject positions. This chapter has considered the macro-contexts, or historical forces of transformation, restructuring the spaces of children's everyday lives in Mexican rural areas. Yet what must be emphasized is that these shifting contexts cannot be understood as simply 'impacting' or 'affecting' identities, as cultural scripts to be explored and enacted by young people. Young people are not passively adapting to these shifting contexts of constraints but actually are embodying these historical forces of transformation in their everyday experiences, and becoming agents in shaping their experiential worlds (see also Schäfer, this volume). Everyday practice is always contextually situated, not entirely conscious, and characterised by improvisation, fluidity, and indeterminacy (Bourdieu 1990; de Certeau 1984; Liu 2000). Embodied practice is the site where the social worlds of children are made and modified, where power relations (between adults and children) are given meaning, lived, resisted, and reshaped. It is through embodied practice that children and youth both build upon their cultural legacies and create new identities or forms of belonging. It is in and through everyday practice—the mundane, repetitive daily tasks and ways of doing—that subject positions and identities are formed and constantly changed. Culture and identity become fluid, constantly changing, living forms.

The social existence of a group is fabricated in the practices of the everyday and is always in a state of becoming. Therefore, it is in the very practice of their daily lives that children and youth become key players (to use Bourdieu's game metaphor, 1990) within processes of change and globalisation. On the one hand, children's work and identities as family members provide important contributions to the maintenance of the household. But they are also entwined in the maintenance of forms of dailiness when migration of parents and older siblings for long periods of time entails a significant historical rupture in terms of social existence in the countryside. Also, youth—and especially migrant youth—have a key role in reshaping practices, imaginaries, and power relations in different realms of current and future village life. Children and youth are 'juggling' and improvising with their own life trajectories as they intersect with rapidly changing social and economic contexts of development, where local, rural-urban, and transnational processes overlap.

Youth in San Matías often expressed a sense of ongoing instability in the lives of their families, and lack of a future in this mountain village. When youth began migrating to the United States in the late 1990s, some of them had previous rural–urban migratory experiences, but not all. With the current neoliberal restructuring taking place, numerous youth who grew up in San Matías have left for the United States just as their parents were returning to the mountain village after losing their jobs in Mexico City. Some returnee families have turned to transient activities such as cattle rising and small stores. This disjuncture, between the migratory movements and experiences of parents and young people, frames intergenerational relations when youth return to the village after working in the north for several years. Francisco, a 19-year-old youth returning to San Matías after three years of working in restaurants in Philadelphia, explained:

> My father was always working in Mexico City....I hardly knew him....Other children would go to Mexico City but I never travelled out of the village before I went to Philadelphia....He [his father] came back to the village and bought bulls. When I returned he wanted me to work with him. But he was an unknown person for me....As the time passed I realized I was bored here [in San Matías] and I began to have frequent fights with him.

When young people in San Matías say, '*llevamos la vida como calcetín volteado*' ['our lives are like a sock inside-out'] they are highlighting the uncertain, messy, unstable nature of their everyday lives, in the face of major economic and social changes in rural Mexico. By fulfilling their responsibilities as family members and workers, Nahua children are learning skills and knowledge for a form of rural village adulthood that might not be possible in the future. Under Mexico's experience of modernisation with the current penetration of transnational capitalism, multiple trajectories can be traced for young Nahua lives. Many teenagers are attending school while waiting for their opportunity to migrate to the north. Numerous youth have returned to the village after two or three years working in the United States. A few of them use this migratory experience and the savings earned to continue studying or to open a small business in Mexico. Others, the majority, perceive their lives are trapped in the back-and-forth nature of the illegal, transnational, migrant labor circuits. When returning to Mexico, migrant youth expect to build up a block house of their own and open a small store instead of working in the cornfields. They soon realise that in order to sustain an improved standard of living it is necessary to have a constant flow of remittances, and thus decide to return to the north.

The most obvious effect of transnational migration in rural Mexico is increasing socio-economic stratification. Transnational migration has also brought newly emerged subject positions and identities for youth and children, and the very intimate domestic conflicts between generations. By means of school attendance and the flow of images and information that accompanies transnational migration, children in rural Mexico are developing an awareness of both the modern, global notion of protected, nurtured childhood (Hecht 1998) and the local conditions of life that prevent them from living according to that ideal. Mexican rural children do not expect to live a modern form of nurtured childhood but rather a particular form of global, consumer-oriented youth. This chapter has examined the multiplicity of youth's life trajectories interweaving local village realities and spaces with wider circuits of migration, employment, and consumption that characterize Mexico's transnational relations. In doing so, it has highlighted the effects of global inequalities of power (deteriorating agricultural possibilities and increasing desires for access to cash and the global consumer market) on experiences of childhood and youth, and the multiple identities young people navigate.

Acknowledgements

I thankfully acknowledge the research support from the Spencer Foundation, the Center for US-Mexican Studies, and the Center for Comparative Immigration Studies at the University of California, San Diego. Views and opinions expressed are those of the author alone.

NOTES

1. After the Mexican Revolution of 1910 millions of hectares of land concentrated in large landholdings or *haciendas* were expropriated and distributed among rural communities. Under the old Mexican Agrarian Law these communal lands or *ejidos* were then divided into small individual plots and assigned to peasants who could work the land themselves without leaving it unused, renting or selling it. Communal farmers only had 'use rights' to the land they worked. The new Agrarian Law of 1992 meant the end of the State's commitment to the legacy of the Revolution through the Agrarian Reform.
2. This included the virtual dismantling of credits, subsidies, and quota protection for agriculture and signalled the withdrawal of the corporatist Mexican state, giving rise to an unstable neoliberal order.
3. This is a pseudonym for the community.

4. Villagers use the term *El Norte* (The North) when talking about migration to the United States.
5. Family-sponsored saint's celebration.
6. Boys and girls between ages of 12 and 20 are taking the lead in emerging patterns of circular transnational illegal migration, seeking low-wage jobs in New York and Philadelphia. Most youth of both sexes work in restaurants and factories.
7. The generic word *fiesta*, as used throughout central Mexico, typically refers to different kinds of events: life-cycle markers, and cyclical religious and agricultural celebrations (see Brandes 1988).
8. Characteristic of most peasant Indian communities in Mexico the *barrio* is equivalent to a neighbourhood association.
9. After the construction of the road and the introduction of public transportation to this mountain village, Mexico City is about a day's journey.
10. School attendance has increased in rural Mexico since the new World Bank's Welfare program for the Mexican countryside, '*Oportunidades*', has made it mandatory in order for families to receive monthly cash aid. However, the cash is also spent by children on diversions such as video games.
11. *Cargo* (literally, burden or charge) is a civil or religious office. Characteristic of rural Mexico, the cargo system is a rotating system of civil-religious office holding in which adults take turns at leadership. The office holder spends considerable amounts of money in sponsoring civil or religious celebrations, and in the construction and maintenance of public buildings such as the school and the health centre.

5 Rural daughters in Australia, New Zealand, and the United States

An historical perspective[1]

Kathryn Hunter and Pamela Riney-Kehrberg

INTRODUCTION

Mercy Bachelor wrote to the *New Zealand Farmer* in 1892 detailing her work around the farm: 'I was cooking, washing, ironing and butter-making. I had to milk three cows at night.' (*New Zealand Farmer* vol.12, 9 September 1892). Other records, including the personal writings of rural women and the letters that girls wrote to children's pages of agricultural papers, illustrate similar duties shared by farmers' daughters who were growing up in locations where family labour was essential to farm operations. They describe the common lot of Australia's, New Zealand's, and the American Midwest's rural daughters, those white, English-speaking girls and young women who were old enough to contribute substantially to their families' agricultural enterprises, but not yet ready to marry and leave the family home. Their words demonstrate that to be a daughter in any of these rural locations was to be an essential part of the economic fabric of the family and the farm.

Recent literature on contemporary rural children has highlighted three areas: the gendered nature of notions of the agrarian ideal or the rural idyll; the tensions between this rural idyll and the diversity of experience of rural children; and debates about the agency of children in constructing their own lives. Geographers and historians have argued that notions of agrarianism, or of the rural idyll, are gendered in their construction and in their impact (Davidoff et al. 1976; Fink 1992; Little and Austin 1996). This is as evident from the study of children's experiences in rural areas as it is from those of women. Scholars have also commented on the strength and durability of the rural idyll and have argued that it serves to reinforce gendered divisions of labour and domesticity for women (Little 1987). An historical perspective can contribute to these discussions, revealing the gendered nature of the rural idyll to be an historical construction, as much as one constructed by place, and to be a construct that is contested.

Here we examine the histories of rural daughters in Australia, New Zealand, and the United States in the years between 1870 and 1920. The exploration of the work of daughters and unmarried women creates another window through which to glimpse the operations of gendered ideologies governing farm labour. This is especially possible at points where discourses surrounding girls' labour came into conflict. An examination of both public representations of girls' labour and their personal writings about that work reveals that over these decades of social and economic transformation the tensions between competing discourses of girls' farm work became more marked. In developing a portrait of the rural economies of Australia, New Zealand, and the United States, and the place of white girls within those economies, it becomes apparent that, throughout these three regions, the value systems within which those girls worked were often at odds with urban, middle-class models of proper childhood and womanhood. Rural girls were workers, although the exact nature of that work varied with family composition, location, stage of settlement, crop mix, and a number of other factors, particularly the availability and affordability of hired labour. Despite those differences, there are a host of similarities in girls' roles between these states and colonies, be it the similar work of small girls, or the growing responsibilities of older daughters. Also evident within these girls' stories is a tension between the values and needs of rural communities and the growing power of domestic ideology. Rural societies were increasingly unsure how their daughters should negotiate the slippery slope between necessary labour and desirable domestic feminine accomplishment. In locations where femininity had been epitomised by 'usefulness,' that usefulness had to be tempered increasingly by young women's attention to their physical duties as future mothers. It was also shaped by state/national desires both to present their female population as leisured as a sign of prosperity, and to promote the continued desirability of rural life.

METHODOLOGY

A challenge to this research is the dearth of historical scholarship about rural girls and young women. This scholarly neglect is more obvious when the significance of the young female population, particularly in colonial contexts, is reflected upon. In the more populous colonies of Australia in 1881, 40 per cent of the female population was under 15 years of age and nearly 70 per cent of females were aged 29 years or younger (*Victorian Year Book* 1900–1930; McDonald et al. 1987). Demographic details from the American Midwest also underscore the importance of girls' experiences to rural history. In the Midwest (defined here as Illinois, Iowa, Kansas, Minnesota, Nebraska, and Wisconsin), girls aged 5 to 19 years were a formidable presence. In each state, girls accounted for more than 15 per cent of the total population, and more than 31 per cent of the female population. In two states, Nebraska and Minnesota, girls made up 35 per cent or more of all females (United States Census Office 1902). The demographic evidence alone would suggest that the time has come to consider seriously the importance of rural girls to the histories of their communities.

Other evidence also spurs on enquiry. Farm girls are made visible in the historical record in a variety of ways. Personal papers, diaries, and letters are key sources in rural women's history because they constitute one of the few bodies of evidence that contain women's words and voices. Young women themselves left personal papers and writings, such as the letters to the rural press used in this study. They are also visible through the writings of their mothers and siblings, as are other young women in the community, friends, neighbours, and workers. Discourses about femininity are also present in the sources produced by 'agents of modernity': that is, within records produced through an increasing awareness of and concern about the welfare of children and young women. For example, concerns about girls' behaviour appear in school records and letters to the rural press about the effects on girls and young women of their strenuous outdoor work. Young white women are also visible in the censuses and hence in debates, now being reinvigorated, about the impact of a disproportionate sex ratio in colonial and frontier situations (Macdonald 1999). The experiences of illiterate and poor white women, indigenous girls, and farm women from other non-Anglo cultures are often more difficult to discern within an historical record dominated by literate English-speaking voices, but there are studies that have specifically attempted this task with varying degrees of success (Jensen 1990; 1991). It is through these varying and often fragmented sources that the experiences of white rural girls and young women can be brought into focus, illuminating alternative perspectives on the colonial, frontier, and rural historical narrative.

Histories of rural girls can illuminate the operation of the discursive threads of agrarianism and domestic womanhood in these decades of social and technological change. In spite of the apparent similarities in the lives of rural daughters resident in these three locales, the project of comparing the histories of farm girls' labour in disparate geographical locations must be undertaken with sensitivity to a range of issues. A focus on white farm daughters allows possibilities for synthesis and comparison while remaining sensitive to the social, environmental, and cultural differences in these girls' lives. Nineteenth-century colonial cultures, as demonstrated by many rural historians, were not homogenous and this cultural heterogeneity needs to be recognised within any comparative study. Placing rural girlhood within the comparative context allows the scholar not only to appreciate the differences between girls' lives in disparate locations, but also to identify and understand the similarities created by such factors as family pressures, cultural expectations and the agricultural economy.

THE FARMING CONTEXT

In the late nineteenth and early twentieth century, New Zealand and Australia were in the midst of economic transformation. These countries were becoming more urban, but their economic foundations still rested firmly upon agriculture. The way in which farmers in both Australia and New Zealand filled their labour needs, was to use their wives, daughters, and sons. As late as the mid-1920s, 60 per cent of New Zealand's farmers worked their lands entirely with the labours of their families (Brooking 1992). In economies where labour was both scarce and expensive, and where few could afford machinery or to hire extra hands, a family-based labour system was the logical, time-honoured solution.

During the same period, farmers in the American Midwest were in a similar situation. While the crop mix on farms in the United States, Australia, and New Zealand was different, the way in which families produced those crops was very similar. In order to grow and raise these cash crops, in addition to providing items for home consumption, farm families relied upon their own exertions. This conformed to an ethic valuing work and a belief in 'making do' or doing without (Neth 1995). Additionally, given the uncertainty of farm incomes, as well as the expense of labour relative to the selling price of farm produced goods, for most families it made more economic sense to make use of the labours of women and children than to hire labourers. Thus, there were similarities between life on farms in the U.S. Midwest, Australia, and New Zealand.

There were, of course, differences in the experiences of farming girls and women in these locations. Very different histories of colonisation and agricultural development underpinned these women's presence on the land. Differences between farming families were also apparent where communities were divided by wealth and by the stage of development of their farms. Levels of hired labour were contingent on wealth, but many farming families relied on the assistance of neighbours and kin, and only occasionally on seasonal labour such as shearers or threshers. The various stages of farm settlement meant that some girls were involved in clearing scrub and forest, hauling logs and cutting ferns, while others lived on farms that had long been cleared.

Those who have studied farm life in these locations have discussed the values that prevailed among farm parents. Neth (1995), in her study of farms in the U.S. Midwest, has found that farm parents valued hard work and usefulness in their children. Through work, they taught their children the values and skills necessary to a career in agriculture. They held these values for girls as well as boys, although there is evidence that ethnicity influenced family adherence to gendered notions of appropriate labour (Neth 1995; Salamon 1992). New Zealand also welcomed, and indeed expected, the contributions of daughters; training for a 'useful life' began in childhood. As a part of an urbanising western world where the womanly ideal generally meant genteel domesticity, and where childhood was increasingly defined as a time of school and play, rather than work, rural New Zealand, as well as the rural American Midwest, ran against the current. In Australia, however, debates in the rural press about the effects on children and threats to farm girls' 'womanliness' resulting from hard physical labour began early. In the early twentieth century, dairying was also singled out as an industry that involved the 'white slavery' of women and children (Lake 1985).

There were further differences in children's lives in these settler frontiers. Differing crop mixes caused a different balance of tasks for children, with dairying causing stresses that cash grains did not. The varying stage of settlement would have placed different strains on girls in different locations, although there might be as much variation within locations in Australia, New Zealand, or the United States as between the United States and the colonies. The legal position of children varied as well, with children in New Zealand and Australia generally being affected by compulsory schooling laws prior to those in the Midwest. Despite these differences, the similarities generated by the family economy and a value system emphasizing the importance and value of work, and hence children's 'usefulness', are worth exploring.

FARM GIRLS' WORK

Comparisons between the work roles of girls on family farms in these countries show an enormous similarity. There was some elasticity in contours of useful farm daughterhood in each location but to be a daughter was definitely to be a worker. The girls themselves seemed to understand that reality, and as one 11-year-old wrote to the children's page of New Zealand's *Otago Witness*, 'as we grow big we do not want to be idle' (*Otago Witness*, 24 August 1893). A daughter's industry did not have to be domestic, although that was often the case. The role of farm daughter was flexible enough to include nearly any work that was necessary, including some stereotypically male tasks, such as planting and reaping. Katie Currie's mother recorded Katie's work with her father: 'Daa clearing out drains, Katie stayed to clear away titree stumps in the swamp, very tired' (Currie, 14 March 1888). Girls' participation in heavy field work was particularly apparent at harvest time, and in homes where there were few sons or where they were absent (Toynbee 1995). Georgina Oswin's 1896 diaries show that the older girls, Fanny and Florry, aged 15 years and 21 years respectively, shared the domestic work, while her younger daughters, Ethel and Edith (often written of as Olive or Pud), aged 11 years and 7 years, worked on the farm and in the fields: 'I washed, Ethel went to Post, met Dada at Bandy, they brought home some horses. Harry, Davey, Erney, Dick and Olive cutting chaff' (Karney 1991). This usefulness began in early childhood, and extended throughout a daughter's years at home, sometimes into her twenties.

Young girls' letters to the children's pages of New Zealand's periodicals provide effective illustrations of the work expected of school-aged girls of eight to fourteen years, and the ways that work was represented in this public forum. On dairy farms, milking was nearly universal. Eleven-year-old Mercy Bachelor milked six cows, 14-year-old Crissy Hemingway milked three, and 9-year-old Gertie Sanders was just learning to milk. Gertie's father was a progressive man, and like some other fathers offered his daughter 'small weekly wages for milking' (*New Zealand Farmer* vol. 12, 2 February 1892; *New Zealand Farmer* vol. 16, 8 August 1896; *New Zealand Farmer* vol. 14, 5 May 1894). Daughters also picked potatoes, weeded, and gardened. Additionally, mothers often asked their daughters to assume child care burdens. Young Agnes Templeton, aged 9, wrote 'I have a pet calf, but I have not much time for petting it, as I nurse the baby for mother' (*Otago Witness*, 18 May 1899). Farm families were larger than average, and older daughters often cared for their younger siblings (Toynbee 1995; Myres 1988).

Greater age brought a proliferation of duties. In New Zealand, most girls left school before or upon completion of Standard Six (roughly equivalent to the eighth grade) and remained at home to help their parents.[2] Being 'at home' meant assuming an ever larger share of the work of the household. Alice McKenzie's diary, begun in her fifteenth year, bears witness to the tremendous amount and variety of work that a young woman might contribute to the family enterprise. Alice McKenzie grew up in Martin's Bay, an extremely isolated settlement on the southwestern coast of New Zealand's south island. She was one of five children, with an older sister and brother, as well as two younger brothers. When Alice was 16, her sister Helen married and moved to another remote settlement. Helen left all of her work to Alice, in addition to her existing chores. The burden was considerable.

Aside from the very heavy task of clearing bush, there was little around the farm or home that Alice McKenzie did not do. Within the household, nearly any task was within her purview. She washed, ironed, cooked, sewed, mended boots, and scrubbed floors and walls. When her brothers brought home fish, she cleaned and smoked them. She participated in dairying, the farm's major source of income, and was primarily responsible for butter making. Her role in the dairying operation included caring for the cattle, milking and churning, and scrubbing the milk house. She also spent hours chasing cows and calves when they inevitably strayed into the bush. Additionally, her outside chores included gardening, gathering wood, tending to the chickens, caring for the sheep and pigs, hauling water, and cutting grass. As an older daughter, Alice's tasks included also caring for her siblings. When her mother was away, she added to her daily routine teaching her brother Hugh his lessons (McKenzie, 4 December 1889).

The stories of New Zealand's girls are mirrored in those of the daughters of Australia. Mothers relied on daughters within farming households, and sisters upon each other, for practical assistance. In Molly McKay's Australian diary, Hannah and Essie were able to go on holidays because they could rely on their sisters to do the work. In the Field family, a large number of daughters in the household meant that the workload was lighter for each of them individually. The Oswin family consisted of eight children, four of whom were girls. The farm diary revealed the interdependence of the siblings. In September 1900, fifteen-year-old Fanny Oswin was keeping house and keeping the diary: 'Mother still in bed been sewing all day. I ironed and baked. Pants [her younger sister Ethel] housemaid.... 29 Sept. Father took Ethel down to the coach. Pud [her younger sister Olive] housemaid today.... Mother pretty bad today' (Karney 1991). The responsibilities of the household soon began to take their toll on Fanny and she wrote, 'I feel knocked up, think I'll collapse'. However, help was at hand: 'Pants came home this morning, much to my delight. She cleaned the house up, I washed, nearly pegged out with pains' (Karney 1991).

Maintaining the household during seasonal increases in farm work required sacrifices to be made. For example, education was often a low priority. In the McKay household, Alice was sometimes required to stay home from school to assist with the work: 'Boys cut chaff today and Alice had to stay at home to drive the horses' (McKay, 27 January 1898). The Oswin children also performed their myriad of duties sometimes at the expense of their schooling: 'Washed to day dont feel well got a pain in my side I kept Ethel home to help sent Olive to school [*sic*]' (Karney 1991). When families were in dire straits their children became vital wage-earners, usually on the farms of neighbours. Dorothy Adams recalled that her mother provided work for the daughter of a miner's wife whom 'poverty and worry' had worn down, but without the desired result: 'One of the girls came and did the washing for mother, spending her meagre wages on a piece of bright print when the Indian Hawker drove his van to the 'creek'.' (Adams nd)

School-aged girls in America participated in the same types of work as those in Australia and New Zealand, and also described their work to children's publications. Many did outdoor work similar to that expected of boys. Annie Getchell of Brockway, Minnesota was proud of her work husking corn, which she had done since she was 9 years old (*American Young Folks*, vol. 3, 11 November 1877). Eight-year-old Margaret Carr of Nebraska herded cattle while her older male and female siblings husked the corn, while 10-year-old Myrtle Jordan and her sister were charged with responsibility for 750 sheep (*Nebraska Farmer*, 2 January 1907). Girls also reported plowing, running a hay rake, milking, and caring for livestock. At the same time as they learned the rudiments of outdoor work, parents also expected girls in this age group to learn the skills necessary to housekeeping so that they would be ready to assume their mothers' burdens if necessary. Eleven-year-old Ruth Landwehr stepped into her mother's shoes during an illness: 'When my mamma was sick of course I had to do the housework. I had to make supper. I also had to do the scrubbing, and thought it was fun to scrub. My papa killed a chicken and I dressed it and made mamma chicken soup. Mamma said it tasted good. She said I was doing pretty well' (*Nebraska Farmer*, 7 February 1912). Many other girls reported the same sorts of experiences with housekeeping, and lives full of work.

As was the case with New Zealand and Australia, American daughters gained responsibility with age. Lottie Norton, a farm daughter in central Kansas, illustrated the degree to which a family might become dependent upon the labour and skills of an older daughter. In 1879, she was 22, but still living at home. Her work included both outdoor and indoor chores. Outside, she gardened, planting potatoes and setting out cabbages. She also helped her father plant corn and sorghum. Corn planting, in particular, seemed to be a task that older girls shared with the men in their families. Although her chores often took her outdoors, Lottie Norton was, however, more likely to work indoors, cooking, cleaning, sewing, and sharing in the many activities necessary to keeping a family of twelve fed, clothed, and clean. Child care was an important part of her tasks, since there were five children between the ages of 1 and 9 years in residence. In addition to these burdensome chores, she also contracted with soldiers at Fort Larned to do their laundry. This brought needed wages to her cash-strapped family; most of her earnings she spent on her siblings and mother rather than herself. The best measure of the value of Lottie Norton's work is that when she married and moved to Illinois, her mother wrote in the family diary 'Nobody knows how much I miss Lottie' (Norton, 21 January 1881).

BOUNDARIES OF 'WOMANLY' WORK

Although young women in each of these places participated in most kinds of work on their families' farms, it is clear that many believed that there were boundaries beyond which white farm daughters' work should not go. After two young women wrote to the editor of the *Kansas Farmer* asserting their ability to do all varieties of agricultural work, and one of them further arguing that it was preferable to stereotypical women's work, a youngster calling himself 'Yankee Boy' wrote to chastise them. While he acknowledged their abilities, 'I have seen women do work that would astonish even this pair of young heroines,' he argued that girls should balance their labours between the home and the field. 'I...believe they should all learn the mysteries of housekeeping. It might come handy to them some time, if they should suddenly conclude to marry some young man that did not know how to cook and wash and bake' (*The Kansas Farmer,* vol. 9: 7, 1 April 1872; *The Kansas Farmer,* vol. 9: 19, 1 October 1872; *The Kansas Farmer,* vol. 9: 20, 15 October 1872; *The Kansas Farmer,* vol. 9: 22, 15 November 1872). Clearly, 'Yankee Boy' placed the value of domesticity to husbands above the value and pleasure of outdoor work to women and their families.

In a New Zealand publication, the debate went even further. A heated exchange carried out on the children's page of the *Otago Witness* illustrated the contested boundaries of acceptable female work roles. The debate carried on for thirteen months, so long that Dot, the page's editor, was forced to refuse to print any further letters on the subject. The catalyst for this discussion was the following letter, included on 21 July 1898. A young woman, later identified as 'Jessie C.', wrote: 'Dear Dot, I live 12 miles out of Gore on a farm, and my father has a lot of sheep and cattle. I can milk, and I often drive sheep. I was driving some the other day, and there was a lot of water across the road, and the sheep all stood still, and I could hardly get them to move. I can drive a team of horses, and I am going to learn to plough this season' (*Otago Witness*, 21 July 1898). If Jessie had limited herself to the previous statements, her letter most likely would have elicited little comment beyond Dot's praise for her industry. Milking and driving sheep were well within the realm of acceptable female occupations. Jessie, however, continued her letter. 'I have only killed one sheep yet, but I intend to kill more. Do you like the country, Dot? —Yours truly, J. (aged 14 years).' This final revelation was entirely too much for Dot. She replied, 'This letter comes from a girl, but I am very doubtful about a girl killing a sheep, whatever she may do as a drover. I keep out her name.—Dot'. Killing a sheep, not to mention feeling a sense of accomplishment for having done so, was beyond Dot's comprehension of acceptable female behaviour. Withholding the author's name indicated her extreme disapproval.

As might have been expected, 'J's' peers dug out their pencils and paper and wrote to 'Letters from Little Folks' overwhelming Dot with their commentary upon Jessie's actions. A young woman, E. D., characterized Jessie's sheep killing as 'most unwomanly, and not at all a thing to boast about' (*Otago Witness*, 1 December 1898). Boys, too, criticised Jessie's behaviour on the grounds that it was unfeminine. A writer who signed his name only as 'BOY' wrote 'Now, I object to Jessie C s stamp—a girl who is proud of being able to kill a sheep. I think it is very out of place and unmaidenly' (*Otago Witness*, 23 March 1899). Young Lindsay agreed, 'It is not right for girls to do such work as that' (*Otago Witness*, 18 May 1899).

These objections to Jessie's confession were perhaps predictable; killing anything larger than a chicken did not seem to be proper female behaviour.[3] Some writers, however, defended Jessie on the grounds of equal rights for girls but most of Jessie's defenders used a different concept to justify her actions: usefulness. Jessie lived in a world where killing a sheep just might be necessary. Irene certainly thought so, although she qualified her defence. 'It shows a girl's pluck when she can kill a sheep...it is not work for a girl, but sometimes a girl has to do such thing. I don't think it a ladylike accomplishment, certainly; still I admire her pluck and nerve' (*Otago Witness*, 25 May 1899). Young Kit perhaps put it best, writing 'Things on a farm would soon become mixed if the girls began to say that certain things were not girl's work. I have killed a poor calf to put it out of pain, when there was no one else to do it, and I don't consider myself hard-hearted' (*Otago Witness*, 15 June 1899).

The lines of womanly behaviour were drawn more firmly as the twentieth century went on. Increasingly young women were finding themselves caught between the material realities of their family's farms and labour needs and modern notions of womanliness. A debate remarkably similar to that in the *Otago Witness* took place in the Australian rural press twenty-five years later, when two unmarried farm daughters, 'Nancy' and 'Trixie', wrote letters declaring themselves a 'first-class farm hand' and 'father's right-hand man' (*Farmers' Advocate*, 26 September 1924 and 10 October 1924). A similar mixture of criticism of and support for these young women appeared in the press over the following months. Critics were concerned about the effects of such strenuous work on the reproductive health of women, reflecting the age difference between these Australian farm daughters and Jessie C, rather than a difference in discourse. One correspondent wrote: 'I venture an opinion that our farm girls' health and happiness is far more valuable to the nation, and their future homes, and careers of motherhood, than trying to imitate a young amazon...' (*Farmers' Advocate*, 24 October 1924).

Jessie C's defence of herself mirrored that of her highly practical peers, in terms of her utility to her family. Jessie had killed the sheep out of 'necessity,' and within a short time had killed another for the same reason: it simply had to be done. Similarly, 'Nancy', 'Trixie', and other young women who wrote in support of these farm daughters, justified their actions in terms of usefulness and a sense of duty to the family and the economic vulnerability of family farms such as these. 'Nancy' wrote: 'Perhaps I am old-fashioned and queer, but I greatly prefer work—even in a cow yard—to worry and fear of foreclosure' (*Farmers' Advocate*, 26 September 1924). Similarly, 'Happy' wrote of her experiences arguing, 'I did not do it to "imitate a young amazon"...I did it for love of mother and father and I would do so again if necessary' (*Farmers' Advocate*, 12 March 1926). These daughters appeared to be able to reconcile their role within the family economy with concepts of feminine behaviour through 'dutifulness'. As vigorous and willing daughters in farming households, it was their responsibility to work in the fields and pastures beside or in place of their fathers and sometimes brothers. If this led the farm daughter into 'unmaidenly' actions, she explained those actions in terms of her duty to the family and to the farm. While their behaviour would not have been acceptable in all families, and certainly raised eyebrows among their peers, it appears to have been permissible in these homes. Most young women did what was necessary and made themselves useful, although within somewhat more restricted boundaries.

This culture of 'usefulness' had its detractors and its disadvantages. Writings that were not for wide public consumption, such as diaries, alert us to the ways the girls themselves mitigated what could be a monotonous and arduous lifestyle. That this lifestyle could be arduous is evident from some women's personal writings. Rose Field wrote in her diary in March

1891 of the 'greatest event' of the year so far: the birth of her niece Ruby. Rose reflected on the baby's future from her own perspective as a 31-year old unmarried woman and the eldest daughter in a farming family:

> I rather pity Ruby being the eldest girl. Whether she will ever have any sisters will not be known for some time to come[.] My opinion is that she will be a fortunate girl if she does not have to[o] many altho they are very nice if there is plenty of money to help and educate them but if she has to work hard and help to sew and cook and work for them she will soon feel worn out and want to get married which will be perhaps out of the frying pan into the fire. (Field, 26 March 1891)

Debates in the rural press about the virtues and detractions of country life appeared as rural communities became increasingly concerned with the 'drift' to the cities. Young people, when asked for their opinions, replied that farm life entailed very hard work usually without economic reward. One farmer's daughter was reported as saying: 'I'd soon tell them why the country girl and boy get to the city as soon as they can! If you had to milk 3 gallons of milk to get eightpence and had to milk 50 cows morning and night because you could not get help, how would you stand it?' (*Farmers' Advocate*, 1 June 1922). As reported in girls' letters to the rural press some families attempted to mitigate this discontent by providing their children with independent incomes, often by setting aside a milk can for each child and children also gained independent incomes from the rearing and sale of livestock. 'Usefulness' and fulfilment of duty were not always their own reward.

CONCLUSION

The cases of young women in New Zealand, Australia, and the Midwestern United States in the late nineteenth and early twentieth centuries lend weight to two assertions: that the gender roles espoused in the rural idyll became more pronounced and rigid as the twentieth century wore on; and that young women contested those gender roles using mechanisms of duty to the family and economic necessity. In the larger United States society, the ideal of separate spheres for women and men seemed well entrenched, yet those in farm country persisted in older beliefs that labour was honourable and right for women, whether it was in the home or the fields. New Zealand, given its unique settlement history, valued the usefulness of its farm women, both young and old. Farm daughters in nineteenth-century Australia, similarly, lived in households that operated on modified ideas of family economy. Their labour, always expected, was sometimes rewarded economically through a small independent income or in larger ways through inheritance. Working within a framework of similar values, girls began to work early, and continued to do so as long as they remained in the family home. Family demands might tie them to the kitchen, or might as easily require that they herd, plant, and harvest. It seems equally clear, however, that usefulness had its boundaries. By the early twentieth century, in all three locations, there were increasing pressures to re-cast young farm women's lives and experiences to fit ideas of modernity and proper women's roles. In colonies where femininity had been epitomised by 'usefulness', that usefulness had to be increasingly tempered by young women's attention to their biological duties as future mothers and by state/national desires to present their female population as leisured as a sign of prosperity. What was expected increasingly was a balance between stereotypically male and female work, and a belief that girls should exhibit domesticity and femininity, even while being willing and able to carry out the most arduous of chores. 'Usefulness' waned as 'dutiful' behaviour became the more acceptable manifestation of farm girls' femininity. The work expected remained, nevertheless, remarkably similar.

NOTES

1. Reprinted in shortened form from *Journal of Rural Studies* vol. 18: 135–143. Hunter, K. and Riney-Kehrberg, P. 'Rural daughters in Australia, New Zealand and the United States: An historical perspective'. Copyright (2002), with permission from Elsevier.
2. Most girls did not receive a secondary education. Even among those who did, and therefore had the option of further education, clerical work, or other trades, a 1925 survey indicated that half went home to help their parents upon completion of secondary schooling (Fry 1985; Wimshurst 1980–1981).
3. For example, when animals, from kittens to cattle, had to be killed on the McKenzie farm, Alice McKenzie's brothers did the job.

6 Reflecting on contexts and identities for young rural lives

Naomi Bushin, Nicola Ansell, Hanne K. Adriansen, Jaana Lähteenmaa, and Ruth Panelli

INTRODUCTION

Complementing the preceding four case studies, this chapter reflects more generally on the formation and articulation of young people's identities in the context of rural places. Salient points from each of the preceding chapters are drawn together, further discussed, and situated alongside wider research. The chapters in this part of the book have shown the diversity of young people's experiences of rurality as well as highlighting differences within and between childhoods. The definition of 'rural' has been shown not to be the most uniformly important defining feature of the places which the young people occupied, and the chapters have demonstrated that young people may perform or be ascribed many identities other than that of 'rural young people'. These matters and wider implications surrounding contexts and identities are expounded in the following sections. The first section revisits the notion of contexts, pointing to the diversity and complexity of rural contexts that need to be appreciated beyond the existing literature. The second section then turns to consider generic observations surrounding identity—noting the ways rural youth studies can be more fully engaged with wider conceptual approaches to identity. The third section then draws these concerns together, recording the interconnections between contexts and identities.

CONTEXTS

Ansell (2005) has highlighted the immediate and wider cultural and politico-economic contexts that shape young people's lives in Majority world countries. This complements Panelli's (2002) identification of local and broader conditions that distinguish the rural settings young people experience across Majority and Minority worlds (viz.: cultural, political, economic, social, and environmental). While great diversity exists across rural settings, this diversity is often overlooked, particularly because of the tendency to contrast rurality with urbanity. Rural locations are regarded as sites of traditional cultural practices, of primary production, of the maintenance of more conservative political structures, and the existence of diverse (sometimes inaccessible) biophysical environments (Giddings and Yarwood 2005; O. Jones 1999; Matthews et al. 2000; Ward 1990). In her discussion of British rural childhoods, Valentine (2004: 23) states: 'The countryside is popularly imagined to be a safe, carefree place that offers a sense of belonging and an escape from the dangers of the city'. This imagining can be seen to pertain to rural areas in diverse settings such as Bolivia, England, and Tanzania, with the countryside being valued and romanticized for the perceived benefits of safety, freedom, space, childhood fun, socio-cultural belonging, and for some, socio-economic status (O. Jones 1999; Klocker; and Punch this volume).

The idealised definition of rural areas is problematic, however, and deconstruction of the category 'rural' has shown that many different ruralities exist (Hoggart and Buller 1987; Mormont 1990; Philo 1992). For this reason, other distinctions are frequently more meaningful; for example, between mountain and lowlands (Ansell and van Blerk, this volume) or desert and delta (Adriansen and Madsen 2004). Moreover, while the biophysical world is often thought to be 'closer' to people's livelihoods in rural areas, the sheer range of environmental conditions that may exist means that young people encounter rural experiences stretching from the extremes of severe winters and long summer days in the high latitudes through to unrelenting tropical heat and associated challenges (e.g. de Bruijn and van Dijk 1995; Waara 2002).

Across this diversity, rural settings are understood as cultural and economic constructions of the wider societies and nations in which young people live. Irrespective of whether they are areas of poverty, agrarian productivity, or bucolic idealism, rural environments reflect the historic and contemporary ways by which rural places are embedded in wider politico-economic processes and cultural systems (Ansell 2005; Elder and Conger 2000; Hunter and Riney-Kehrburg this volume; O. Jones 1999; Katz 1991). A striking example is provided by the 'New Lands' in the Egyptian desert (see Box 6.1). These lands reflect Egypt's interconnected goals of economic and environmental development, as well as the aspirations of graduate parents wishing to provide a space of opportunity for their offspring. The Egyptian case, together with those documented in Chapters 2 to 5, reveal a variety of contexts like those shown in Table 1.1 (Chapter 1). Together, they show that physical environments shape young people's lives by providing material resources for food and shelter, as well as specific challenges based on distances, seasonal weather, and rural demographic/service issues that often result in less access to services and opportunities (see also Dunkley and Panelli; Schäfer; and Punch this volume). Secondly, economic processes in local rural settings—and their connection with wider, uneven political–economic relations—produce a continuum of work and material experiences for rural youth ranging from agricultural and exchange/

market labour (Ansell 2005; Elder and Conger 2000; Punch 2000; Wallace et al. 1994), through to their participation in cultural consumption and advancement via education, recreation, and technology (Carpena-Méndez; Laegran; Dunkley and Panelli; Schäfer this volume). Thirdly, social and cultural dimensions shape young people's experiences of subjection to both adult values and expectations, as well as their institutional roles (for example, to support the household; adhere to gender relations; advance themselves educationally; or conduct themselves in appropriate behaviour). Together (and as demonstrated in the previous four chapters) these contexts provide the fabric with which young people generate their lifeworlds: navigating migration; creating a sense of identity through their passion for cars; or exploring existing and future gendered lives.

The settings and systems contextualizing young people's rural lives cannot be neatly disaggregated for analysis, nor can they be assessed either as contexts of poverty and need, or of productivity and affluence. Rather, continua of contrasting axes must be recognized in order to develop nuanced understandings of the conditions that young people experience. The ways in which these axes of environmental attributes, economic processes, social structures, and politico-cultural systems intersect in composite ways must also be acknowledged. One example of this is Laegran's discussion of how relative affluence and diverse transport and technological infrastructure in mid-Norway provide opportunities for somewhat socially marginalized young men to build identities and skills via a specific youth culture that is car-based. In contrast, Ansell and van Blerk have shown how the exigencies of rural production, household structure, and cultural origin produce emotionally charged and actively performed lives, with children experiencing belonging or loss. Moreover, this latter example highlights the dynamism and fluidity of contexts.

For future nuanced analyses of young rural lives, a deeper appreciation of dynamic contexts is required. Hunter and Riney-Kehrburg's chapter reminds us that these issues will have nuanced historic forms and, even in current rural settings, contextual dynamism may have diverse origins, for example: bio-physical processes; local socio-demographic change; or wider politico-economic processes—such as Carpena-Méndez's chapter has shown. Nevertheless, greater attention is needed to understand the complexity and fluidity of the rural conditions young people encounter. When a dynamics-oriented analysis of rural contexts is made, it is possible to identify the intersecting nature of diverse contexts and implications. The case of Kaustekko and Kivivaara in Finland highlights this possibility (Box 6.2). Finnish rural contexts are shown to be diverse and fluid; the contrasts between Kaustekko and Kivivaara indicate how differing economic conditions, cultural life, and social connections have produced contrasting histories and contemporary contexts for young people. In the case of Kaustekko, young people draw on the intersecting economic and cultural dynamics that are producing contemporary agricultural productivity, cultural heritage,

Box 6.1 Rural childhoods in Egypt's 'New Lands'—Hanne K. Adriansen

Egypt is primarily a desert land but due to the Nile River the area has had a long history as a prosperous agricultural country. The arable land along the river and in the delta only makes up 4 per cent of Egypt's land area. As this is also where the 70 million Egyptians live, the fertile arable land is very densely populated and agricultural land is decreasing due to encroachment from urbanisation. Consequently, the government has tried to expand the arable area for the past fifty years by reclaiming desert land primarily on the fringes of the delta (see Figure 6.1). Since 1987, the 'Mubarak Youth Project' has been responsible for land reclamation and community development in desert lands. This complex politico-environmental undertaking has created the 'New Lands'—a unique rural landscape with a specific socio-cultural group. Only young adults who are graduates and have an agricultural background are eligible to settle in this area. This requirement produces a homogenous demographic group (in a country marked by class, gender, and other social differences) and settlers' children are growing up in a highly planned environment.

This example illustrates an extreme version of culturally constructed rural contexts for children, yet also it resonates with rural experiences in other cultures. Although there were quite diverse perceptions of life in the 'New Lands', research identified three core descriptions: there is space; the air is clean; and it is peaceful and quiet. This contrasts with the old lands, which are described as crowded, dirty, stressful, and noisy. Furthermore, many settlers noted their higher material standard of living in the 'New Lands'. All aspects were valued for raising children. The 'New Lands' were narrated as a 'space of opportunity' (Adriansen 2003). In this way, the 'New Lands' compare with many of the idyllic perceptions of rural childhood noted in Britain (O. Jones 1999; Little and Austin 1996; Valentine 1997a).But, realities in the Mubarak villages are more complex than the ideal imaginings. Although the settler graduates gain an opportunity to own their own land, they have to live in a physical and socio-economic context that is very different from where they originate. For instance they live in nuclear families far away from relatives who would traditionally share childcare responsibilities. This, together with women's involvement in paid employment, means kindergartens are regularly used. Thus 'New Lands' children are exposed to new experiences and to values, norms, and behaviours that differ from those in the old lands. In addition, school-aged children also face some of the same issues experienced by other rural populations. Schools with

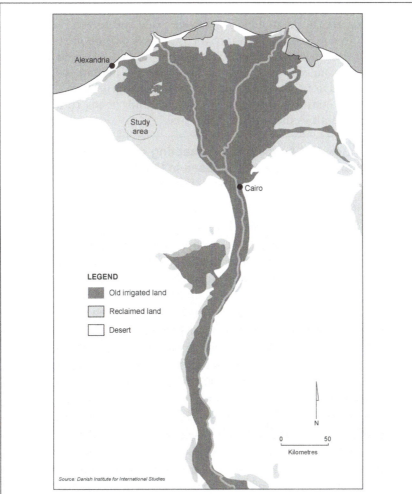

Figure 6.1 'New Lands' study area.

too few teachers and a lack of good teacher–pupil interaction are wide-spread problems in Egypt (Elkamel 2005), and in the 'New Lands' the high value placed on education means that parents regularly report a lack of good schools and absentee teachers. In some cases households subsequently divided to enable mothers and older children to return to the old lands in the hope of the children gaining better education. This contrasts sharply with the aspirations of settling in the 'New Lands' where many settlers value the environment and opportunities in this created rural space. In short, while the 'New Lands' become a 'space of poverty' for some parents, many still perceive the desert villages as a 'space of opportunity' especially for giving their children a good start in life (see also Adriansen [2003] and Adriansen and Madsen [2004]).

and a healthy tourism sector. They narrate their area as a vibrant, living, and growing area—one in which they have pride and to which they attribute value. In contrast, in Kivivaara the processes of economic and social decline and the loss of a lively political history produce a layered landscape of loss, pessimism, and even shame. This example reminds us that even within broad Majority or Minority world categories, rurality is a dynamic and complexly constituted context which surrounds young rural lives and textures the identities they are given, or take.

Box 6.2: Aspects of intersecting contexts and identity formation processes in the lives of young rural Finnish people—Jaana Lähteenmaa

Finland is the world's northernmost agricultural country, with the lowest population density in Europe. The winters are cold and long, and the length of the growing season is much shorter than in Central Europe. The number of people living in rural areas and obtaining their livelihood from agriculture shrank considerably in the 1960s, and has been declining gradually since. In northern parts of rural Finland especially, inhabitants have to rely on one local centre. However, they have access to several cities within a few hours' drive. Young people in these rural areas have access to television, the Internet, and telephones, and thus are more aware than ever of the lifestyles and career possibilities in big cities (Helve et al. 2000; Waara 2002.). Recent research has explored young people's desire to remain versus their desire to leave marginal rural areas of Finland and Sweden; especially those areas that are experiencing high levels of depopulation (Waara 1996; Soininen 2001; Tuhkunen 2002). This evidence suggests that an overwhelming majority of rural young people move to locations where they perceive there to be opportunities for self-development, work, and a 'better future'. Typically, young people in rural areas are dissatisfied with available education and employment opportunities, which are quite unevenly distributed, especially in marginal regions of eastern and northern Finland. Interestingly, girls often desire to move away more than boys (Waara 1996; Helve et al. 2000; Tuhkunen 2002). Both vibrant and declining rural localities occur in Finland and young people in Kivivaara and Kaustekko respectively show the implications of these conditions when describing their thoughts Lähteenmaa (2006). Kivivaara (in central eastern Finland) has experienced out-migration since the 1960s, resulting in an uneven demographic profile and severe economic problems for the municipality. Located over 100 km from the nearest city, Kivivaara is surrounded by vast forests, and young people note that it is too 'far from everything'. However, young people also love their home parish and are worried, even anxious, for its future: '...this place will disappear, and at last its name, also. It disappears not just from the map but also from the minds of people [...] it makes me sad.' In contrast, Kaustekko (in central western Finland) has better economic prospects than Kivivaara. Less out-migration has taken place here and agriculture is more viable for geographical reasons. The cultural sector is also vital, with a strong folk music tradition and international folk music festivals every summer. Many of the young people aged 15 to 16 years have a vision of Kaustekko expanding in population terms in the future—although its population is fairly stable. The majority of young people in Kivivaara are not proud of their area: some say they 'hate' it or 'feel ashamed' of it. However, some young people did express pride when referring to its very pure nature and its good hunting and fishing possibilities. In Kaustekko, young people's pride comes from other sources: many note the famous folk-music festival, and report that most local people play musical instruments. In Kivivaara, young people express anxiety about the bad public image of their area whereas in Kaustekko young people mention its good public image. These two cases illustrate the diverse contexts surrounding one's local identity as well as the emotions that may affect their future decisions to stay or leave the areas (see also Lähteenmaa 2006).

IDENTITIES

As well as recognizing rurality as complexly constituted, others have noted that meanings of childhood and youth also vary over space and time (Jenks 1996). There have been calls to recognize differences within and between childhoods (Philo 2000b; Valentine 2003), and the preceding four chapters address this call. They highlight the diversity of rural childhoods and have shown that there is no 'one' rural childhood identity but that children and young people develop and negotiate their identities in different ways and at different times in rural places. Processes of identity formation have been explored in the previous chapters, the limits to young people's agency have been recognized (see also Part II of this volume) and, building on the work of Valentine (2003), the ways in which other social identities such as gender, class, and race intersect with youth identities has been highlighted. Liechty (1995: 167) points out that individual identities are multiple, and may be claimed or ascribed; lived or imagined; thus: 'a person may have many identities encompassing many ways of being, within and between which there is no necessary consistency or logic'.

While Part II of this volume will note that there are limits to young people's agency, children and youth nonetheless actively engage in constructing identities for themselves. For Giddens (1991: 53): 'Self-identity is not a distinctive trait, or even a collection of traits possessed by the individual. It is the self as reflexively understood by the person in terms of his or her biography'. Young people are believed to make their own biographies by deliberately engaging in 'identity work' (Cohen and Ainley 2000; Hall et al. 1999). This process is reflected in the previous four chapters. In Laegran's chapter, for instance, young men performed masculine identities by working on their cars and racing up and down the street outside the Internet café where they did not feel welcome. This example, and Dunkley and Panelli's chapter, suggest how some 'biographical projects' can include uneven power relations, even marginalisation (Valentine 2000). Nonetheless, identity construction is a dynamic process, and in postmodern societies many individuals strive deliberately to avoid fixity of identity (G. Jones 1999).

Ackroyd and Pilkingon (1999: 447) point out that 'a process of representation is central to identity formation'. Young people construct their identities in part through the discourses that are available to them. Somers (1994) describes four dimensions of narrative that people draw on in undertaking identity work: ontological narratives (used by individual social actors to make sense of their lives); public narratives (used by institutions varying from family, workplace, church, government, nation); metanarratives (e.g. progress, decadence, enlightenment—built on concepts that are themselves abstractions); and conceptual narratives (constructed by social researchers). The latter three sets of narratives are constructed principally by adults, and they are also employed by adults in projecting identities onto the young. This makes it particularly important to engage with young people and explore their lifeworlds from their own perspectives. It is also significant that these three forms of narrative are widely exported from Minority to Majority world contexts, thus the narratives through which young people come to understand themselves and their place in the world may conflict with the discourses through which others in their society interpret their lives. Pribilsky (2001) and Hollos (2002) chart the changing expectations relating to childhood among rural families in Ecuador and Tanzania. While neither study presents direct evidence of how imported Minority world discourses inflect children's own accounts of their subject positions, both highlight the impact of changing practices on children's engagement with, and sense of belonging to, their households and communities. They provide examples of identity as deeply interwoven with immediate and wider contexts.

As Ansell and van Blerk's chapter noted, identity is not entirely an outcome of reflexively constructed biography or external dynamics. Instead, the significance of action/performance, and the role of the body in identity construction among young people has attracted attention (e.g. Dwyer 1999; Frost 2003; see also Hunter and Riney-Kehrberg; and Jones this volume). Furthermore, affective place relationships also influence children's emerging sense of self-identity (Spencer and Woolley 2000). This has been shown in G. Jones' (1999), and Ansell and van Blerk's studies (this volume)—where children's pleasures are acknowledged as they play or work and build a sense of place or belonging (in England, Malawi, and Lesotho).

Children's identification with other people has also been shown to be important. Bagnoli (2003) proposes a relational model of identity construction, observing that young people construct their identities as much through relationships with others as through deliberate differentiation. Whilst adults may cling to the notion of childhood through postmodernity (Beck 1992), children's relationships with their peers often lie at the heart of their childhood experience, with group affiliation supplying emotional security, a source of status and of reputation (Cotterell 1996). Thus friends and social networks are very important in young people's development of identity: 'As they grow up, young people move from a situation in which their identity is ascribed or derived from their families of origin, to a situation where identity is negotiated between the self and the other' (G. Jones 1999: 2). This can be seen in the chapters on Ansell and van Blerk's, research (Chapter 2) and Laegran's study (Chapter 3), with people (and peers) being more important than physical places. It was not necessarily a distinctive rural identity that young people sought to develop but rather a sense of connection and identifiable life with both people and rural places, thus enabling them to develop a sense of social and local belonging. Identity development also may be a mutual process whereby young people consciously or subconsciously alter their behaviours and identities in relation to one another. Ansell and van Blerk discuss migrant children's everyday ways of 'getting used to' a new place. These children had not consciously changed their behaviours or identities in order to 'fit in' with their peers; rather identifying with 'country ways' had been a gradual and sub-conscious process through everyday practices.

RELATIONSHIPS BETWEEN CONTEXTS AND IDENTITIES

As Dixon and Durrheim (2000: 27) remark: 'questions of "who we are" are often intimately related to questions of "where we are"'. The chapters in this first Part, show that contexts greatly affect the construction of identity among young people. Identities are prescribed, resisted, and reconstructed in multiple and dynamic ways by young people, but always in relation to contexts that are complex, multi-scalar, and changing. Carpena-Méndez's analysis of Mexican youth is a graphic example of these diverse interconnections. But each of the past four chapters has indicated how young people's identities in rural contexts reflect the bio-physical and socio-economic realities of the environments, as well as their cultural (or imagined) geographies, and the emotional ties that they hold.

The physical environment is a notable feature of most rural settings, and forms a backdrop against which rural young people live their lives. The great distances between human settlements inspire in some young people in Finland (Box 6.2) a sense of isolation (all the more acute when distance is partially overcome by technologies such as television, mobile phones, and the Internet). In addition, 'encountering nature' is often important to children's lives (e.g. Matthews and Limb 1999; Jones, this volume). For herdboys in Lesotho, learning to negotiate the harsh mountain conditions, particularly in winter, is fundamental to their identity as residents of particular rural communities (Ansell and van Blerk this volume).

Superimposed on, and partly determined by the biophysical environment, are a variety of socio-economic processes that again shape young people's lives. In some contexts there is no option but to take on the role of worker at a young age. This is more common among the rural youth of the Majority world than among urban youth—and even for young people in the Minority world, work is more often a feature of rural life than it is for those in urban settings. In the Minority world, however, it is more common for young people to practice particular patterns of consumption to mark out their identities as similar to, or different from, their peers, as among the 'råners' and Internet users in Laegren's chapter. The availability of commodities for consumption in rural settings can be more restrictive, and is very often distinct from that in urban environments.

The patterns of production and consumption that are found in rural settings reflect socio-economic processes taking place at a range of scales from the household to global level institutions and financial transactions. They also reflect cultural expectations: young people migrating to rural communities in Lesotho are expected to work, in part because there is a widespread social expectation, particularly in rural areas, that children should contribute materially to their households. Similarly, Hunter and Riney-Kehrburg (this volume) show the historic ties between productive and reproductive work and gendered kinship relations, where identities as 'daughters' have been articulated with diverse labour expectations.

Many children in rural areas may have spatial and symbolic freedom in the countryside, as a response to the widespread discursive construction of a 'rural idyll' (see Jones, this volume) and this allows them to build their own identities and geographies. A close relationship to nature is considered to be part of an ideal childhood (Gullestad 1989, cited in Wiborg 1999) and the countryside has been held up as the ideal environment in which to raise children (Bunce 1994; Short 1991). Indeed, it has been posited that families migrate to the English countryside 'for the sake of the children' (Little and Austin 1996; Woods 2005). This notion can also be seen in Adriansen's discussion of migration to the Mubarak villages, Egypt (Box 6.1), with families seeking a better life. But the chapters in this section have shown also that children are able to develop their own identities through their interactions with each other and rural spaces. Children may develop their own identities 'under the cover' of adult construction of rurality, and thus challenge the constraints of rural areas by creating their own spaces and identities in rural places (Jones this volume; Nairn et al. 2003; Panelli et al. 2002). Young people's identities in rural places have been shown to be fluid and not necessarily coherent with adults' imaginings of country childhood identities. Thus the need to explore children's and young people's own experiences of rurality and how this influences the formation and development of their identities from their own perspectives have been shown to be paramount.

Feelings of belonging to place also can be seen to be important in young people's formation and negotiation of identity: attachment to place fulfils people's emotional needs and helps people to develop and maintain their identities (Kaiser and Fuhrer 1996). For example, the children in Chapter 2 identified strongly with their villages; and in Chapter 3, 'råners' associated with the local garage forecourt, whereas other young people identified with the Internet café. Differences between childhood and youth identities can be seen with young people operating their own exclusionary spatial practices according to the spaces with which they identified both collectively and individually.

Experience of place is itself dynamic, not constant (Hart 1979), and young people's identities have been revealed as dynamic and changing depending on dimensions of both time and space. Mobility, too, is important. As well as questions of 'who we are' being intimately related to 'where we are' (Dixon and Durrheim 2000) it may also be crucial to consider 'where children are from' or 'where children have been'. Individuals, worldwide, are less tied to places than was the case in the past, and 'place-based identities among migrants cannot be reduced to one's current geographic location' (Silvey and Lawson 1999: 125). Thus 'the ethnic absolutism of 'root' metaphors, fixed in place, is replaced by mobile 'route' metaphors' (Pile and Thrift 1995b: 10). Migrant children may develop feelings of 'multi-belonging' (Parr and Philo 1995; Kaufmann 2002; van Blerk 2005) and even experience both assimilation and marginalisation simultaneously (Lawson 2000).

The instability that some of the children discussed in Ansell and van Blerk's research has some parallels with youth migration intentions in rural Scotland. There, G. Jones (1999) reveals that a family history of migration can increase young people's likelihood to out-migrate, whereas a family history of rootedness can increase young people's desire to remain living in a rural area. Identifying with their rural places was not simply a matter of personal choice for these young people but also depended on being accepted by the wider community. Young people who dissented from the norms of the community tended to out-migrate, whereas those who conformed remained. Thus young people's identities are mutually constituted and, although they may have an opportunity to express agency, are also constrained by external factors.

Ní Laoire (2000) states that if migration is part of long-term biography formation, then migration decision making by rural youth must be conceptualized as being bound up with all other transitions and decisions that occur in youth. Similar to Laegran's study of masculinity in rural Norway (this volume), differences between masculine and feminine identities can be drawn out from youth migration studies. Irish young women in Ní Laoire's (2000) research out-migrated to escape the male-dominated 'pub, football and church culture'; similarly, in Helve et al.'s (2000) study, Finnish and Swedish young women were more anxious to leave their rural villages than were the young men. Some children and young people may want to identify with where they are, others may not, and further still, young people may develop identities that are hybrids of places.

CONCLUSIONS

This chapter has drawn together the discussion of young people's contexts and how these relate to their identities. It has also shown the importance of exploring young people's experiences of rural places and their sense of attachment to these places from their own perspectives. Adultist constructions and imaginings of both childhood and rurality may obfuscate rather than clarify. Thus the need to research with children, ensuring that we attain their own perspectives, is paramount if we are to appreciate their rural (and other) lives and performed identities, and if we are to adequately acknowledge the multiple and dynamic contexts they navigate. But attention to contexts and identities will be but one part of a more nuanced research agenda, for as young people negotiate their contexts and explore the possibilities (and limits) of diverse identities they actively create everyday actions and experience, more or less constrained forms of agency. Thus, it is to questions of agency and action that Part II of this volume turns.

Part II
Agency and everyday action

7 An example of 'thin' agency
Child domestic workers in Tanzania

Natascha Klocker[1]

Child domestic workers are children 'under the age of 18 who work in other people's households doing domestic chores, caring for children, and running errands, among other tasks' (UNICEF 1999: 2). They can be paid in cash or kind and are employed by (and usually live in the homes of) adults who are not their parents (Kifle 2002: 3–4). Domestic work undertaken by children (abbreviated here as CDW) is particularly prominent in Majority world countries where it thrives because of its informal and unregulated nature. Although child domestic workers are usually employed in urban areas, their lives represent a face of rural childhoods in the Majority world because most are born, socialized, and educated in rural areas, and it is the poverty of this rural 'lived space'[2] that overwhelmingly drives them into child labour.[3]

This chapter focuses on recent research centered on 'employing' three former child domestic workers (aged 14, 16, and 18) to be researchers and to undertake an investigation into CDW in the Iringa Region of Tanzania (see Figure 7.1). It draws predominantly on qualitative material gained from ethnographic observations; focus group discussions (FGDs) with rural primary school students and former child domestic workers; written 'essay' responses elicited from the focus group participants; and information gained during various exercises (including a questionnaire) undertaken with the three young researchers.

At the outset, I wish to clarify that I am cognizant that my own perceptions of children's rights, gender, and child labour have been formed in a Minority world context. I did not go to Tanzania with the goal of eliminating CDW, or of holding onto the 'northern myths of childhood as a time of play and innocence' (Robson 2004a: 228). Rather, my intention was to work with these young researchers towards a locally relevant and workable approach to addressing situations of abuse and exploitation within this type of employment. The objective of this chapter is to begin to unravel the complicated ways in which rural Tanzanian girls experience their context and assert their agency in their everyday actions and, more specifically, in the various stages of 'becoming' and 'un-becoming' child domestic workers.

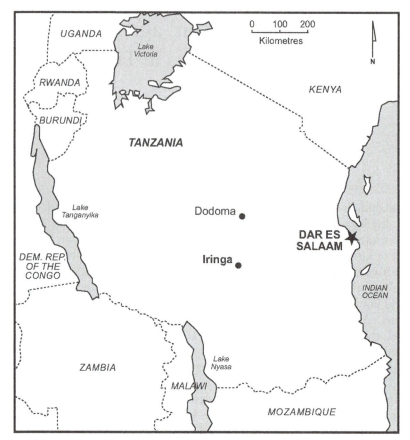

Figure 7.1 Location of study area (Iringa) in Tanzania.

The focus of this chapter is on girls because CDW is highly feminized in the Tanzanian context.

'THICK' AND 'THIN' AGENCY

Throughout this chapter, the terms 'thin' and 'thick' agency are referred to.[4] This distinction fits within Giddens's (1984) structuration theory, as it avoids the creation of a structure/agency dualism; and within a Foucauldian perspective of power, as it acknowledges that power is relational and that even the seemingly disempowered possess an ability to act (Foucault 1982). The distinction between 'thick' and 'thin' agency has been adopted because of my reluctance to be dismissive of the pressures placed on rural Tanzanian girls, by poverty and various socio-cultural factors, to enter (and to stay in) potentially appalling employment situations. At the same time, their agency in this process cannot be completely denied, as they understand and actively negotiate the expectations and power relations that surround them while making decisions aimed at improving their own lives and those of their families (Holloway and Valentine 2000b; Punch 2002b). Set against this background, 'thin' agency refers to decisions and everyday actions that are carried out within highly restrictive contexts, characterized by few viable alternatives. 'Thick' agency is having the latitude to act within a broad range of options. It is possible for a person's agency to be 'thickened' or 'thinned' over time and space, and across their various relationships (see also Bell and Punch, this volume). Structures, contexts, and relationships can act as 'thinners' or 'thickeners' of individuals' agency, by constraining or expanding their range of viable choices. Between 'thick' and 'thin' agency there is a continuum along which *all* people (including rural young people) are placed as actors with varying and dynamic capacities for voluntary and willed action. These terms are preferred (rather than referring to constrained or expanded capacities to exercise agency) because they convey a sense of the 'layering' or 'eroding' effects of the multiplicity of factors that affect young people's agency.

WHAT 'THINS' THE AGENCY OF TANZANIAN CHILD DOMESTIC WORKERS?

In this chapter, age, gender, 'tribe',[5] and poverty are identified and discussed as 'thinners' of Tanzanian girls' agency—before, during, and after their engagement with CDW. It is important to keep in mind that all of these categories inevitably overlap and reinforce each other in complex ways, 'weav[ing] together a series of relations and expectations' that must be negotiated (Panelli 2002: 116). Significantly, 'rurality' is omitted as an independent category because all of the other categories are *automatically* examined through the lens of rural life, which is the 'norm' in Tanzania where only 23 per cent of the population lives in urban settings (Government of Tanzania 2002). While acknowledging that many of the socio-cultural and economic issues discussed in this chapter are also present in other Majority world settings, analysis here is restricted to Tanzania.

Age: Respect for elders and intergenerational responsibility

In Tanzania, it is expected that a younger person (of any age) use a specific, respectful greeting (shikamoo) for those who are older. When a young child says 'shikamoo', it is often accompanied by an action whereby the adult bends down towards the child who then places his or her hands on the adult's head. This greeting and action are symbolic of a powerfully hierarchical age-structure:

> Children in Tanzania have extremely little power or say in negotiating their relationships with adults...children know that there is no place for their views or feelings—they are to do what they are told and accept what comes without question. (Rajani 1998: no page number)

Various childhood literatures, referring to both the Majority and Minority worlds, are rich with discussions of hierarchical adult–child relationships and of the seemingly universal[6] age-based marginalization of young people (Fyfe 1989; Mabala and Kamazima 1995; Rwezaura 1998). In this volume alone, there are abundant examples of the ways in which Majority and Minority world rural children and young people are exposed to inequitable intergenerational power relationships. In the case of Tanzania, the submissiveness with which children *visibly* carry themselves vis-à-vis adults, signals an adult–child relationship in which it is difficult for children to assert themselves—even when harmful actions are being perpetrated against them (Kopoka 1999; Rajani 1998, 2000). 'Silencing' of children and denying them agency is apparent at all levels of Tanzanian society. Although the United Nations Convention on the Rights of the Child (UNCRC Articles 12 to 16) and African Charter on the Rights and Welfare of the Child (Article 7) unequivocally state that children have a right to participation in matters affecting their lives, the Tanzanian Government (a signatory to both conventions) stated in its June 1994 report to the United Nations Committee on Children's Rights that 'generally these Articles are not covered by law mainly owing to society's belief that...a child...cannot be left to make decisions concerning his or her own life' (CRC/C/8/Add.14, 1 June 1994, para. 37; cited in Rwezaura 1998: 58). Children and young people are acutely aware of such perceptions. During FGDs with 19 female and 12 male Standard VII[7] students in a rural primary school in the Iringa Region, we[8] spoke to the participants about their ability to execute decisions and act as 'agents' in their everyday lives. With the exception of one student, all respondents insisted that they do not have freedom to participate in decision making about their lives because 'I'm still under my parents'[9] (FGD1, 15 June 2005). In a ranking exercise,[10] the majority of these students positioned themselves as only the fourth or sixth most important decision maker in their *own* lives. The prevalence of such unequal adult–child relations influences Tanzanian girls to become child domestic workers, their subsequent position within the households where they work, and their ability to leave employment. During a discussion with the young researchers, they told us that employers prefer to hire children as domestic workers because '"it is easier to make children do work quickly than adults"..."children are not able to oppose...[or]they will be beaten"'[11] (Discussion, 7 July 2005).

Another 'thinning' factor relating to age is the strong sense of intergenerational responsibility prevalent in Tanzanian culture. Although the former child domestic workers in our FGDs emphasized that they had *not* been directly pressured to enter CDW, their guardians' reactions to their decision to do so are indicative of the importance of family obliga-tions as a driving factor. One girl commented that: 'My mother herself was feeling happy [about the decision] because she was separated from my father...Mother knew that if I go to work, I'll be helping her.'[12] (FGD3, 21 June 2005), and another:

> I was living with my grandmother. After telling her that I want to go to work, she agreed with me because the life was very hard. We didn't have money for soap, sugar, salt and she told me to go to look for money in order to help her. (FGD4, 21 June 2005)[13]

Migrating to cities and engaging in CDW is a key means for Tanzanian girls to fulfill responsibilities towards their rural families.

Gender: Disempowerment of Tanzanian girls

The following discussion seeks to elucidate the ways in which social con-structions of gender relations in Tanzania are 'embedded and visible in ideologies, structures and practices [that] shape children's lives' (Robson 2004a: 208), thereby 'thinning' the agency of Tanzanian girls. Of all countries for which statistics are available, Tanzania has the lowest rate of secondary education, at approximately 6 per cent of eligible children (UNICEF and United Republic of Tanzania 2001: 4, 79). It is a reality that most children will never continue on to higher education, and the educa-tional opportunities for (rural) girls are slimmest.[14] Scarce family resources are preferentially spent on the education of male children, because 'tran-sient' daughters will eventually leave to become part of their husbands' families (Mabala and Kamazima 1995: 8–9). Furthermore, socializa-tion into domestic roles may affect the academic performance of girls, as domestic chores consume much of their study time and often lead to poor school attendance (Mabala and Kamazima 1995). This domestic burden has become even greater with the impact of HIV/AIDS[15] in Tanzania as female children are often required to take on an even greater number of domestic chores while simultaneously caring for their sick parents, or tak-ing responsibility for parentless households (Robson et al. 2006).[16] Career options are few for female primary school graduates or 'dropouts'—they can either stay in rural villages to help on the family farm (although they are unlikely to inherit family property); become seamstresses, child domes-tic workers, or bar workers; or engage in commercial or survival sex. All of the primary school girls we spoke to indicated that they hope to become seamstresses if unable to continue with secondary education (FGD1, 15 June 2005) but realistically, vocational training and sewing machines are much too expensive for most rural families. Because they have been social-ized into a domestic role, CDW seems to be a 'natural' option for girls who want to work outside their rural villages (see also Rubenson et al. 2004).

Furthermore, because there is nothing unusual about girls doing domestic work, CDW is normalized and often not even recognized as 'real work':

> [I]n societies where it is normal to hire a young girl to help around the house, the practice commands such social acceptance that it takes a leap of imagination among researchers, social scientists, social workers and NGOs to think in terms of enquiring into it. (UNICEF 1999: 10)

Such normalization thins the agency of child domestic workers because it is unlikely that adults will listen to any complaints they might make about their treatment. CDW, unlike mining, prostitution, or plantation labour, is not one of the headline-grabbing forms of child labour. 'Child work' and 'child labour', in general, are very difficult to differentiate and define, such that acceptable, unacceptable, hazardous, and exploitative types of work (and the transitions between) are not clearly demarcated (see Fyfe 1989; Rodgers and Standing 1981; and Schildkrout 1981 for further discussion). As CDW is about girls working in the 'female' space of the home, it is even more difficult to highlight.

Another obstacle facing Tanzanian girls is that children's socialization often leads to 'the boy internalizing his superiority and the girl internalizing her inferiority' (Mabala and Kamazima 1995: 21). It is interesting to observe the ways in which Tanzanian children themselves are cognizant of such differences. One boy explained to us that girls from his rural village enter CDW because: 'Women are very easy to be convinced so if anyone comes to convince them they could not disagree.'[17] (FGD2, 15 June 2005); while a former child domestic worker commented:

> Boys are very arrogant, even when their mother talks to them, they answer back. Boys can come home at 7p.m. without mother asking them anything, but if a girl returns home at 5p.m., mother asks 'where are you coming from, do you think you are like a boy? Eeh!'[18] (FGD3, 21 June 2005)

Boys and men are often given more and better food within the family (see also Beazley, this volume); daughters and widows are usually unable to inherit property; and the male head of the household generally controls the financial resources (Mabala and Kamazima 1995). Ongoing customs and practices (such as female genital mutilation [FGM],[19] polygamy, bride-price, forced early marriage, widow inheritance[20] and the expulsion of pregnant school girls[21]) also influence the context within which Tanzanian girls exercise their agency, and impact profoundly on their ability to assert themselves and safeguard their own rights. Mabala and Kamazima (1995: 113) view the practice of bride-price as one of the major factors limiting the agency of Tanzanian girls, arguing that 'the girl is reduced to a thing, an object rather than a subject'. In Kiswahili, the verb 'to marry' even varies according to gender. While the man actively marries (kuoa) the woman is passively married (kuolewa), symbolizing her parents' agency in the marriage arrangement.

The disempowerment of Tanzanian girls also manifests itself as a lack of sexual agency. The first sexual experiences of many Tanzanian girls are coerced, and sexual harassment is commonplace: 'Male sexual dominance is pervasive and rarely challenged by community leaders, teachers, parents or other authorities.... Intimidation and harassment of girls is seen as normal, and girls have little recourse to protection' (UNICEF and United Republic of Tanzania 2001: 83). This lack of sexual agency was evident during a role-play exercise conducted with the young researchers, during which they were asked to show how they would resist the sexual advances of a male acquaintance (played by a female research assistant). All three girls looked down at their feet, adopted a submissive posture, allowed 'the boy' to touch them and smiled shyly when 'he' asked them to engage in sex. When 'he' continued to pressure them, each girl succumbed and agreed to meet 'him' later that night. Sexual disempowerment has important implications for the sexual agency of child domestic workers. Indeed, over 60 per cent of those interviewed in a Tanzania Media Women's Association study (Dickinson 2003) indicated that they had been forced (either physically or coerced) into having sexual relations with male members of the households in which they worked. Furthermore, sexual abuse and harassment within Tanzanian schools (often by teachers) is widespread and encourages many girls to drop out of school and begin working (Kuleana Centre for Children's Rights 1999). Gender based disempowerment clearly 'thins' the agency of Tanzanian girls and has important implications for their everyday actions.

Do some 'tribes' produce better child domestic workers than others?

The 'tribal' background of Tanzanians remains enormously important, despite the nation-building exercise famously undertaken by the first President, Julius Nyerere. When meeting for the first time, Tanzanians almost always inquire about a person's 'tribe'. This is significant to the lives of Tanzanian girls, because a raft of stereotypical characteristics is attached to them depending on their 'tribe'. The predominantly rural Iringa Region is occupied by the Wahehe people and is commonly identified as Tanzania's leading 'source' area for child domestic workers (Mosha 2005). It is commonly acknowledged (and has been documented by Forrester-Kibuga 2000), that employers throughout Tanzania prefer to employ Wahehe girls for CDW because they are reputed to be subservient, submissive, tolerant, hard-working, and pliant. Importantly, these social constructions have a very specific 'thinning' effect on the agency of Tanzanian girls from this region—they not only play an important role in their recruitment to CDW, but affect the expectations placed on them once employed.

Poverty

It is clear that poverty is a key factor pushing Majority world children into the workforce and motivating parents to pressure (or at least not prevent) their children from doing so at a young age (see Robson 2004a). Poverty also encourages rural-to-urban migration among Majority world children and youths. Tanzania is one of the world's poorest countries and residents of Tanzania's rural areas are 'disproportionately poor' (see Research and Analysis Working Group 2005; UNICEF and United Republic of Tanzania 2001: 5). Within the context of the research reported here, poverty is a key 'thinning' factor influencing the agency of rural Tanzanian girls, pressuring them to enter (and stay in) CDW.

At the outset of researching CDW, I believed that rural Tanzanian girls would stop entering CDW if they were educated about the risks. Through this research, it has become apparent that Tanzanian girls *do* know the dangers inherent to CDW, but their families' financial circumstances leave them with few alternatives. A female primary school student commented:

> They come to take us in a good way and promise us a lot of things, the result is that he/she uses you as an income earner, dresses you up and sends you into commercial sex....I don't like it at all. I don't want to get diseases. (FGD1, 15 June 2005)[22]

Furthermore, a male student observed:

> They [the girls who join CDW] know [about the problems] but...they have been here [in the village] for a long time without anything to do, so if they hear about a job in town they think it is better to go instead of continuing to stay here. (FGD2, 15 June 2005)[23]

Not only do rural Tanzanian girls know the risks of migrating to cities to enter CDW, they also know that continuing with their education would provide them with a better future. Every single primary school student in our FGDs expressed a strong desire to continue on to secondary school, but they were also aware that it is beyond the means of their families. None of them expressed a desire to become a child domestic worker.

CDW clearly has financial benefits for the poor rural families from which these girls come—indirectly, because there is one less child to support in the household and directly because child domestic workers usually send money home. Furthermore, once girls are involved in CDW, poverty continues to 'thin' their agency and prevents them from leaving abusive or exploitative employment situations. The working conditions of the former child domestic workers who participated in the FGDs had involved physical abuse, verbal abuse, excessive working hours, tasks that were too strenuous or beyond their age, being denied freedom to leave the house or to visit relatives, and not being given enough food. They tolerated this mistreatment in the expectation of being paid, a clear indication of the desperate economic circumstances from which they had come. They finally made the decision to leave CDW *only* when they realized that they were never going to receive their wages.[24] However, even after they have made the difficult decision to leave, poverty continues to 'thin' child domestic workers' agency as many cannot even afford the bus fare home:

> Another time she [the boss] said 'in your home there is extreme poverty that's why you came to work for me'. I tolerated all of this. I told her I wanted the fare to go home, she told me she hasn't got it [the bus fare] and if I have it I should return home to the poverty, because even if I go home I would come back to her house again. (FGD3, 21 June 2005)[25]

A particularly cruel side illustrated in the above comment is that the employer used the child domestic worker's poverty to belittle her, to exacerbate her sense of powerlessness, and to emphasize her lack of alternatives. Poverty is both a material and symbolic 'thinner' of agency in the everyday lives of prospective, current and former child domestic workers.

AFTER SO MUCH 'THINNING' IS THERE ANY AGENCY LEFT?

There are clearly numerous motivations and pressures causing rural Tanzanian girls to enter CDW. One element common to all of the girls' stories gathered in this research was their desire to take responsibility for their entry into CDW. When asked whether they had been pressured to become child domestic workers, *all* of the girls replied unequivocally that they had decided for themselves. This finding mirrors Jacquemin's (2004a: 385) observation that 'even in situations where they have few choices, these working children reject being made an object'. Thus, although the research reveals that Tanzanian girls do not generally *want* to become child domestic workers (but end up in CDW because of their socio-cultural and economic contexts), it *also* suggests that their lives should not be placed unproblematically into a box labelled 'object'. Indeed, focusing only on the down-trodden elements of the Tanzanian child domestic worker's character, her strengths, abilities, and knowledge are either overlooked, or considered insignificant in relation to her context. This strength is readily apparent when former child domestic workers say: 'I am doing [sewing] exams in November....I would like to be able to build my own life myself'[26] (FGD3, 21 June 2005), or 'That's why I joined domestic work, because of extreme poverty, I joined in order to fulfill our very small needs at home....I knew that if I get a wage it will help us in our poverty. (Written response, 21 June 2005).[27]

This research with Tanzanian child domestic workers has led me to the conclusion that Tanzanian girls do not enter CDW (or stay in it) because they are weak or ignorant, they do so because they honestly believe that this decision will produce the best possible outcome for themselves and their families—it is a coping strategy, an active and 'rational' response 'in the face of a crisis of social reproduction' which characterizes their life worlds (Robson 2004a: 208; Robson 2004b: 239; Schäfer, this volume). Tanzanian girls' work-oriented migration from rural areas into CDW is crucial to the survival of their household units and although 'born into economic and cultural circumstances which cannot be explained away' (Qvortrup 2000: 79) their lives involve a 'synthesis of structure, culture and agency' (Davis et al. 2000: 218). When their agency is identified as 'thin', rather than as being non-existent, this enables acknowledgement both of their difficult circumstances *and* their efforts to survive and to build better lives.

Spending time in the field with research participants whose agency has been thinned through their various contexts and relationships, led the research team to feel a strong sense of obligation to use the research process itself as a thickening influence. The ways in which this research endeavored to thicken the agency of research participants is discussed in Robson et al. (this volume). An approach to working with young researchers in ways specifically intended to strengthen their agency arises out of a concern that professional researchers have questioned the lack of 'authentic' opportunities for children's participation in the decision-making structures of local governance, within schools and within the family (Hart 1997; Johnson 1996a; Juckes Maxey 2004), while continuing to guard our own field. Can we not relinquish some control and make space for young researchers? After all, they have *personal* experience of the issues we are researching, and the highest stake in the research outcomes.

NOTES

1. The 2005 Thenie Baddams Bursary from the Australian Federation of University Women assisted the author with the expenses of fieldwork on which this chapter is based.
2. See Matthews and Tucker (this volume).
3. For more extensive details about CDW see: Forrester-Kibuga (2000) or Lugalla and Madihi (2004) for Tanzania; Jacquemin (2004) for Cote d'Ivoire; and Camacho (1999) for the Philippines. See also the various ILO International Programme for the Elimination of Child Labour (IPEC) rapid assessments of CDW for example in Sri Lanka (Kannangara et al. 2003).
4. The initial idea for using 'thick' came from Geertz's (1973: 3) reference to 'thick description'.
5. The term *tribe* is widely used in Tanzania in a non-pejorative manner. The terms *tribe* and *ethnicity* have separate meanings in Tanzania—people perceive their ethnicity to be 'Bantu' while 'tribe' has a much more localized and specific meaning.

6. 'The biological dependence of children on adults is universal and inevitably leads to an asymmetrical authority relationship between adults and children' (Schildkrout 1981: 81–82).
7. Standard VII is the last year of primary school and compulsory education in Tanzania. The children participating in the FGDs were 13 to 16 years old.
8. 'We' refers to the author and a female Tanzanian research assistant (not a former child domestic worker).
9. 'Bado nipo chini ya wazazi'. All research was undertaken in Kiswahili and the original Kiswahili of all quotations is provided.
10. A total of eight decision makers were listed: older siblings, younger siblings, parents/guardians, 'myself', teachers, community leaders, religious leaders, and friends.
11. 'Ni rahisi kuwafanya watoto wafanye kazi kwa haraka kuliko watu wazima' and 'Watoto hawana uwezo wa kukataa...[au] watapigwa'.
12. 'Mama mwenyewe alifurahi kwa sababu alitengana na Baba. Mama alijua kuwa kama nitaenda kufanya kazi nitamsaidia'.
13. 'Nilikuwa naishi na Bibi yangu. Baada ya kumwambia kuwa nataka kwenda kufanya kazi alinikubalia kwa sababu maisha yalikuwa magumu sana. Tuli-kuwa hatuna pesa ya sabuni, sukari, chumvi na aliniambia mimi nikatafute pesa ili nimsaidie'.
14. More girls than boys fail primary school leaving exams and there is a sub-stantial gender gap in enrolment to upper secondary school, with girls only constituting one third of total enrolments. The net (primary school) enrol-ment rate in urban areas is 72.3 per cent compared to only 57.2 per cent in rural areas (UNICEF and United Republic of Tanzania 2001: 42, 45, 79).
15. According to the Tanzania Commission for HIV/AIDS (TACAIDS) approxi-mately two million Tanzanians are living with the disease and the President of Tanzania has declared it a 'national disaster' (TACAIDS 2003: 1). UNAIDS (The Joint United Nations Programme on HIV/AIDS) estimates that there were up to 1.4 million AIDS orphans in Tanzania in 2003 (UNAIDS 2004: 2).
16. The impacts of parental death on rural Tanzanian children's lives are mark-edly similar to those of parental migration on 'Malaysian Orphans' (Beazley, this volume).
17. 'Wanawake ni rahisi sana kushawishiwa kwa hiyo kama mtu yeyote atakuja na kuwashawishi hawatakataa.'
18. 'Wavulana wana viburi sana, hata wakisemeshwa na mama wanajibiza. Wavulana wanaweza kurudi nyumabani saa moja usiku bila mama kumuu-liza chochote, bali msichana akirudi saa 11, mama anamuuliza 'umetoka wapi, wewe unajifanya mvulana? Eeh!'
19. FGM remains common practice among certain tribes in Tanzania, including in the Iringa Region. The reasons given for FGM include 'training and social control' of the girl-child (Mabala and Kamazima 1995: 54–56).
20. Widow inheritance refers to the practice whereby a widow is inherited by one of her husband's relatives.
21. The expulsion of pregnant schoolgirls (and the boys who impregnated them) is stipulated in Tanzanian law. In practice, the boys are rarely punished.
22. 'Wanakuja kutuchukua vizuri na kutuahidi mambo mengi, kumbe matokeo yake anakufanya wewe kitega uchumi, anakuremba, na kukutumia kwenye ukahaba...mimi sipendi kabisa. Nisije nikapatwa na magonjwa'.
23. 'Wanafahamu lakini...wanakaa hapa kwa muda mrefu bila kitu cha kufanya, sasa wanaposikia kuna kazi mjini wanafikiri ni bora wakafanye kuliko kue-ndelea kukaa hapa'.

24. Almost all of the former child domestic workers spoken to were not paid at all while employed.

25. 'Muda mwingine alisema 'nyumbani kwenu kuna umaskini uliokithiri na ndio maana umekuja kufanya kazi kwangu'. Nilivumilia yote hayo. Nilimwambia nataka nauli ya kurudi nyumbani, alisema hajapata na kama ninayo nitarudi nyumbani kwenye umaskini, kwa sababu hata kama nitarudi nyumbani nitarudi tena nyumbani kwake'.

26. 'Nafanya mtihani mwezi wa kumi na moja...ninapenda kujijengea maisha yangu mwenyewe'.

27. 'Ndio maana nilijiunga na kazi za ndani, kwa sababu ya umaskini, nilijiunga ili kukidhi mahitaji madogomadogo ya nyumbani...nilijua kwamba kama nitapata mshahara utatusaidia katika umaskini wetu'.

8 On both sides of the tracks

British rural teenagers' views on their ruralities

Hugh Matthews and Faith Tucker

INTRODUCTION

Within the Minority world, notions of the 'rural idyll' abound. The notion of a rural idyll stubbornly persists as a common conception of the British countryside, particularly with regard to issues of family life. Rural children are popularly understood to be able to run freely across fields and through woods, being able to explore distant hills and forests (Aitken 1994), where they develop a close association with the 'natural' environment in which they live. For many onlookers, rural places are conceived as safe, risk-free, community-rich spaces in which parents can bring up their children away from the turmoil and social dangers that are seen to be part of urban living today (see Valentine 1997a). O. Jones (1997; 2000) draws attention to a substantial body of literature, whose re-reading by successive generations, portrays the countryside as a haven of 'primitive innocence', the last refuge of a state of humanity defined by a 'wholesome naturalness' that enables children to develop in pure, unblemished, almost perfect ways (Matthews, Taylor et al. 2000: 141). Nature is seen to provide spaces and materials for play, and rural young people are understood to be free to explore their local area and able to use spaces apart from the ordered adult world (Shoard 1980). The countryside in these (re)presentations is typically that of well-organized, pastoral, Middle England and not that of remote, desolate, wild Britain, whose essence equates instead with degradation, deprivation, and dehumanization (Ward 1990). Commodification of this Romantic ideal reinforces a view that the rural package is an entity that is worth buying into, especially for those who have the well-being of children in mind (Bunce 1994).

In this chapter we critically consider the countryside as a place for growing up as a young teenager. In so doing we mobilize the notion of 'psychogeography', a term particularly associated with the situationist Guy Debord (1970; 1998). Psychogeography draws attention to the 'specific effects of the geographical environment, consciously organised or not, on the emotions and behaviour of individuals' (Knabb 1981: 45). Originally conceived to accommodate the emotional or psychic aspects of the urban experience, we extend its application to (re)consider 'everyday life' within rural spaces. The construct of 'everyday life' is itself closely linked with another figure often associated with situationism, Henri Lefebvre (1991a; 1991b). Lefebvre distinguished three types of space: the 'perceived space' of everyday social life, the 'conceived space' of planners and speculators, and a sphere of 'lived space'. Brooker (2002: 97), drawing upon Shields (1999), defines the latter as a symbolic (re)imagining 'of [urban] space that reconfigures the banality of the first'. In this chapter we utilize these constructs to provide new productive meanings that challenge the representation of a rural idyll for rural youth in the Minority world.

In addition, we introduce the concept of 'moral *terroir*' in an attempt to disentangle the everyday realities of rural living. We have argued elsewhere that there is neither one rural childhood nor one group of rural children (see, for example, Matthews, Taylor et al. 2000; Tucker and Matthews 2001; Tucker 2003). In this chapter we extend this theme by examining the 'outdoor' rural geographies of young teenage girls to uncover the significance of outdoor places as social sites of contestation, transition, and rites of passage. We draw upon and (re)consider a series of empirical studies[1] carried out between 1998 and 2002 with teenagers aged 11 to 15 years resident in South Northamptonshire, among the most accessible and affluent of English counties.[2] Yet, amidst this affluence there are pockets of relative deprivation—defined by high rates of unemployment, a large proportion of single-parent families, low social class, poor levels of educational attainment, and a high proportion of public sector housing—from which we also drew our participants. A multi-method approach defined each study—typically, semi-structured interviews, in-depth discussion groups, child-taken photographs, and video tours. In order to get as close as possible to the 'everyday' worlds of these young people, wherever possible their narratives are incorporated into the text.[3] What emerges are complex micro-geographies (Matthews et al. 1998) infused and loaded with the agency of young people.

RURAL PSYCHOGEOGRAPHIES—THE
NARRATIVES OF TEENAGERS

Barker and Wright (1955: 55), in their seminal ecological study of children living in the U.S. Midwest, discuss how certain aspects of an environment exert a 'coercive influence' on perception and activity. For example, they noted that when Midwestern children see an open level surface free from obstruction, they remember these places not for their designated purpose (for example, the Courthouse lawn, the football field) but as potential sites for vigorous activity, such as 'running and romping'. From this perspective, the configurational setting of an environment is overwritten by sets of ecological affordances relevant to particular groups in time and space (Gibson

1979). To some extent these ideas resonate with those of psychogeography, which draw attention to the emotional or psychic aspects of concrete space. Both approaches encourage reflections on how the physical makeup of a (rural) setting may impact on the ways in which young people encounter (conceived space), make sense of (perceived space), and live out (lived space) their everyday lives.

In the Minority world context of England, for many adults among the perceived benefits of a rural upbringing is that children can grow up and develop in settings that enable a close association with nature (Little and Austin 1996; Valentine 1997a). Many studies have shown that younger children value the outdoors (Matthews 1992; Valentine 1997b; Ward 1990), and there are many accounts that draw attention to the virtues of meeting and playing in 'natural spaces' (R. Hart 1979; Moore 1986; Kong et al. 1999; Kong 2000; Percy-Smith 1999). However, within our studies we found that teenagers rarely commented upon the intrinsic worth of natural settings. Rather ironically, opportunities for young people to access natural spaces were often very limited for, as Davis and Ridge (1997) have pointed out, in many rural areas of the Minority world there is very little land that is not in private ownership, either farmland or, with an increasing number of affluent incomers, personal property. Somewhat paradoxically too, without access to farmland, most rural villages possess very little public land, and what little there is, is often fiercely defended by adults (Davis and Ridge 1997). Within rural South Northamptonshire, teenagers repeatedly bemoaned how vigilant adults routinely curtailed their attempts to access 'open spaces'.

We can't go there [a field on the edge of a new housing development].... There's a big sign saying KEEP OUT, TRESPASSERS PROSECUTED. We went there once and this guy comes out and starts giving us some verbal.... It's not worth it.... We didn't really want to go there in any case.... (Boy, aged 13)

I was walking along with me mates down by the little stream and this old geezer starts shouting at us 'GET OFF MY LAND'.... Stupid old fool, who does he think he is! It's just a path by a house.... (Girl, aged 14)

There's a man who lives near the park. He shouts if people play in the trees because 'IT'S COUNCIL PROPERTY', but there's nothing else to do in this boring old park so we just do it anyway.... (Girl, aged 13)

We're not really allowed to go on the greens at the golf course. There's this man, and he told my brother off for leaving his rucksack there.... (Girl, aged 11)

In our studies we found that for a significant proportion of teenagers, their lived experience of the countryside often contradicted the social construction of the idyll. The routine practices of daily existence within a rural place are not, for many young people, filled with infinite prospects. Instead, their psychic experience is more likely to be a shared sense of ennui, boredom and languor. Typical complaints revolved around the lack of things to do and the paucity of settings to hang out, particularly away from the adult gaze. Although claims such as these have a universal resonance for teenagers (Corrigan 1979; James 1986; James and Prout 1992), given the declining service structure of rural places, poor public transport provision, and the expense of private alternatives, rural teenagers typically reside within opportunity-poor environments:

> [So what sorts of things are there for people your age to do in the village?] There's no parks. There's just the field behind the trees over the road.... There's no shops.... The bus only goes on a Saturday or a Wednesday, and then it doesn't go to where my friends live. There's no clubs or anything here.... (Girl, aged 11)

Moseley (1979: 37) has argued that the 'lack of a car is probably the biggest single factor in any identification of those rural people who are disadvantaged in access terms'. Levels of car ownership are high in South Northamptonshire, yet whilst high levels of independent mobility may be experienced by many adults, young people are a disadvantaged group and one particularly vulnerable to the effects of the rationalisation and centralisation of many services in this area (Nutley and Thomas 1995; Storey and Brannen 2000). Problems are further exacerbated if a family lacks a car or if another family member is using their only car for another purpose, such as access to work during the school holidays. As Davis and Ridge (1997) have noted, there appears to be an age—especially during the early teenage years—when living in the countryside can seem particularly restrictive and inhibiting.

These experiences, when taken together, define situations and events that in turn stimulate various shared mentalities or common psychogeographies amongst teenagers (Christensen 2003). In our studies, this is represented by a cacophony of negative emotions and feelings. We often found that when talking (thinking) about their localities, teenagers provided accounts full of frustration and restlessness. Indeed, many stated a strong preference for commercial leisure spaces such as cinemas, leisure centres, shopping centres, coffee shops, and so on, and much of the dissatisfaction they expressed with leisure provision in their home village was related to the lack of access to such spaces. Rather than being content to spend their leisure time within their own communities, for many teenagers, especially girls, there existed a strong desire to leave their home village to take advantage of facilities elsewhere. For these young people, their residential location deprived them of easy, independent access to desired leisure spaces.

[What's it like here?] Boring. It's pretty quiet...you need transport to get out of the village...there's not a lot of buses. There's about three buses a day.... We often go out on a Friday or Saturday night and we phone up a taxi...it's eight pounds from here to Milton Keynes but if you get a black cab...it would cost you a tenner. Too expensive.... There's no jobs, like, going in the village. You have to be over 16 and we're just coming up to 16 and we got restrictions. You need transport to get out of the village to get a job.... (Girl, aged 15)

Nothing ever happens here...it's gross, really bad...so we try to make things happen by meeting together...but then we get moved on.... (Boy, aged 15)

There's nothing to do here, and it's not as if you can get a bus to any-where else. There aren't many buses, and those that there are don't go where we want. And you can't get a bus anywhere at night.... (Girl, aged 15)

[What's this place like?] There's nowhere to go and nothing to do.... (Boy, aged 13)

Among the considered benefits of living within small, discrete, relatively remote, rural places are that they facilitate a sense of belonging and commu-nity. Many studies (for example, Lewis and Sherwood 1994; Lewis 1989; Valentine 1997c; O. Jones 2000) have shown how rural adults—especially incomers—rely upon these constructs to authenticate their experience of the rustic. Yet for many teenagers, symbolic imagining of this kind has lit-tle meaning for them. Rather, when surmising about their localities strong feelings of angst and anger were commonplace. Several causes trigger such disaffection. First, in the absence of dedicated meeting places, teenagers often congregate together in the village core or in other venues where their presence is highly visible. In so doing, they transgress the sensibilities of those adults who define the public realm as an extension of their own pri-vate domain (Matthews 2003; Matthews, Limb, and Taylor 2000) and who seek to admonish and castigate all those who enter within. Teenagers frequently recall how they were asked to move on when simply hanging around together. Secondly, in most places, parish life and its affairs are car-ried out in the absence of young people. Accordingly, teenagers frequently lament that no one listens to their needs and in any decision-making their views are either ignored or tokenized. Feelings of powerlessness, exclusion, and frustration were commonplace.

We got promised loads of things would happen in the field in summer holidays. There's nothing up there now. [Who made these promises?] We were down the primary school and we were all going in the pool.

We weren't supposed to but we were. And she came down, there's two of them and we were thinking, 'oh we'd better make a move', and they stopped and they were asking questions like you are now...going on about what we do, how we do it and everything and they started saying that they'd be in the village and they were going to do archery and everything. [Where were they from?] I can't remember now. That was about two years ago.... (Girl, aged 15)

We have an adults' council in our village for people who decide what's going to go on in the village and I don't think they have ever had a children's say in it.... (Girl, aged 13)

The council spent a lot of money, like half a million pounds, on doing up the place. They've re-done the pavements and put in new benches and stuff. They never ask us [young people] what we'd like. Half a million pounds—that was just a waste of money. With that money they could have built a leisure centre or a community centre or something. They could have built something that everyone could use, you know, something for families.... (Girl, aged 13)

Sentiments such as these highlight the 'profound emptiness' of rural places for many teenagers and the falseness of the consolation of the myth of the idyll. For them, the concrete dimensions of rurality define an emotional landscape (or psychogeography) of 'othering', 'otherness' and 'marginality'. Space is thus simultaneously objective and subjective, material and metaphysical, a medium and a construct of everyday life. The ideas of Genette (1982) are of interest here. Drawing upon the anthropological work of Lévi-Strauss (1966), Genette proposed a distinction between two social beings: that of the 'engineer' and the 'bricoleur'. 'While the engineer uses the appropriate tools and designated parts for the job, the bricoleur makes do, putting together the left-over, extracted and borrowed pieces at hand so as to compose a new whole' (Brooker 2002: 22). We interpret the ways of (rural) adults as those of the engineer, persons always in charge, manipulating the mythic and the real for their own gains and benefits. On the other hand, (rural) teenagers are the bricoleurs, living with and within the oddments and cast-offs of adult endeavour and working with these scraps through their own agency to carve out a variety of social and cultural bricolage. As Soja (1996) surmises, social reality then is not just coincidentally spatial, its essence is moulded by and in physical space.

THE 'MORAL *TERROIR*' OF RURAL TEENAGE GIRLS

When looking and attempting to understand the lives of young people, there is a continuing need to recognize the importance of diversity and agency. The notion of sub-cultures, each with its own particular 'stamp' of behaviour(s), dress, manners, and moral territories, goes only part way to encapsulate the essence of difference. What our study and many others have shown, is that within a locality there may be groups of young people who share common ways of seeing and who—from the outside looking in—may be labelled as representative of particular sub-cultures and yet—from the inside looking out—distinguish themselves from others around them. From this perspective, sub-cultural distinction is an inadequate descriptor and an (in)convenient sociological badge. What is needed is a better means to capture the variety and variation that inevitably exists between groups of young people who share common localities. The French word *terroir* is useful in this respect. There is no adequate translation for this construct in English. It refers to the way in which a disparate range of micro-conditions combine to produce a physical landscape that enables wines of different quality to spring from their locations and surroundings. Thus, every place has its own peculiar *terroir*, which will—sometimes sharply and sometimes much less so—distinguish wines from the same grape. We suggest that the metaphor of a 'moral *terroir*'—whereby elements of social (e.g. age, sex, social class), cultural (race/ethnicity, lifestyles, patterns of parenting etc.), and environmental (neighbourhoods, streets, sides of the road) properties come together in unique 'moral' topographies, provides a step towards understanding differences of this kind. However, it is how young people work with and within these structures and power relations that gives rise to subtle yet profound variations in their identities and the outcomes that ensue.

Thus, using this idea of the 'moral *terroir*' we can better understand those differences in the everyday experiences of a group of young people growing up in the same locality, at the same point in time, subject to the same structures, and from similar backgrounds in terms of ethnicity and family structure—a group who appear 'from without' to be similar, and yet who exhibit diversity with regard to behaviour and lifestyle, largely through their own agency. To demonstrate this, we consider the differences between groups of young people growing up on different sides of the tracks—that is, on the one hand, within well-defined, relatively affluent enclaves with parents who own their own properties, typically large, single, detached dwelling units and, on the other hand, children from less prosperous families, living nearby in another morphologically distinct area of local authority-owned properties.

Lucey and Reay (1999) have argued that middle-class children's horizons extend beyond their local area since their families have the funds and ability to travel more widely. Middle-class children, according to Lucey and Reay, develop 'nomadic' identities through these high levels of mobility. In affluent South Northamptonshire, many young teenagers relied on their parents providing transport to commercial leisure spaces, having to reach a compromise between their wishes and the mobility needs of their parents (Pavis et al. 2000). The parents of teenage girls interviewed in one of the empirical studies (see Tucker 2003) did not complain about having to provide transport in order for their children to gain access to leisure facilities. Indeed, many parents welcomed the opportunity to provide transport because in this way they were able to regulate their children's behaviour, and were able to influence where they went, who they went with, and at what time they were to return. In some cases a network of parents became established, enabling several adults to keep track of who their children were socialising with, whilst the strong links between particular adults made it easier for young people to meet with those friends more regularly.

> You always have to [sort out travel arrangements] between friends. Like one parent will take and another parent will bring back. It's quite organized. And my parents have taken us quite a lot so another parent will come forward and say, 'Well I'll take this week'.... (Girl, aged 15)

> I think the disadvantages of living in a village are...you have to take them to do anything they want to do as they become teenagers. But I don't mind that at all.... There's a network of parents who are spending all their time shunting their kids from one place to another. And I think that's part of, you accept that. And I don't dislike doing that anyway. I think that's quite nice.... (Mother of two, two-parent family)

> [Daughter] has got a lot of friends in villages actually. So we drive her there.... The bus services here are appalling. I mean, if you've got a friend who's three miles away in Northampton you can just get on a bus and get to them, but you can't here. But on the other hand, I feel that's OK...whilst I'm driving them places I know where they are and who they're with. I would prefer to live in [village] and do that than live in Northampton and have them have a free rein really.... (Mother of two, two-parent family)

Although many of the parents spoke about the advantages of rural living—and specifically about the freedom the rural offers as opposed to urban living—this did not tie in with the limited spatial freedom experienced by these young people. In order to access those leisure spaces that they particularly valued, the girls were reliant on their parents 'approval'. For some, this involved a series of organized events or activities, with parents escorting their children and keeping control on their use of leisure time. For others, this involved visits to specific (indoor) locations, with curfews and guidelines structuring their time.

> On Mondays I go swimming. There's an athletics club after school on Tuesdays. I play the piano and I have lessons usually on a Thursday. That's in town. Then there's 'Wave Rave' [activity at local leisure

centre] on Friday nights and music school in town on Saturday mornings.... (Girl, aged 11)

I usually go out round somebody's house. There's a bloke up my street that I go and see, either to do my homework or just to sit and chat with him. But we're in a house, so we're not walking around at all...which my parents like, and I only live nine doors down...so I'm only yards away. We just sit and listen to music there and chat.... (Girl, aged 15)

I'm not allowed just to wander 'round the village. I have to go somewhere specific. Like, I'm allowed to go to my friend's house, but we have to stay there.... I have a curfew and if I'm not home then I'm in real trouble. Sometimes I 'phone to say that I'm just coming down the road.... (Girl, aged 11)

My parents always check up to see where I am. If I say that I'm going to so-and-so's house, my mum rings to check that I'm there.... (Girl, aged 15)

Although Northamptonshire is one of the most affluent counties of England, pockets of deprivation exist. For some less affluent young teenagers, such escorted geographies were uncommon aspects of their everyday lives. On the other side of the tracks, lack of access to a car or limited funds for leisure and recreation, led to many young people feeling disenchanted with rural living, disheartened by the lack of facilities and services, problems of accessibility, and feelings of 'missing out' on aspects of youth culture portrayed through the media.

People who decide where...[leisure facilities are located] don't think of young children. They just think 'Oh yeah, they can get their mums and dads to drive them there', and they can't. Most people only have one car and most people go to work. And with that one car gone then you need to walk there and risk your life, probably, going across the roads.... (Girl, aged 13)

We've got two cars but both my mum and dad work.... They just don't get time to take us out apart from at weekends.... (Girl, aged 13)

There's not much to do here that you don't have to pay for. And my mum doesn't have lots of money to spend on that sort of thing.... (Girl, aged 11)

We could do with a teenagers' café or something...like the one in 'Neighbours' [a popular television programme].... We haven't got anywhere to go.... (Girl, aged 13)

From these observations, rural spaces take on a fluid, paradoxical meaning for teenage girls. While many parents are keen to invoke rhetorical eulogisms that play up the empowering, liberating, and enriching worth of rural living, in practice, the very act of residency in a rural place closes down what young girls are able to do. We suggest that the everyday lives of young teenage girls can be symbolized by a 'lived space' that is characterized on the one hand by 'displacement' and on the other by 'resistance'. Identity formation then is played out amidst these dialectic tensions and spatial dilemmas.

Furthermore, on each side of these tracks it was also evident that other more subtle differences were clear, with different groups of girls distinguishing themselves from their immediate counterparts through a complex social network of gang membership. Each of these gangs was keen to stamp out its own identity through the use of their own appellations. Thus, among the less well off were the 'Spicer Girls'—a play of words on a well known girl band of the time—and the 'Barley Crew'. From the outside these groups looked little different to each other, comprised girls of a similar age with an interest in the same kind of fashions; yet fierce loyalties divided each group from the other. Within the village each group had marked out its own territory, where they met up to chat and smoke. Rarely did members of either gang transgress these social spaces and if doing so, they talked about feeling uncomfortable and 'out-of-place'.

> We don't like going down there [a member of the Barley Crew pointing down the street] it's where the Spicer Girls hang out. We don't like them, they're slags, up to no good. 'Good riddance to them' is what we say.... (Girl, aged 15)

Within the more affluent parts of the village, too, some girls drew attention to how they differed from other girls of a similar age, attending the same school as them.

> Groups of people [hang out at the recreation ground]. They intimidate you.... They just, like, sit there and stare at you. Or they come up and say something horrible.... (Girl, aged 13)

Other friends talked about how members of this girl gang were perceived to be 'hard people' and 'people with attitude'. For these reasons certain parts of the village were avoided, especially at particular times of the day when it was known that different groups would be out and about.

Through our brief encounters with these young people it was evident that a complex mosaic of social worlds had been mapped out through their own agency and superimposed upon where they lived. The canyons and crevasses of this cultural landscape were defined by and signified through a moral *terroir* of difference and diversity.

CONCLUSION

In this chapter we have considered what it is like to be a young teenager growing up in a part of the English countryside today. In so doing, we have looked critically at the imagining of the rural as idyll and the ways in which children are central to this configuration. Implicit within these constructions are notions that 'pastoral' equates with a state of purity, innocence, and stability, where childhoods are happy and carefree. However, in common with a growing number of other studies, our investigations have shown that, far from being idyllic paradises, many rural villages in the Minority world are desolate places for young people, characterized more often by spatialities that exclude, marginalize, and persecute. Drawing upon the notions of psychogeography, we have considered how residency in such places, which are generally bereft of opportunities and where young people are always within the adult gaze, impacts upon teenagers' interpretations of their rural childhoods. Typically, what emerge in their narratives are feelings of frustration, alienation, and anger that play up the negative psychic and emotional aspects of the rural experience. We suggest that within these milieux children carve out their own embodied geographies in the manner of cultural bricoleurs, working imaginatively, but mostly with the scraps of adult endeavour. The new concept of the moral *terroir* is useful for understanding some of the worlds of difference and diversity that define these experiences. Through its application, we demonstrate how young people growing up closely together, who from the outside appear to share common experiences, are residing in worlds that are sharply differentiated from each other. In essence, even within one locality there are many practices of everyday life.

NOTES

1. For a full discussion of these populations and a review of the ways in which each young person was recruited see Matthews, Taylor et al. (2000a), Tucker and Matthews (2001) and Tucker (2003).
2. For reviews of 'other rurals', especially from the perspective of young people, see Vanderbeck and Dunkley (2003) and Panelli (2002).
3. For reasons of confidentiality, the 'voices' of the young people are anonymized. At the outset of every interview or discussion group assurance was given that the views to be recorded would not be attributable to any individual or to any specific location—this guarantee was provided so that the young people would be secure in knowing that they could talk openly about matters close to their everyday lives, without fear of repercussion.

9 The 'Malaysian orphans' of Lombok

Children and young people's livelihood responses to out-migration in eastern Indonesia

Harriot Beazley

INTRODUCTION

This chapter describes the responses of children and young people left behind in rural areas when their parents migrate overseas. In particular it examines the conditions, experiences, and livelihoods of children and young people in East Lombok, a rural and remote district of Eastern Indonesia, and how their everyday lives have been affected by the phenomenon of trans-national migrant labour. The chapter explores how these young people actively respond to the impact of international migration, in terms of their everyday actions, and their plans for the future. Also considered is how going to Malaysia to work on plantations for boys, or Saudi Arabia to work as domestic servants for girls, is increasingly being understood as a 'rite of passage to adulthood' for young rural Indonesians (see Punch 2002b).

International migration is a global priority issue, and Indonesia is a major contributor to trans-national labour flows (United Nations Economic and Social Council [UNESC] 2005; Bryant 2005). During the 1990s it was estimated that 4 million Indonesians were living abroad (Rahman 2002). Since 2000, population mobility within and outside of Southeast Asia countries has escalated (UNESC 2005). Migrants from Indonesia are mostly overseas contract workers working in Malaysia, Singapore, China, Hong Kong, South Korea, and Taiwan. The Middle East, especially Saudi Arabia, has increasingly been a favoured destination for Indonesian women, who go to work as housemaids (Hugo 2002; Rahman 2002).

While the economic benefits of remittances from migration are well documented, most studies of the social costs of international migration have focused on the migrants themselves, their health concerns, labour conditions, and treatment by employers (Rahman 2002; Nasution 2001; Hadi 2000; Sukamdi et al. 1999; Robinson, 1991). For example, the movement of female workers overseas has sparked major protests from labour unions and women's organisations in Indonesia, due to the increasing number of sexual harassment cases and human rights violations against female Indonesian workers, particularly in Singapore, Hong Kong, and the Middle East (Hugo 2002).

Figure 9.1 Location of study area in Indonesia.

Much less attention has been paid to the socio-cultural impacts of migration on the families of migrants who are left behind (see Hugo 1995; 2002 for an exception). Research on the effects of international migration on the children of migrant workers has been particularly limited, and there is a need for careful investigation into this issue (Dwiyanto and Keban 1997 cited in Bryant 2005: 8; UNESC 2005).

This chapter outlines the main findings from Participatory Rural Appraisal (PRA)[1] data gathered from adults, children, and young people in the hamlet of Naukek, a remote hamlet in East Lombok (Figure 9.1).[2] Topics explored included the impact of male and female out-migration in relation to infant mortality as well as children's health, livelihoods and well-being.

Lombok is an arid and remote island situated in the Eastern Indonesian province of West Nusa Tenggara. The province is one of the most isolated and impoverished parts of Indonesia due to its mountainous terrain and archipelagic fragmentation (G. Jones and Raharjo 1999). Lombok has long experienced poor communications, grave health indicators, a lack of access to and quality of health services, inadequate sanitation facilities, and insufficient education provision (G. Jones and Raharjo 1999). It has also acquired the undesirable reputation of having the highest recorded rate of infant and child mortality in the country (Hull et al. 1999: 21). As an indicator of social and economic well-being, the infant mortality statistics reveal numerous concerns associated with poverty, culture, livelihoods, and traditional practices.[3]

OUT-MIGRATION

In Indonesia, it is important to consider the lives of young people in light of the country's increasing participation in global trade and commerce, the

financial crisis of 1997 to 1998, the impact of the subsequent political turmoil, and the 'democratisation' process since then (Vickers 2005).

Since the economic crisis the numbers of young migrant workers leaving
Indonesia, including Lombok, through official and unofficial channels has
risen sharply (Bryant 2005). Many of these migrants are as young as fifteen
years, having managed to secure false birth certificates and travel documents, which state that they are eighteen years old or over. Most migrants
from Lombok are young men—known as TKI (male Indonesian overseas
workers)—although there is a growing number of young female overseas
workers (TKW), usually going to work as domestic servants.[4] The out-
migration of TKW from Lombok to Saudi Arabia to work as housemaids is
sponsored by an official government program with three-year contracts, for
girls over eighteen years old, but young women below eighteen years old are
also departing through unofficial channels (Hugo 2002). The government
of Indonesia supports the expansion of the country's overseas workforce in
order to reduce the ranks of its unemployed (officially at 40 million), while
simultaneously boosting foreign remittances.[5] Between 1995 and 2000 the
1.6 million documented Indonesian overseas workers sent home a cumula-
tive US$5 billion (M. Cohen 2000: 28).

Recent research indicates that from a purely economic perspective, the
prevalence of migrant workers has had a positive impact on families in
the sending regions, which are predominantly rural (Bryant 2005; Nasution 2001; Tamtiari 1999). In Lombok, however, out-migration has also
had negative impacts on poor families, especially women, infants, and children. Some initial calculations suggest that in Indonesia there are over 1
million children left behind by their parents and older siblings when they
migrate overseas (Bryant 2005: 3).[6] However, these figures may be higher
as the significant movement of undocumented 'irregular' or illegal migrants
from Indonesia, particularly Lombok,[7] makes it difficult to know the real
numbers of children who have to cope with the phenomenon.[8] From a socio-
psychological perspective it has disrupted family life, led to increased stress
for family members left behind, and to a steep rise in rates of divorce and
separation.[9]

IMPACT OF OUT-MIGRATION

The hamlet of Naukek is physically isolated up a rough, steep track, in the
foothills of Indonesia's largest volcano, Mount Rinjani. At the time of the
research in 2000 it had a population of 76 families, approximately 400
people. Due to its geographical location Naukek is subject to flash floods,
and is characterized by poverty and frequent incidence of infant mortality. It is typical of a remote rural area in the Majority world in that the
hamlet lacks sanitation or electricity, has poor community access to health
services, no public transport, no access to clean drinking water, and no secondary school (Ansell 2005; Potter et al. 2004; Punch 2004). The people

of Naukek call themselves *orang-hutan* ('people of the forest'), as that is where they spend most of their time, gathering resources (firewood, leaves, grass, birds, fruit, and wild plants) to survive.

> When we first walked into the hamlet of Naukek, we were greeted by dozens of curious children, some of them carrying their younger brothers or sisters on their hips in a sarong sling, *gendong* style. There were no adults in sight. 'Where are your parents?' we asked. 'Ibu (Mother) is in the fields', they answered. 'And Bapak (father)?' 'In Malaysia' they said. At lunch time the women came back from the *sawah* (rice fields) to prepare lunch for themselves, their children, and their own parents, and to listen to the *sandiwaran* (local soap opera) on the radio.[10] They explained that most of them were *Jamal*, an acronym from *Janda Malaysia*, which means, 'Malaysian Widow'.[11] This is the local term given to women who are married but whose husbands are working overseas, usually in Malaysia, on the plantations and in the factories. (Field Notes, May, 2000)

A number of consequences of out-migration were identified by the villagers as impacting on the socio-economic makeup of Naukek. As well as the imbalanced gender ratio resulting from the out-migration of men, a further noticeable concern is that migration has altered the community's age pyramid, as sixteen to forty-five-year-olds (especially men) are essentially missing. The only men present in the village were returned migrants (who had come home for a visit after Ramadan or in between contracts), older men, and boys under the age of sixteen.

Discussions with *Jamal* revealed that some had been waiting for years for their husbands to return, and they had not received news or money for months. Some women were *ditalak* 'divorced' by their husbands on the phone (permissible in Islamic law) and had remarried. This custom has led to a rise in polygamy—a legal but discouraged practice in Indonesia—which is associated with the greater number of women available in the village, relative to men. Men described how they moved between two or three households, with wives and children in each. The high rates of divorce and re-marriage has also had an impact on the limited resources in the household, and on children's well-being. In addition, women spoke of how their new husband did not accept their children from their previous marriage, and that they were forced to neglect them, or to leave them with their parents or neighbours.

EFFECTS OF OUT-MIGRATION ON
CHILDREN AND YOUNG PEOPLE

The difficulties faced by children and young people as a result of out-migration in Naukek were identified as: an increase in household tasks; pressure to earn an income; increased school drop-outs, especially girls; decline in infant and child health; increased infant and child malnutrition; and higher infant mortality. Children also reported feelings of loneliness and of missing their parents, and other family members, and of having to take on more responsibilities as a result of their absence. I refer to these children as 'Malaysian Orphans', when both of their parents are away working overseas, either in Malaysia or elsewhere.

In Naukek, older women looked after their grandchildren—infants and toddlers—while their daughters were working overseas. One grandmother was caring for a three-year-old boy who had been left by his mother when he was a few weeks old. His father had been in Malaysia since he was born. The grandmother had not received any news or money for over a year. She said that she had a hard time finding enough food to feed herself, let alone her grandson, and that she was too old and weak to capably look after him. As a result, neighbours looked out for the boy and offered him food. In another household a young woman gave birth to a baby boy, but he died a few days later. Her husband was also in Malaysia, and she did not have enough money to take her baby to the village midwife when he became sick with a respiratory infection.

All villagers stressed the negative effects of out-migration on child rearing, and a few children were not properly cared for once their parents left. Some children, most of them boys aged seven and over, actively respond to their impoverished and marginalized position by developing a 'repertoire of strategies' in order to survive (Beazley 2003; Bell this volume). One strategy involves leaving the village and going to the local market to scavenge, beg, busk, or shine shoes, which is acceptable for boys, but not for girls (Fetter 2006b). Others go further a field and live on the streets in the provincial capital city of Mataram, or they travel to the nearby islands of Sumbawa, Bali, or Java. There they live with communities of street children, appropriating urban niches in the city, in which they were able to earn money, feel safe, and find enjoyment (see Beazley 2003; Fetter 2006a).[12]

Work

With most of the men overseas, women have to adopt the tasks traditionally done by men. Their daughters help them by performing household chores such as food preparation, cooking, washing clothes, childcare, and cleaning. This has led to more girls dropping out of school before completing primary school in Naukek, so that they can help their mothers (see also Ansell 2005). In Lombok mothers consider being skilled in housework as a benefit to their daughters when they marry (Bennett 2005). Girls in Naukek are also responsible for working in the fields and for collecting water at the river; a long walk down a steep track. They make the trip four times a day as water is required for washing and cooking, and they can only carry one large bucket on their head each trip (see Figure 9.2). Boys do not collect water as it is considered a female task. Collecting water is the one

Figure 9.2 Girls carrying water.

opportunity girls had to be away from the parental and adult gaze, and for combining play with work (see Katz 1993; 2004; Punch, this volume). For their own diversion and amusement the girls make the most of these trips, by playing with their friends in the waterfall and swimming in the river (see Figure 9.3).

Boys' tasks include looking after livestock, hoeing in the gardens, cutting grass, collecting and carrying stones from the riverbed (see Figure 9.4), which they then sell to construction workers for cement, and collecting firewood, grass, and birds from the forest. They rise early in the morning to go to the forest, and spend several hours away, thus enhancing their environmental knowledge through work and play (Katz 2004). This knowledge was evidenced in the mobility maps the children drew. The maps showed that as they get older the boys' geographical knowledge grows outwards into the forest and surrounding villages and towns of the island, and that a more complete mental image of their physical environment develops over time (see Matthews 1984; Beazley 2003). The girls, however, have a much more limited knowledge of their environment, even as they grow older, and many girls have not even left the hamlet by the time they are fifteen. Boys, however, find opportunities to go the village centre, to earn money, to visit friends or holy graves on the island, or to visit the seaside resort town of Senggigi for the weekend. These are all activities which girls are not permitted to do.

Figure 9.3 Girls playing with friends at the waterfall.

Education

Education in Indonesia, although nominally free, places a heavy economic burden on families (G. Jones and Nagib 1999). Children in Naukek only stay enrolled until the end of primary school, when they are eleven years old. The main reason is that there is no secondary school within walking distance of the hamlet, and transport costs are too expensive. Many

Figure 9.4 Boys collecting stones for construction.

children drop out earlier, and it is usually the girls who do so, particularly those who have fathers working overseas. Girls in particular are more likely to leave school when their household has limited financial resources, or when there is a need for them to work. The research in Naukek derived similar findings to those of Jeffrey and McDowell (2004) and Punch (2004) in rural Bolivia, where parents and children perceived education as having little value, and parents wished their children to leave school as soon as possible in order to start working. Children also described how they dropped out because they were bored at school, they did not learn much, and that they wanted to work in order to help their parents.

From the perspective of the teachers at the primary school, it was reported that a serious problem was the lack of concentration of the children in class. The teachers reported that this was particularly true for children who came from families where one or both of the parents were overseas, and who they believed came to school hungry and tired from extra chores.

Nutrition

During interviews with the village nurse and local *dukun* (traditional healer), they confirmed that children of migrants were often neglected and malnourished. Observation at the local village health post also evidenced low nutritional status of many children under five. Older children frequently told of having headaches, a sign of nutritional deficiency, and women said that some children experienced night blindness, a sign of Vitamin A deficiency. It was also reported by village respondents that very young babies were given *nasi papak* (chewed up rice rolled into a ball with salt) if they cried. Women believed that this would stop them from being hungry where 'thin' breast milk from malnourished mothers would not.

Other cultural practices which may also impact on a child's nutritional intake include taboos related to what food children cannot eat, as it is believed that children should not eat water spinach, young papaya, chillies, seafood, guavas, or mangoes. Further, preferences are given to the men in the family, who take a higher priority in the allocation of protein and nutritious food intake than their children and grandchildren (see also Ansell 2005). As a result boys often only obtain their protein from whatever they manage to catch in the forest, while women and girls fulfil their calorie needs through eating heaps of rice mixed with water, salt, and chilli paste, and leaves collected from the forest.

Health

Health and sickness was clearly related to malnutrition, poverty, and external factors, including out-migration. Geographical and environmental factors included remoteness from medical services, a lack of sanitation and clean water, living in closed smoky houses, the proximity of cow pens to houses, and the poor diet of all the inhabitants, especially children and women. During interviews it was discovered that most small children related to sickness in terms of pain, and appraised toothache as the most severe sickness that they experienced. Scabies, skin diseases, mumps, colds, and coughing are very common among the children of Naukek, but were not considered to be very serious and were accepted as a fact of everyday life.

The deaths of infants left behind by migrant mothers were also described by village respondents. One eight-month-old baby left in the care of her grandmother died of malnutrition. The frequent occurrence of infant death in the village meant that women saw the loss of a baby as an inevitable event, and women reported that they expected to lose their first and second baby as it was '*Kehendak Tuhan*', or God's will (Rusman et al. 1999; see also Scheper-Hughes 1992).

The belief and acceptance that infants 'simply die' (Hull et al. 1999) was reflected in the declared ambivalence towards modern health services when a child is sick. This was due to poverty and geographical factors, as well as a lack of trust in modern medicine. In Naukek infants and children had the lowest priority in getting access to health services, and villagers reported that they are rarely taken to see a nurse or a doctor. This they said was particularly true for infant girls, and boys are more likely to be taken to a health professional and to be given medication (see also Ansell, 2005). However, this rarely occurred as the medical services were so difficult to access and the cost of medicine was prohibitive (Fetter, 2006a).

MOBILITY AND ASPIRATIONS

Even in the most remote villages, the integration of Indonesia into the global economy, including its participation in trans-national migration, has led to increased individualism and consumerism throughout society. At home, children consume radio and other media images and are strongly influenced by global messages of modernity, individuality, freedom, and 'goods associated with a proper childhood' (Nieuwenhuys 1994: 275). There is only one television in Naukek, powered by a generator, but that is enough to give young people a glimpse of *sinetron* (television drama) and a sense of another life (Widodo 2002). They listen to *sandiwaran* on the radio, and have occasional access to magazines and newspapers. They also watch publicly screened films, shown in the village centre.

All these images have the power to increase a young person's desire for symbolic consumption and 'life styling' (see Shipman 2004; Widodo 2002). Leaving the village and working in the city or going overseas is regarded as a source of liberation, offering many more attractions and a greater freedom than village life (see also Ansell 2005). As G. Jones (1997: 39) asserts:

> Villagers these days are bombarded by images of the urban middle-class, not to mention of the great world beyond national boundaries... these images help to fuel the migration of young people from rural areas....

The research found that children and adolescents in Naukek are influenced by the changing expectations created by globalisation, and appear to be dissatisfied with their village lives and the boundaries and restrictions enforced on them. They do not want to work in the fields like their parents and eat rice. They want to participate in cultural practices which they see other young people doing on the TV (Ansell 2005; Utomo 1998; Widodo 2002). For this reason many children actually chose to drop out of school and work (see also Punch 2004; Beazley 2003). It is also a strong reason why adolescent boys and girls choose to migrate: either to meet their increased materialistic needs and improve their family's 'symbolic consumption', or to earn their own money to spend as they please (Shipman 2004).

Increasingly, young men and women are migrating from Lombok as young as fifteen or sixteen years old. During focus group discussion eight adolescent boys aged twelve to twenty were asked '*Pingin ke Mana?*' ('Where would you like to go'?). One young boy, Muliyah (aged 12), spoke for all of them when he replied:

> I want to go to Malaysia, to look for work as a construction labourer or in the plantations. When I am bigger for sure I will go to Malaysia.[13]

Ari (aged 14) said: 'I want to leave. My village has been left behind by Indonesia'.[14] Another young man, aged twenty, who had already been to Malaysia replied: 'America, to work'.

Going overseas to work is becoming a rite of passage in Lombok and a means to gain power and prestige in the community. Departing and returnee migrants from Malaysia are treated like movie stars, and everyone comes to welcome them back and bask in their success. It is little wonder, therefore, that these young men are influenced by such euphoric responses and want to participate in the excitement, despite the negative stories that returnee migrants bring back of exploitation and terrible working conditions.

The boys indicated that they were acutely aware of the restrictions on them to succeed if they stayed in their village, but were determined to change their futures. They felt that they could escape the poverty trap and their powerless position in their remote community by going overseas. They had witnessed their parents, aunts, uncles, and neighbours return home with enough money to buy consumer goods and in some cases to build brick houses. As traditional houses are made with rattan walls and thatch roofs, the brick houses are a sign of wealth and prosperity. These houses are known locally as *Rumah Malaysia* (Malaysian Houses) because they are built with money from working in Malaysian plantations. Returnees also buy motorbikes, TVs, parabola (satellite dish), and land (see Hugo 2002). They show off their newfound wealth to their neighbours by buying clothes and jewellery, and other material possessions (see also Punch this volume). The villagers told us, however, that the wealth is often frittered away on gambling and buying liquour, or through obligations to extended family. They also said that once the cherished house was built, those inside were often *masih lapar* ('still hungry').

Overseas migration is also a way for girls to negotiate their circumscribed role in Lombok society. Going overseas offers them many more attractions and opportunities than the village, and is increasingly perceived by them as a source of emancipation. Traditionally in Indonesia, young unmarried girls have restricted mobility, are excluded from public life and are forbidden from going far from the house, where they are expected to be a 'good girl', perform domestic duties, and to be a good daughter and wife (Suryakusuma 2004; Beazley 2002; Bennett 2005). This is particularly true in Lombok, where the placenta of a baby girl is buried near the house as a symbol of hope that she will always stay nearby, as parents rely on them for support in times of crisis and old age. Further, early marriage and pregnancy among adolescent girls is common practice in Lombok, and girls are often married as young as twelve or thirteen. Culturally there is considerable social pressure for girls to marry by the age of fifteen, or they are called derogatory names, indicating that they are no longer desirable in the marriage market (*Darmos* or 'on the shelf'). Similarly, unmarried males are called *Termos*, but not until they are twenty years old.

To compensate for their social and geographical exclusion young girls listen avidly to the radio. They are fascinated by soap operas, and consume the media images of glamorous 'Western' lifestyles of free and independent women (see Ansell 2005; Widodo 2002). These are far more persuasive than the state or village community's construction of femininity, and much more appealing as an agent of socialisation.

Traditionally, therefore, there is a high expectation for girls to take on marital and family obligations at an early age. This trend is changing, however, as a result of the opportunity to work overseas, earn an income and escape the traditional expectations and gendered power relations in the village. An increasing number of unmarried girls want to go to Saudi Arabia, to work as domestic servants. These TKW are treated as heroines as long as they remain invisible and send regular money home to the extended family. If they come home, however, the community acts ambivalently toward them, suspicious of how they have 'changed' as a result of their experiences. This suspicion is partly due to a belief that TKW are raped or involved in prostitution, a rumour that has begun to circulate and gain currency in Lombok. Such talk results in problems with the re-integration of the young women back into their communities upon their return, including their chances of being able to marry. They become regarded as outsiders and often face physical or verbal abuse, and bestow shame upon their family due to the scandalous gossip. In most cases a new contract overseas is the solution to the social stigma.[15]

In spite of this stigma, however, girls' desire to go overseas for the perceived benefits continues to compel them to actively navigate such risks, in order that they may earn money, gain independence, and escape their restricted roles in the family and village (see also Hugo 2002). There is also the tantalising possibility that they will meet a man to marry, so that they never need return. In this way the girls may also be perceived as active agents, organizing their lives and negotiating the gendered power relations around them (Punch 2000).[16]

CONCLUSION

This chapter has shown how in spite of their circumscribed and marginal lives, young people in rural Lombok are dynamic negotiators, who are able to challenge and subvert the circumstances produced around them by adult power relations and external global forces. In this way they challenge the existing ways of doing things, and make effective judgements about their play, work, and everyday actions. This includes their ability to make informed decisions about their future activities, including acting upon their desire to work overseas.

Overseas migration is a trend that is set to continue in Indonesia, and to expand with the growth of illegal *calo* and female migration. In Lombok, the rise in the numbers of legal and illegal TKI and TKW has had a dramatic impact on both the structure and survival strategies of family households, including the health, well-being, and livelihoods of children and young people. In spite of its negative effects, however, children left behind by their migrant parents are able to cope with and benefit from the changed circumstances in their villages, and to find ways in which to blend work, school, and play.

Nevertheless, due to their disadvantaged rural village environment adolescents do find it difficult to fulfil their leisure and work aspirations though locally available opportunities. Further, the endemic poverty of Eastern Indonesia is no longer accepted as passively as it has been in the past (Bandiyono et al. 1999).[17] With the pervasiveness of communication into the villages, almost all young people have been exposed to the powerful and glamorous images of the global youth culture. Increasingly they are defying the power relations and limited opportunities available to them in their village, and leaving.

These young people, particularly boys, choose to seek their fortunes elsewhere, either as street children or as overseas migrants. This is because going away offers many more opportunities and a greater freedom than is available in their impoverished village. Increasingly, girls are also going overseas to work, as their only alternative is early marriage, childbirth, and hardship. Working overseas provides them with the opportunity to escape the poverty trap and the impact of the ongoing economic crisis, to take control over their own lives, and to actively resist their restricted role in society.

Acknowledgements

I am grateful to Alison Murray, Joy Reynolds, Michelle Carnegie, and the editors for their detailed and helpful comments on earlier drafts of this chapter. The data for this chapter were gathered in 2000 while I was the Community Participation Adviser on an Australian Agency for International Development (AusAID) funded 'Women's Health and Family Welfare Project' (WHFWP), a joint cooperation between the Indonesian and Australian governments, which had the objective of improving maternal and child health in Eastern Indonesia. I am thankful to both AusAID and the Overseas Project Corporation Victoria (OPCV) for giving me the opportunity to work on the project. I am also indebted to Kate Bunbury, Terry Hull, Laurel MacLaren, Lenny Setiawati, and Yang Suwan for sharing with me their knowledge and expertise, and to the PRA team in Lombok (Ibu Suwan, Ibu Rohanna, Ibu Beauty Erawati, Ibu Nurgina Wahyuni, and Pak Mintarjo Adi) for their assistance during the data collection period. I must emphasise, however, that the views and opinions expressed in this chapter are mine alone and do not reflect those of the Commonwealth of Australia, AusAID, the Indonesian Government, or any other organisation or individual involved in the WHFWP.

NOTES

1. Data were collected while working on an AusAID (Australian Agency for International Development) project aimed at reducing infant and maternal mortality in the region. To analyse the community-based factors influencing maternal and infant health at the village level, the project utilised PRA methods, aimed to engage communities in qualitative research that identifies and analyses their situation. Examples of PRA exercises include mobility maps; resource maps; time-lines; transect walks; seasonal calendars; causal flow diagrams; and sickness rankings. The emphasis of participatory research is on generating knowledge from the perspective of those being researched, not from the perspective of the researcher (see Chambers 1990; 1994; 1997; Cornwall 2003; Cornwall and Pratt 2003; Beazley and Ennew 2006). See also Johnson et al. (1998) and Johnson (1996b) for a discussion on participatory research with children.
2. In order to protect the identity of the hamlet, the name has been changed.
3. In 1992 Lombok's infant mortality rate was recorded at 100 deaths per 1,000 live births (compared to 32 per 1,000 live births for Indonesia as a whole). See Rusman, Djohan, and Hull (1999) for a full discussion on the complex issue of infant mortality in Lombok.

4. The term *TKI* stands for *Tenaga Kerja Indonesia* and specifically refers to men (as an individual or as a group) working overseas. *TKW* or *Tenaga Kerja Wanita* is the term used for international migrant women workers.

5. Unemployment figure from United States–Indonesian Society (2005).

6. Bryant (2005) makes this estimate based on official figures of total number of overseas migrants and recent UNPD 2002 fertility rates, which estimates that the average woman will have 1.5 children by the time she is thirty years old.

7. Lombok is favoured by recruiters because it is a poor, predominantly rural island with few avenues for generating income and because the people of Lombok, the *Sasak*, are considered to be hard workers. Lombok is also well-known as 'the island of a thousand mosques', and the inhabitants are devout Muslims, which is regarded as an added advantage to employers in Malaysia and the Middle East.

8. Although official migrants to Malaysia are relatively few, due to strict immigration and employment laws, the business of illegal migration, conducted without legal work visas, is huge. Many studies have shown that the number of illegal Indonesian workers (who are assisted by middlemen or *calo*) exceeds the number of legal workers (Bandiyono et al. 1999). Illegal migration is often preferred by employers as they can exploit the situation by paying lower wages and offering appalling living and work conditions.

9. This fact was reported by the village head, the village midwife, and the village health staff, who all attributed the rise in divorce rates to the rise in overseas migrations.

10. All Indonesian soap operas and *sinetrons* (Indonesian television dramas, many imported from Mexico and Brazil) depict women and girls as wealthy, powerful consumers. See Widodo (2002) for an analysis.

11. The status of being a *Jamal* in Lombok is not an easy one. *Jamal* are targets of male jokes and seen as easy prey for an extra-marital affair.

12. In January 2006 Yayasan Peduli Anak, a street children NGO based in Mataram, Lombok, conducted a study of 200 street children who had dropped out of school and left home (personal communication, Fetter, 2006a). Most of the children were aged from nine to fifteen years old , were from Lombok, and from broken homes: 'many times the mother went to Malaysia to work there and left their children with the father, family or just alone' (Fetter, 2006b). An additional reason for leaving home given by the children was that their mother had remarried, and the child was not accepted by the step-father and was subsequently rejected or neglected. Other children were sent to the street to earn money by their impoverished parents (see also Beazley, 2000a).

13. Cita cita saya pingin ke Malaysia untuk menjadi kuli bangunan atau kerja perkebunan. Kalau saya sudah besar pasti saya akan ke sana (translated from the Sasak language by fieldworker).

14. Saya mau keluar. Desaku adalah desa tertingal di Indonesia (translated from the Sasak language by fieldworker).

15. These conclusions raise important debates around gendered power relations in the village as well as the well-publicized abusive conditions the girls often face when working overseas. Thus, young women may find that having escaped the stifling conditions of home life they are faced with even harsher and exploitative conditions with their new employers. This issue clearly points to the necessity for further research.

16. See also Williams (2005) and her analysis of how young women from Eastern Indonesia use transnational migration as a means of seeking a 'new subjectivity'.

17. As justly noted by one of my reviewers, according to Scott (1985) it is questionable if the rural poor have ever accepted their poverty passively.

10 'I mean, it depends on me in the end, doesn't it?'

Young people's perspectives on their daily life and future prospects in rural East Germany

Nadine Schäfer

INTRODUCTION

Children and young people have been identified as one of the groups most severely affected by declining standards of welfare and by the rise of socio-economic inequalities in post-socialist societies (Brake and Büchner 1996; Kollmorgen 2003; McAuley 1995). However, there has been limited research to date on the ways in which young people negotiate their life circumstances and develop strategies for building meaningful and purposeful lives (see Côté 2002; Jeffrey and McDowell 2004). This chapter begins to address this gap by analysing the way rural young people in the East German state of Mecklenburg-Vorpommern negotiate and seek to challenge structural disadvantages through a range of everyday practices. It follows a wider call in the study of childhood and youth to acknowledge both structural conditions that characterize young people's lives, as well as young people's agency (see Holloway and Valentine 2000a; James, Jenks, and Prout 1998).

The chapter is based on research into the daily life and future prospects of rural East German youth, which was carried out in 2004 and 2005 and adopted a qualitative, participatory approach. Here, I focus on group discussions conducted with two mixed gender groups of 15- to 16-year-olds from rural communities. Each of the groups consisted of eight participants who were recruited through local schools. The narratives of young people's daily lives and hopes for the future that are presented here give an insight into the diverse ways in which young people experience, cope with, challenge, and resist forms of disadvantage and social exclusion related to their location in rural East Germany. They also show a need for greater recognition of the creative and resistive practices of people's everyday lives in post-socialist societies (Burawoy and Verdery 1999; Hörschelmann 2002; Pilkington et al. 2002; Pilkington 2004; Pilkington and Johnson 2003; Stenning 2005).

Research on young people's lives in post-socialist countries (see Hörschelmann and Schäfer 2005; Machacek 1997; Pilkington et al. 2002; Pilkington 2004; Pilkington and Johnson 2003; Riordan et al. 1995; Roberts et al. 2000; Smith 1998) indicates that values and norms developed in the past, as well as in the context of transformation, continue to be relevant for how people experience and interpret present conditions, thus challenging the perception of post-socialism as 'a temporary, transitional category with no power beyond a limited historical and geographical moment' (Stenning 2005: 113; see also Hörschelmann 2002). The importance of recognising post-socialist difference when researching youth is also voiced by Smith (1998), who argues with Pilkington (1994) that 'simply analysing youth cultures in eastern Europe as a poor relation of western youth cultures is to miss their significance in reflecting the forces that shaped them and shaping their societies' (Smith 1998: 290). Yet, young people in post-socialist societies also do not fit easily with the category Majority world, as it is employed in this book (see also Penn 1999; Punch 2003; Woodhead 1998). While I agree that this category is useful for subverting the privileged, western-centric perspective that underlies divisions between first world and third world, I am concerned that replacing these categories with a new binary division between Majority and Minority world risks overlooking the lives and experiences of those who, like young people in eastern Germany, do not fit easily within either conceptual sphere. The concepts are useful insofar as they offer an alternative to the peripherality implied by the term *third world* and draw attention to the power relations that sustain Minority world privileges. However, we need to remain reflexive about the binary constructions on which these terms rest (Punch 2003) and use them as strategic devices rather than as frameworks that define people's experiences and perceptions in all their complexities. Young people in rural East Germany draw benefit from their residence in a Minority state and yet are disadvantaged by their structural marginality within it.

MECKLENBURG-VORPOMMERN AS A SITE OF STUDY

The research project was conducted in the Landkreis Müritz, a region which is located in Mecklenburg-Vorpommern (MV), one of five 'new federal states' that formerly belonged to the German Democratic Republic (GDR) (see Figure 10.1). MV is situated in the northeast of Germany and is characterized by agriculture, with more than 60 per cent of the land used for arable farming.

Since unification, MV has suffered from radical economic changes and has been classed as an EU 1 region, confirming that it is one of the poorest regions in Europe (Bundesamt für Bauwesen und Raumordnung 2000). This is reflected in its poorly developed infrastructure, low population density, and unemployment rates that are more than twice the national average (see Table 10.1).

Furthermores the region has to cope with low birth rates and high levels of out-migration, (Fischer et al. 2002; Kröhnert et al. 2005) so that

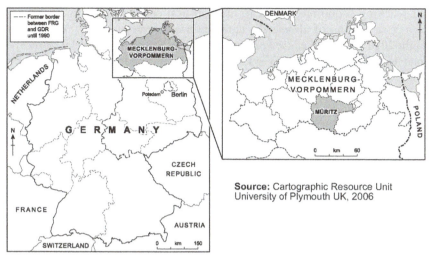

Figure 10.1 Mecklenburg-Vorpommern and the Landkreis Müritz.

Mecklenburg-Vorpommern's population is becoming one of the oldest in Germany (see Kröhnert et al. 2005).

YOUNG PEOPLE'S RURAL LIVES IN MECKLENBURG-VORPOMMERN (EAST GERMANY)

Rural regions, compared to urban areas, in both the Minority world (see Ansell 2005; Punch 2004) and the Majority world (see Jentsch 2004; Jentsch and Shucksmith 2004; Vanderbeck and Dunkley 2003), suffer from poorer choices in terms of education and higher unemployment rates. Scholars have highlighted the specific disadvantages of rural East Germany compared with West German regions, due to the dramatic loss of services and facilities since reunification (Baur and Burrmann 2000; Brake and Büchner 1996; Kollmorgen 2003). The collapse of state socialism has had

Table 10.1 Key statistical comparisons

	Federal Republic of Germany (FRG)	*Mecklenburg-Vorpommern (MV)*	*Müritz (in MV)(specific research area)*
Population density	231/km²	75/km²	40/km²
Unemployment rate	9.8%	20.0%	22.9%
Youth unemployment rate (≥ 25 years old)	9.4%	12.5%	18.7%

Source: Statistisches Landesamt Mecklenburg-Vorpommern 2003

far-reaching economic, political, and cultural consequences that have led to a re-definition of almost the entire fabric of everyday life' (Young and Light 2001: 942) and caused new uncertainties as lives and worlds of meanings 'lost their moorings' (Verdery 1999). Young people in East Germany are growing up in a time that is characterized by uncertainty and the need for re-orientation.

A prime example of the radical changes that have affected people's everyday life in rural areas is the restructuring of the 'Landwirtschaftliche Produktionsgenossenschaft' (LPGs); large-scale agricultural cooperatives that fulfilled important social functions in addition to their economic roles during the GDR. LPGs were the institutional outcome of the collectivisation and industrialisation of socialist agriculture (Wilson and Wilson 2001; Wilson and Klages 2001). These cooperatives were responsible for a wide range of social and administrative functions in villages, offering childcare, community services such as libraries, bars, and shops, and organising cultural and social events (see Rudolph 1997: 450; van Hoven 2001:41). In addition, the Freie Deutsche Jugend (FDJ; Free German Youth) offered young people a wide range of leisure facilities and organized social activities. It was the only official youth movement in the GDR; an instrument of the state that most East German youths joined at the age of 13 or 14. In 1988, 99.4 per cent of eligible school pupils and 92.5 per cent of university students were members (Schefold 1995). The FDJ monopolized organized youth activities and ran holiday camps, discos, and youth clubs for rural as well as urban young people.

Differences between rural and urban areas in the GDR were generally small, since state policies followed the ideological aim of eliminating structural inequalities between agricultural and industrial societies (see Beetz 2004). Since reunification in 1990, however, socio-economic differences between rural and urban areas have re-emerged strongly in East Germany (Bundesamt für Bauwesen und Raumordnung 2000; van Hoven 2001; 2002). The restructuring of cooperatives has led to a major decline in agricultural employment (see van Hoven 2001: 42) and to the loss of social services associated with them. In addition, the FDJ lost nearly all its members and the number of youth clubs declined rapidly. Out of 9,620 state-run youth clubs that were registered in MV in 1988 only 312 such clubs existed in 1991 (Schefold 1995).

As the number of schoolchildren in Mecklenburg-Vorpommern has declined by 45.2 per cent since reunification (Statistisches Amt Mecklenburg-Vorpommern 2006), due to out-migration and dramatically falling birth rates, services and facilities for young people have closed, making access to education and training and employment increasingly difficult. Young people growing up in rural East Germany are facing problems associated with changing schools and travelling further to school as well as fewer training options (see Baur and Burrmann 2000; Brake 1996; Brake and Büchner 1996; Kollmorgen 2003). Partly in response to this, skilled young people often leave the region. Such trends reinforce rather than reduce the differences between East and West Germany. Comparative research suggests that young East Germans have experienced more dramatic changes than their West German counterparts, and are more likely to perceive their future as bleak (Brake 1996; Brake and Büchner 1996; Werz 2001). In regard to this rural young people living in East Germany are still referred to as the 'losers' of reunification (see Baur and Burrmann 2000; Brake 1996; Brake and Büchner 1996; Kollmorgen 2003).

While such a characterisation recognizes the multiple disadvantages faced by East German youth, it also contributes to the perception that young people growing up in these rural regions are 'a "problem", in relation to crime, drugs, political extremism' (Smith 1998: 297). This negative and one-sided picture of East German youth dominates public and academic discourses and fails to acknowledge the heterogeneity of young people in East Germany. The construction of East German youth as 'different' and 'other' may also have a negative influence on East German young people's own socio-spatial identity construction, thus contributing further to feelings of exclusion.

In order to challenge the perception of East German youths as either deviants or victims, more attention needs to be paid to discourses *by* rather than *about* them. In particular, it is important to understand the lifestyle strategies adopted by young people in response to challenges or changes that *they* view as affecting *their* lives (Hörschelmann and Schäfer 2005). The following sections aim to achieve this through an analysis of qualitative data that was produced through participatory research. The project enabled young people to define their own priority issues and to conduct much of the research themselves.

YOUNG PEOPLE IN RURAL EAST GERMANY: CONCERNS ABOUT THE FUTURE

Young people identified limited job prospects and high unemployment rates as the main disadvantage of their rural and East German residency:

> Anja (15) :1 Yeah well, I think the only disadvantage we have living in the countryside is that there are not enough jobs for us. I mean, this is not only the case for [the village she lives in] but for the whole region. It is different in West Germany, though.[2]

This perception had a major impact on young people's day-to-day lives resulting in an often expressed fear of becoming unemployed themselves. A large number of the young people who participated in the research were thus worried that if they failed to achieve high or exceptional results in their final exams they would have little success in the job market.

This concern arose from young people's firsthand experiences of unemployment. They often had witnessed close family members becoming unemployed and were aware of the negative financial and emotional impact of unemployment on the individual. This led to a feeling of vulnerability that they too would be at risk from a lack of work. However, although young people draw a connection between their rural and East German residency and the risk of being unemployed, they described it as a personal risk which they tried to overcome as individuals.

This corresponds with Beck's (1992; 2000; Beck and Beck-Gernsheim 2002) description of the perception of social inequalities in today's world. Beck has argued that although the reunification has led to increasing unemployment rates and poverty, these social inequalities are now explained through personal failure and are reduced to personal experiences, rather than through broader social structures, thus overlooking the structural causes for social inequalities that still exist (Beck 2002: 47). This means that social exclusion is 'collectively individualised' (see Beck 2000), which corresponds with the empirical results of Furlong and Cartmel's (1997: 7) work on young people's life experiences in modern industrialized societies as 'a wider range of pathways to choose from', which gives young people the impression that their own route is 'unique'.

The majority of the young people interviewed felt that they were responsible for their own future:

> Sven (16): Well, when I come home with bad marks, how then is my mum supposed to help me? She can't do anything because it is my future.[3]

Similarly, Maren describes how her job prospects mainly depend on how hard she works at school.

> Maren (16): I mean it depends on me in the end, doesn't it? My marks in school are not so brilliant at the moment, so I really need to do more schoolwork if I want to get a job. I think I just need to study harder for it.[4]

Given this sense of responsibility, many young people developed their own strategies to avoid future unemployment. These strategies are described below.

Strategy 1: Getting a good school-leaving certificate

Some young people developed strategies to overcome, for example, personal learning difficulties or difficulties with particular teachers, which the following extracts demonstrate:

Tobias (16): It all depends on your own motivation, I think. If you really want to get a good job, then you have to work harder for it. But there are lots of people who don't care. And just being good is not good enough any more.

Nadja (16): That sounds so easy, but I really try hard and still get really bad marks in maths. I don't know what to do any more. I just don't understand it.

Tobias (16): Well, then I would repeat the class because if your final exam results aren't really good, nobody will take you.[5]

Tobias argued that Nadja should repeat a year in school to get better results which, from his point of view, would improve her chance in the job market. Tobias made a similar decision himself since he changed schools due to problems with two subjects. He argued that he will have better chances on the job market with brilliant exam results taken when aged 16 than with higher level results, and that a change in schools would allow this. Tobias describes that he asked his parents to let him change school because he saw his future job prospects were in danger. Although his parents would have preferred that their son aimed for higher academic qualifications (taken when aged 18) he succeeded in persuading them to change his school. In doing so, Tobias accepts a much longer journey to school than before and a loss of nearly two hours of his free time everyday due to bus travel.

This example shows that young people reacted to the wider socio-economic circumstances they grow up in and developed their own strategies to overcome risks of disadvantage and to improve their own situation.

Strategy 2: Getting additional qualifications

Young people argued that it is not only essential to do well in school, but that it is also important to get some additional qualifications, which help them to develop new skills and give them an insight into different jobs. Futhermore, they felt that securing additional qualifications helped them to build networks with potential employers. Nearly all young people placed high value on school organized work placements which allowed them to work for two weeks during term time. These job experiences were perceived as very important because they offered insights into jobs available regionally and helped them to clarify in which field they wanted to work later on:

Martin (16): I never really knew what I wanted to be, so when we had to do our work placement I did not really know what to go for. I worked in a garage finally and it was really fun. Now I am trying to find a place to train as a mechanic.[6]

In this context, participation in the research project also became important for the young people. The project was designed to be participatory and to be beneficial for the participants, so they were offered a certificate (in English and German) that acknowledged their engagement in the project and described the skills they learned as useful for their future lives.

Anna (15) and Tim (16) for example, were doing some teamwork related to training in research methods.[7] Tim suggested that he could videotape Anna's attempt to interview so that they could analyze it together afterwards. Anna, however, did not want to be filmed and said she would feel very uncomfortable and would not know what to say when other people were watching her. While Tim did not further insist on filming her, he responded:

Tim (16): Well OK, we don't have to, but I think this is pretty good training for future job interviews. We can't start training for this early enough, don't you think? And here we get pretty good feedback as well.[8]

Strategy 3: Being informed

Another way that young people actively tried to improve their job opportunities was through consulting the job centre. While a lot of young people made their own appointments and reported that they got helpful information once they had decided which job they wanted to pursue, they also described how limited the support was they got from the job centre. They found it problematic to get an appointment as the job centre was open only once a week in the next bigger town. The quality of information and assistance they received depended strongly on the consultant who was running the office. Furthermore, young people complained that they were mainly referred to job opportunities in West Germany.

Young people argued, however, that they did not want to rely on the job centre alone but searched for further options to find their own 'unique' ways of getting the information they needed. Susan (15), for example, explained that she had spent hours searching the Internet to compile a list of hospitals that train nurses. When asked if she could not get such a list from the job centre, she replied:

> Susan (15): Well, perhaps they have a list, but you know, there may be 30 people asking about training opportunities for nurses and they all get the same list so they all send their applications to the same hospitals.[9]

The internet was seen by a lot of young people as a way to improve their opportunities to find job vacancies and to be more independent of institutional career services. Information was seen as key to improving job prospects. Consequently, some young people used participation in the research

Fotografin:

Als Fotograf/in arbeitet man in einem Atelier oder macht Freilichtaufnahmen, Pass- und Bewerbungsbilder, Portrait-aufnahmen (Baby, Kinder, Mann, Frau, Geschwister, Pärchen, Haustiere, Hochzeiten, Einschulungen, Jugendweihen, Jubiläen usw.), digitale Bildbearbeitung (Retusche, Korekturen), Kundenberatung und den Verkauf von Fotozubehör.
Für die Ausbildung braucht man einen guten Realschulabschluss. Perfekt wäre Abitur.
Eine besondere Anforderung bei Fotografen hier in Röbel ist, dass man ein einjähriges Praktikum absolvieren muss, bevor man eine Ausbildung beginnen kann.
Weitere Anforderungen sind dann noch gute Noten in Mathematik, Deutsch, Physik und Chemie. Das Mindestalter wäre 16 oder 17 Jahre und wenn man einen Führerschein besitzen würde, wäre das noch mehr von Vorteil.
Im Gespräch konnten wir auch noch erfahren, dass der Betrieb ausbildet. Wir fragten die Fotografin auch, wie sie zu ihrem Beruf gekommen ist. Darauf antwortete sie, dass es ihr Wunschberuf sei und dass sie am liebsten mit Babys arbeitet und Freilichtaufnahmen (Hochzeiten etc.) macht.

Figure 10.2 Interview project on local job opportunities conducted by six young people aged 15–16 years.[15]

project as an opportunity to investigate which kind of job training was available for them in their own town. A group of 15 and 16 year old girls thus interviewed fifteen different local employers about the kind of qualifications needed to get a job and the possibility of being given training by these local firms (Figure 10.2).

Young people felt that this project not only contributed to their own future prospects, but also for those of the younger pupils in their school because it gave an insight into the *local* job situation. The project was exhibited in the school auditorium for several weeks and was thus an example of how young people use personal engagement to find a way of overcoming the disadvantages they face.

Strategy 4: Being flexible

The young people who participated in the research highlighted the importance of being flexible. They argued that it was not enough to decide which job they liked best, but that it was more important to think of alternatives that might increase their chances of getting any job at all.

> Anna (16): I believe the worst is when you come up with *one* profession you want to follow and you do not think of any alternatives. Because if

you do not get this one job, which is quite likely, then you are really dis-appointed and you are not able to come up with anything new quickly. If you have two or three alternatives, however, that can't happen so quickly and you have much better chances.[10]

Anna therefore described flexibility as an essential quality to improving opportunities in the job market. Geographical flexibility was also important:

Markus (16): To me it's all about the same. I will go where there is a future for me, where I can find a job.[11]

Lena replied similarly:

Lena (15): It's all the same where I go. I would just like to find a job which enables me to pay my rent every month and perhaps save some money to go on holiday or suchlike. I just want to be sure that I earn enough money to pay for my own living expenses.[12]

The majority of the young people being interviewed were prepared to leave their region in order to increase their chances of finding a secure, well-paid job. The teenagers often emphasized that they aimed to move to West Germany because it offered better job opportunities and salaries than the East. Thus, some young people seemed surprised when it was suggested that they were 'forced' to move to find a good job:

Sven (16): What does that mean 'being forced'? No, I really want to leave and you know, to get a good job you have to be willing to give something up.[13]

Maja (15): When you have the idea of a special job in your head, well, then it is a great chance to go to West Germany. I mean, you have to decide what is more important: the career or to stay here and prob-ably just get a badly paid job or even get no work. I mean, for me it is very clear, I want a job so that I earn enough to pay for my own living expenses.[14]

This shows that young people perceived the possibility of leaving their region as a way to improve their job opportunities rather than something that they were forced to do. It means that these teenagers did not per-ceive themselves as 'losers' but rather, the prospect of moving was seen as part of a self-empowering strategy they could employ to improve their prospects.

CONCLUSION

This chapter elaborates the multiple ways in which young people in rural East Germany aim to overcome their perceived disadvantages. While these young people are described in the academic literature as the 'losers' of reunification, I argue that rural young people growing up in East Germany do not only perceive themselves as victims, but also as agents who can actively improve their future prospects in finding their own 'unique' way to overcome disadvantages.

In highlighting young people's agency, I aimed to challenge the one-sided image of rural East German young people who are often described as passive with regard to the post-socialist transformation process. Such a perception, however, neglects to acknowledge the multiple ways in which young people experience and respond to transformation processes. I therefore argue that more research needs to be done on rural young people's lives in post-socialist countries.

While this chapter has focused on young people's agency and the strategies they employ, it does not argue that they can easily and equally overcome the structural disadvantages they have to face. Nor does it imply that developing such strategies will actually improve young people's job prospects (see Jeffrey and McDowell 2004: 131). Rather, it should be critically questioned which young people are more likely to develop successful strategies and the extent to which social class, gender, ethnicity, and spatiality impact on their decisions and their outcomes.

Much more research needs to be done to uncover why some young people are more successful than others at overcoming disadvantages, benefiting from opportunities, and creating their own opportunities. Specifically, attention should be paid to the extent to which rural residency acts as a restrictive factor.

However, in accordance with Panelli (2002) and Opitz-Karig (2003), I argue that the negative image of the rural and of rural residency needs to be challenged. Rural spaces are not only spaces of marginalization, but also spaces of possibilities 'where landscapes of youth can be read as terrains of creativity, conflict and change, flexing over the broader topography of political-economic processes and socio-cultural systems' (Panelli 2002: 121). That means, while socio-spatial and economic disadvantages of rural residency still need to be investigated in more detail, a more complex and heterogeneous understanding of young people's lives in rural areas of social, political, and economic transition needs to be elaborated. That is why it is all the more important to listen to young people who are living in these spaces and to analyse the multiple ways in which they challenge and resist forms of exclusion or marginalization.

While it has to be critically questioned where young people growing up in a post-socialist region fit into the concepts of Minority and Majority worlds, I have stressed that these concepts need to be understood as contextual frames which help us to understand the broader life conditions, power-relations, and structures that may affect people's lives in these countries or regions. We have to be aware, however, that terms are often implicitly connected with particular constructions of the 'rural' or 'youth' that narrow our views and understandings (see Punch 2003). It means that we have to be more reflexive about the underlying construction which these terms refer to.

Acknowledgements

I would like to thank the young people who participated so enthusiastically in the research project. It could not have been achieved without them! Furthermore I want to thank the editors of this book, as well as Kathrin Hörschelmann and Richard Yarwood for valuable comments on earlier drafts of this chapter. I am grateful for financial support from the University of Plymouth, the Seale Hayne Educational Trust, and the Foundation for Urban and Regional Studies that enabled the doctoral research which this chapter draws on. Thanks also go to Jamie Quinn from the Cartographic Resources Unit in Plymouth, for drawing the map.

NOTES

1. The names of the research participants have been changed in order to maintain anonymity and confidentiality. The pseudonyms used represent the gender of the participants. Information about their age is added in parentheses.
2. Anja (15): Na, also ich glaube der einzige Nachteil ist, dass es nicht genug Arbeitsplätze für uns gibt. Ich meine, das ist ja nicht nur hier [Name des Dorfes in dem sie lebt] so, sondern in der ganzen Region. Naja, das ist eben anders in West-Deutschland.
3. Sven (16): Also, wenn ich mit schlechten Noten nach Hause komme, wie kann mir meine Mutter denn da helfen? Sie kann doch gar nichts tun, ist ja schliesslich *meine* Zukunft.
4. Maren (16): Ich mein, am Ende liegt es doch an mir, oder nicht? Im Moment sind meine Schulnoten nicht so toll, also muss ich mehr für die Schule tun, um einen Job zu bekommen. Ich denke ich muss einfach mehr lernen.
5. Tobias (16): Es hängt letztlich alles von deiner Motivation ab, denke ich. Wenn du wirklich einen guten Job bekommen willst, dann musst du eben hart dafür arbeiten. Aber vielen ist das einfach egal. Und gut sein ist eben einfach nicht mehr gut genug.
   Nadja (16): Naja, das klingt so einfach, aber ich tue wirklich alles und hab immer noch super schlechte Noten in Mathe. Ich weiss wirlich nicht, was ich da noch tun kann. Ich verstehe das einfach nicht.
   Tobias (16): Naja, ich würde dann halt die letzte Klasse nochmal wiederholen, weil wenn deine Abschlussnoten nicht gut sind, wird dich keiner nehmen.
6. Martin (16): Ich wusste nie so richtig, was ich werden will und hatte keine Ahnung, wo ich mein Schulpraktikum machen sollte. Ich hab dann in einer

Werkstatt was bekommen und das hat richtig Spass gemacht. Deshalb suche ich jetzt eine Lehrstelle als Mechaniker.

7. This training took place at the second meeting I had with this group. At the early stages of the research project Anna did not want to be filmed or to interview other people. However, at the end of the project she did the main work for a video project on their everyday lives within which she interviewed several adults and other peers on different topics. It demonstrates that she became much more confident during the research process and enjoyed practising the new skills she developed during the three months of research participation.

8. Tim (16): Naja gut, müssen wir ja nicht, aber ich denke das ist ein verdammt gutes Training auch für zukünftige Job-Interviews. Ich denke, damit kann man gar nicht früh genug anfangen, meinst du nicht? Und hier kriegen wir auch noch gutes Feedback.

9. Susan (15): Naja, vielleicht haben die ja eine Liste, aber weisst du, da gehen vielleicht 30 Leute hin und fragen nach Ausbildungsmöglickeiten für Krankenschwestern und dann haben die alle die *gleiche* Liste und schicken ihre Bewerbungen alle an die gleichen Krankenhäuser.

10. Anna (16): Ich glaube das Schlimmste ist, wenn du dich auf *einen* Beruf versteifst und dir keine Alternativen ausdenkst. Weil, wenn du *den einen Job* nicht kriegst, was ja ziemlich wahrscheinlich ist, dann bist du total enttäuscht und dann fällt dir so schnell nichts Neues ein. Wenn du aber zwei oder drei Alternativen hast, kann dir das nicht so schnell passieren und du hast viel bessere Chancen.

11. Markus (16): Mir ist das wirklich ziemlich egal. Ich will dahin, wo es eine Zukunft für mich gibt, wo ich einen *Job* finde.

12. Lena (15): Es ist eigentlich egal, wohin ich gehe. Ich möchte halt nur einen Job kriegen der es mir ermöglicht meine Miete jeden Monat zu zahlen und vielleicht auch noch etwas Geld zu sparen um mal in Urlaub zu fahren oder so. I möchte halt sicher sein, dass ich genug Geld verdiene, um über die Runden zu kommen.

13. Sven (16): Was soll das bedeuten: gezwungen werden? Nee, ich will ja weg und weisst du um einen guten Job zu bekommen man muss eben auch bereit sein etwas aufzugeben.

14. Maja (15): Wenn du dir einen bestimmten Job in den Kopf gesetzt hast, naja, dann ist es doch eine grosse Chance nach West-Deutschland zu gehen. Ich mein, man muss sich schon entscheiden, was einem wichtiger ist: der Beruf oder hier zu bleiben und dann eben vielleicht nur eine schlecht bezahlte oder vielleicht auch überhaupt keine Arbeit zu bekommen. Ich mein, für mich ist ganz klar, dass ich einen Job haben will, bei dem ich genug verdiene um gut über die Runden zu kommen.

15. Translation: Photographers work in a studio or outdoors to take pictures. It is their job to take pictures for passports or job applications, as well as portrait pictures (of babies, children, men, women, siblings, couples, pets, weddings, school enrolment, Jugendweihe which can be understood as youth consecration, anniversaries and so on). In addition to this they edit digital pictures (retouching, correcting) and are involved in customer service as well as in selling photo-equipment. To get an apprenticeship one needs to have good marks in school leaving exams, preferably higher level.

A special requirement in the photo-shop in our town is that one needs to do a one-year work-placement before starting the apprenticeship. Further requirements are good marks in math, German, physics and chemistry. You have to be at least 16 or 17 years old and it is beneficial if you already have a driving license.

We were informed that this shop offers an apprenticeship. In addition to this we asked the photographer, why she had chosen this job. She replied that being a photographer was always her dream and that she loves to take pictures of babies and outdoor-pictures like wedding-pictures.

11 Conceptualizing agency in the lives and actions of rural young people

Elsbeth Robson, Stephen Bell, and Natascha Klocker[1]

INTRODUCTION

This chapter aims to build conceptually upon the accounts of young people's actions in specific rural settings outlined in the preceding chapters. Like the wider body of ongoing research on young people's everyday lives across the world, the foregoing chapters clearly demonstrate how the shift to viewing young people as individuals with the capacity to act and shape their own lives, i.e. to have agency, rather than seeing children simply as 'adults in training' (Dunne 1980), passive and innocent dependents, or victims[2] has become firmly established in children's and youth studies. This volume illustrates some of the many ways in which young people are creative and competent actors in a diversity of rural settings across Minority and Majority worlds. In this chapter we consider the agency which young people show in their everyday rural lives, identifying different spheres and types of agency as well as the limits to agency; we conclude with some suggestions for future research directions. What follows outlines conceptual frameworks for addressing (and critiquing) agency in present and future research on rural young people.

CONCEPTUALIZING AGENCY

Agency is understood as an individual's own capacities, competencies, and activities through which they navigate the contexts and positions of their lifeworlds, fulfilling many economic, social, and cultural expectations, while simultaneously charting individual/collective choices and possibilities for their daily and future lives. As agents, young people negotiate the institutions and rural spaces they encounter while creating their own experiences (Panelli et al. 2002). Conceptualising young people as agents, i.e. competent social beings, means viewing them as 'doers' and 'thinkers', rather than as 'human becomings' (Valentine 1996). 'Thinking' and 'doing' are important components of any definition of agency, and there is much evidence of young people as thinkers and doers throughout this book.

The 'discovery' of children as agents is relatively recent, and within sociological studies of childhood has led to '...a call for children to be understood as social actors shaping as well as shaped by their circumstances' (James et al. 1998: 6). Thus, many scholars across diverse disciplines have increasingly focused on how rural young people negotiate social relations, actively create their own cultures, and construct understandings of their environments (e.g. Leyshon 2002; Matthews et al. 2000; McCormack 2002; McGrath 2001; Panelli et al. 2002). When young people are conceptualized as 'social actors in their own right' and 'active research subjects', their views and actions are more meaningfully incorporated. Parallel shifts have occurred in policy arenas where the participation of young people in decision making about matters which affect them is being advocated and legislated for.

Reflecting these developments we can argue that young people are not merely figures in rural spaces where they experience obligations and restrictions, but they actively define, produce, and reclaim space as well. Thus, notions of agency challenge the view of children as essentially powerless, changing the emphasis from weak minors to active empowered young people. In furthering this perspective we suggest broad conceptualisations of children's actions, resistance, and innovations in terms of situated agency. There are diverse conceptual approaches to agency reflecting various theoretical traditions, the most prominent of which are examined briefly below.

Materialist approaches to agency, rooted in political economy (and Marxist theory), emphasise the role of children as workers in both productive and reproductive spheres. For example, Katz (2004) focuses on young people growing crops, tending animals, preparing meals, and minding younger siblings, while Robson (2004a) highlights young people's roles in farming, marketing, and domestic work. Materialist approaches stress the limits of structure and tend to be favoured by those researching young people's lives in Majority worlds. Closely allied to structuration perspectives, young people's actions and agency are considered in consort with the material realities, social rules and regulations that texture how and where their everyday lives are enacted.

Cultural theory[3] also provides a number of lenses through which to view agency, particularly used amongst scholars working with Minority world young people. For example, Matthews and Tucker (this volume) describe teenagers as 'bricoleurs' drawing on the approach of Gennette (1982), whereby teenagers make do, and live with and within the left-overs of adult endeavour. The wealth of cultural theory provides many unexplored avenues for conceptualising children's agency in new ways.

Some academics draw on the conceptual resources of both structuration theory and Foucauldian perspectives, thus trying to avoid the binary structure/agency dualism. For example, Klocker (this volume) provides us with the thought-provoking concepts of 'thin' and 'thick' agency, contending that factors such as age, poverty, gender, and ethnicity can enhance or reduce ('thicken' or 'thin') young people's agency. The notion of 'thin' agency is particularly useful for avoiding portrayals of young people simply as victims when conceptualising children's agency in marginalized situations.

Recent reactions to the 'cultural turn' have seen a shift towards the re-materialisation of social and cultural geography by considering both human and non-human (e.g. technology) actors. This is exemplified by Laegran's (this volume) study of young men's use of cars and the internet to assert their agency. Likewise Jones (this volume) portrays the physicality of young people's actions when playing in the English countryside. In these cases, culture is undoubtedly relevant, but the substances and fabric of young people's actions also take an observably sensate and material form.

In contrast to structural approaches, understandings of children's agency drawing on poststructural and feminist theory recognizes (at least) four elements that shape, influence, and constrain rural young people's agency (Figure 11.1).[4] Feminist and poststructuralist approaches to agency are useful in two ways. Firstly, they emphasize the social constitution of daily life through social/gender relations or discursive terrains that position young people in diverse (and often unequal) ways with dynamic capacities.

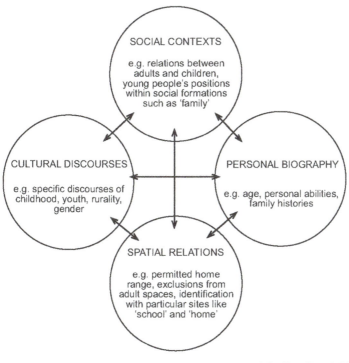

(after Panelli *et al.* 2005: 499)

Figure 11.1 Elements of agency: With rural children's examples.

Secondly, these approaches comprehend the ambiguities and contradictions of children as simultaneously both dependents and agents.

Researchers working across a range of scholarly approaches conceptualize and prioritise the agency of young people in various ways. Each philosophical tradition and theoretical approach to agency has its own strengths and weaknesses for investigating young people's everyday lives and capacity to act. We contend that it is valuable to continue theoretically diverse research so that attention can be given to the equally important effects on young people's agency of individual meaning, behaviour, material conditions, socio-cultural positions, and possibilities. In some accounts, however, agency remains invisible, denied, or claimed as severely suppressed by restrictive circumstances; but where there is oppression there is resistance (Foucault 1979b: 95). Evidence of agency, while difficult to find, is often there and should not be overlooked or ignored. There are several approaches to the idea that populations generally considered powerless do not entirely lack agency, but maintain alternative forms of power constituted in complex webs of informal (invisible) networks of resistance put up (quietly) against prevailing restrictive power relations (e.g. Desai 2002; Scheyvens 1998; Scott 1985; Sharp et al. 2000: 3; Rahnema 1992). These ideas could usefully be applied to young people, and would seem worth further exploration to help develop understandings of how they resist or negotiate adult control in their everyday actions (e.g. Beazley 2002; Bell, this volume).

OUTLINING AGENCY IN EVERYDAY ACTIONS

The creative, active agency of young people is common across rural settings in both Majority and Minority worlds, albeit in rather differing ways, depending on particular circumstances and contexts shaping the limitations within which they find ways to act. This volume highlights some of the constraints and contexts in which young people live and which affect the scope of their agency. Across the chapters we see young people whose ability to act is not just simply constrained by structural forces, yet neither are they entirely free and competent actors. Rather, they are seen to have and to be able to exercise some kind of (albeit sometimes negotiated) agency on their own. While this collection of case studies highlights the varied contexts and forms of agency initiated by young people across diverse Majority and Minority world contexts, we can identify some common threads which are elaborated below.

Safe spaces for agency

Rural youth constantly engage in the creation of 'safe' spaces within which they can act, whether creating play spaces in a rural Bolivian school when the teachers are teaching split classes (Punch, this volume), making tree houses and dens (Jones, this volume), or meeting girlfriends/boyfriends secretly in banana plantations (Bell, this volume). Young people's creation of 'safe' places allows them to feel as though they can act, as well as allowing them (limited) space to do so. More broadly we find parallels with similar examples of the development of spaces where marginalized groups can develop positive self-dignity and solidarity, acting on their own, as well as with others, identified variously as 'homeplaces of resistance' (hooks 1991), 'Third spaces' (Bhabha 1994; Ruddick 1998: 343), 'offstage social sites' (Scott 1990: 119), or 'urban niches' (Beazley 2000b: 484).

Agency in leisure, school, and work

A common theme across this volume is the attention given to young people's agency within their leisure activities, actively filling social time, forming or joining cliques and social groups in the Minority world (Dunkley and Panelli; Laegran; Matthews and Tucker, this volume). This contrasts with a focus on agency within everyday spheres of labour and work in the Majority world (Beazley; Carpena-Méndez; Klocker; Punch, this volume). To a certain extent this dichotomy may largely reflect the material realities across the global North and South. Unsurprisingly, the highlighted activities of young people in the former East Germany (Schäfer, this volume) and last century in the United States, Australia, and New Zealand (Hunter and Riney-Kehrberg, this volume) who may be conceived as sitting somewhere between the present-day Majority and Minority worlds, focus on their current and future working lives. Work rather than leisure dominates their concerns, giving them perhaps more in common with their contemporary peers in the Majority world.

However, it is certainly not the case that Majority world young people do not have leisure activities; rather their time and space for leisure may be more limited than their counterparts in the wealthier Minority world. Similarly, it is worth bearing in mind that many young people in the Minority world also work, although they are more likely to work part-time and to start working at a later age than their peers in the Majority world (see Mizen et al. 2001). Furthermore, we should be wary of over-emphasising distinctions which may result from Minority world researchers focusing more on work as it affects youth in Majority world contexts because this differs from their own childhood experiences and expectations. Many researchers also discuss ways in which work and play are often combined for Majority world children (e.g. Punch; Bell, this volume). The integration of, and overlap between work, school, and play for rural young people is a common theme in research from diverse settings including Bolivia (Punch 2003), Sudan (Katz 2004), Nigeria (Robson 2004a), and among the Canadian Inuit (Briggs 1990).

Agency in relation to adults

Other forms of agency identified in this volume include actions that conform to adult expectations, such as working to earn money for school fees, pocket money or to support the family (Punch, this volume), ending parties when dispersed by police (Dunkley and Panelli, this volume), and meeting parental curfews (Matthews and Tucker, this volume). In contrast, there is what might be termed 'reactive agency' that includes subtle resistance of adult expectations and bargaining (Bell, this volume). Reactive agency includes responding to both people (young and old) and place, as well as what is bound up in young people's experiences of different places, e.g. lack of opportunities. Conforming and reactive agency are not a strict dichotomy, but overlap. In some scenarios young people conform to what is expected by carrying out work and errands, in order to resist in secret, by playing or seeing girlfriends and boyfriends (Bell; Punch, this volume).

Migration is a recurrent theme in rural young people's agency and provides a lens through which to study agency in relation to adults, whether conforming to or resisting adult expectations. Young people may migrate conforming to or resisting adult expectations; of their own volition, or against their will (Klocker, this volume). Some rural young people are desperate to come of age and exercise their agency as soon as possible by leaving their villages to work in another country (Beazley; Carpena-Méndez, this volume). Such migration may not be permanent. For example, in rural Bolivia young people are keen to migrate as a rite of passage to adulthood, to access a cash income and a more consumer-based lifestyle, but do not necessarily intend to leave forever when they first migrate (Punch 2007). Others in the Minority world, like the råners, while not dependent on their parents in terms of, for instance, staying in the village, on the other hand they have (more or less) still chosen to live with their parents (Laegran, this volume). They feel a strong affinity for the place and ties to people and the landscape (conforming agency) which makes it important for them to use public spaces like petrol stations and the car to assert for themselves a place of their own (reactive agency). Not all young people want to leave the rural—the East German youth may not want to, but could not imagine any alternative way to find better opportunities (Schäfer, this volume).

The link between young people 'coming of age' and their agency is an interesting one, and migration is not the only way this is achieved. Some young people may have no opportunity or inclination to leave their rural areas, and achieve coming of age in other ways. Cultural transition ceremonies (Bell, this volume) highlight the transition from child to adult with similar personal gains of increased respect. Where migration is not an option, young people may attempt to assert independence and agency in other ways to gain personal, emotional, and financial empowerment, by engaging in personal relationships for money, or negotiating wages, gardens, and animals from parents (Bell; Hunter and Riney-Kehrberg; Punch, this volume). Lack of economic opportunities also leads to alternative strategies of agency to build self-esteem in other ways, such as through forbidden friendships.

Agency in relation to peers

It should be recognized that there are differences within generations so that groups of young people may have different degrees of agency vis-à-vis their peers, and other young people of different ages, ethnicity, class, birth order, gender, or other aspects of social differentiation. The question of whether rural young people in Majority or Minority worlds have more or less agency is not a helpful one. While everyday actions for the materially privileged may be dominated by education and leisure rather than work, young people everywhere are constrained by a number of structural limitations simply because they are not yet adults (Mayall 2002). The situation of child domestic workers in Tanzania (Klocker, this volume) is of a different kind, constrained by extreme poverty, than that of the råners living in Norway where the human development index is the highest in the world (Laegran, this volume; UNDP 2005). However, there are few circumstances in existence where young people feel able to negotiate with adults on an equal footing.[5] The cases in this book highlight the fact that in both Majority and Minority world settings young people engage in complicated webs of unequal relations where differences in power relations occur between and within generations in ways that generally limit their agency.

There are a range of different actors involved in these unequal power relations that shape socio-cultural norms, all of whom have a varying degree of impact on young people's abilities to become agents in their own lives and communities. Those who 'set the rules' for young people, determining what is acceptable use of space and acceptable behaviour include parents (the most commonly mentioned in many chapters); community members; peer groups, cliques, youth cultures, friends, or 'agemates'; partners (boyfriends or girlfriends); teachers; researchers; NGOs; the police, clergy, elders, and other authority figures. Part III of this book explores in more detail young rural people's positioning within relations of power.

An important point we wish to emphasize is that agency and young people's negotiation of unequal power relations is not static, but changes over time and space, especially over the life course, whereby older siblings tend to exert more agency than younger ones, and this may change as older siblings leave home. Furthermore, cultural ceremonies like male circumcision (Bell, this volume) increase young men's opportunity for agency in rural Uganda, and migration allows young people to access more money, social agency, and status (Beazley, this volume).

CONTINUUM AND CONTEXT OF AGENCY

As we consider rural young people globally there are interesting links between (opportunistic and constrained) contexts, created and expected identities (see Bushin et al., this volume), realms and strategies of agency (outlined above), and negotiation of unequal power relations (see Punch et al. this volume). Initially there appears to be a clear similarity across places in two respects. Firstly, in order to deal with, negotiate, or resist unequal/restrictive power relations vis-à-vis adults and peers, young people must utilize, or initiate, agency to do so. Secondly, agency appears to be inhibited or encouraged by young people's (constrained/opportunistic) locational contexts; identities they are expected to fulfil, and alternative identities they choose to portray; their position of power/lessness; their state of emotions and well-being at a particular time; their stage in the lifecourse and other factors.

Thus, there are several relevant aspects relating to a young person's in/ability to act which are considered in a little more detail here. Firstly, the importance of understanding young people's feelings, emotions, and state of mind when exploring their ability, or willingness, to act as social agents is indicated (or at least hinted at) throughout both Minority and Majority world case studies within this volume and is associated with examples of agency and negotiation.[6] (Success of) agency would appear to be related to an individual's perceived sense of being able, and to his or her confidence. Thus, Punch (this volume) refers to Antonio, who experienced feelings of control, independence, maturity, and pride when he had negotiated his own plot of land. Child domestic workers in Tanzania appear to feel a lack of control and sense of resignation to their current situation, although these feelings are combined with a sense of hope that they will bring improvements to both their own and their families' situation (Klocker, this volume). Rural teenage girls in Northampton express a mixture of despair, exclusion, boredom, frustration, and restlessness alongside their limited agency (Matthews and Tucker, this volume). A young person's state of mind, confidence, and perceived ability to act is also affected by the influence of other people, illustrated in cases of parental discipline, social distancing from peers, exclusion from friendship groups, and parental decision making in relation to curfews.

Secondly, an individual young person's ability to act is related to the constraints she or he faces on a daily basis. Most of the chapters in this volume focus on scenarios of 'constrained contexts'. In Minority worlds, these are created through limited accessibility and mobility, a lack of jobs and income generating opportunities, and limited finances, whereas Majority world studies focus on poverty, and restrictive socio-cultural norms and expectations. A lack of income-generating and employment opportunities are also an important constraining context for Majority world young people, acting as an important stimulus for migration.

Another factor inhibiting young rural people's agency, not explored in these chapters, is personal (dis)ability. Box 11.1 considers how disability is reproduced or transformed within 'inclusive' schools, home, and 'leisure spaces' in rural areas of England (Holt 2004, 2007). The agency of disabled young people is an important under-researched area in the Majority world too, where strong prejudice associated with mind and body differences is widespread, and where there are even fewer means or networks of support, meaning that disabled young people in rural areas may miss out altogether on school and income generating opportunities.

Box 11.1 Agency and rural young people with mind–body-emotional differences—Louise Holt

Young people with special educational needs, impairments, mental illness, or learning disabilities living in rural areas of England are labelled 'vulnerable youth', and because of severe social and educational exclusion, experience limited agency, or are denied agency by powerful actors such as teachers and social workers. The 'inclusion' of young people into mainstream, rather than segregated special schools, is a form of de/re-institutionalisation occurring in many nations (United Nations 1994; cf. United Nations 2004), albeit interpreted heterogeneously given diverse institutional contexts. This process is expected to automatically transform young people's performances of disability. However, young people are social agents and therefore their practices must be explored to question how (dis)ability is reproduced/transformed. This is crucial to young people's present lives and their adult futures, given the exclusions tied to dominant representations of disability (Kitchin 1998; Morris 1991). Some specific issues for young people with mind-body-emotional differences arise in rural contexts. The socio-spatial reproduction of (dis)ability within schools is influenced by the spatiality of the school location, and rural/urban location may be an important factor here. Furthermore, other specific issues relating to the (re)production of school-based relationships beyond the school, pertinent in many contexts, may be exacerbated in the rural arena. Transport and access to a car and driver have been raised as concerns by rural young people (Matthews, Limb, and Taylor 2000) living further from the school and in rural areas. Parents' concerns over the competence of young people with mind-body-emotional differences to negotiate public transport safely (R. Butler, 1998) intersect with the increased distances travelled by many (rural) young people who attend either 'special', or 'special resource' mainstream schools, with facilities aimed at young people with specific impairments. These issues, which will have significant influence on young people's inclusion and, potentially, representations and performances of disability, require further exploration within various (rural) contexts.

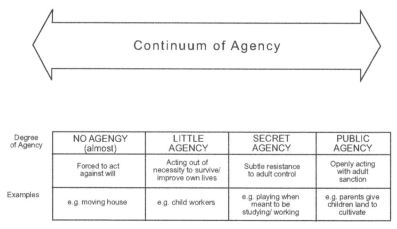

Degree of Agency	NO AGENGY (almost)	LITTLE AGENCY	SECRET AGENCY	PUBLIC AGENCY
	Forced to act against will	Acting out of necessity to survive/ improve own lives	Subtle resistance to adult control	Openly acting with adult sanction
Examples	e.g. moving house	e.g. child workers	e.g. playing when meant to be studying/ working	e.g. parents give children land to cultivate

Figure 11.2 Continuum of rural young people's agency.

In considering the lives of rural young people across both Minority and Majority worlds we identify a continuum in young people's agency, or power/control over their agency (Figure 11.2). For example, young people appear to have almost no agency when forced to do things against their will, such as to move house and have to find new friendships (Ansell and van Blerk, this volume). Similarly, when forced to do things out of necessity to improve their lives and futures young people appear to have very little agency; such as child domestic workers initiating their transition from school to work (Klocker, this volume), or girls finding boyfriends and husbands due to parental neglect (Bell, this volume). Moving up the scale of agency comes subtle resistance by children, whereby all attempts to exert agency are secretive. These might include playing when they are supposed to be working (Punch), seeking forbidden companionship or finding condoms to ensure forbidden sex is safe (Bell, this volume). More obvious exertion of agency includes the small public displays of power whereby improvements are made in their personal lives; for example, where rural young people negotiate land and animals from their parents to generate an income to fulfil basic necessities (Punch, this volume).

The chapters in this book illustrate that young people's experiences of agency change depending on who they are with, what they are doing, and where they are. A young person may experience a lack of agency in some areas of their lives, but can exercise agency in other areas, and an individual moves along the continuum accordingly, over time and in relation to decisions that are made (e.g. Bell, this volume). Thus, agency is dynamic.

Explorations of young people's agency differ between that which is self-initiated, and other circumstances where children's actions might be automatic, expected, requested, or forced. Understanding these differences along a continuum of degrees of agency in more detail may be achieved through deeper examination of the reasoning behind the agency, the outcomes of such agency, and whether different forms of agency are enjoyed or resented. It is important to develop a thorough understanding of the decision-making processes behind actions in order to conceptually develop the links between context, agency, and young people's position within and negotiation of unequal power relations.

INCREASING YOUNG PEOPLE'S AGENCY
VIA THE RESEARCH PROCESS

It is argued by some that a key responsibility of researchers investigating childhoods, especially marginalized childhoods such as those of child domestic workers, is to interact with their young participants in ways that not only avoid further reducing or 'thinning' their agency, but which also endeavour to act as 'thickeners' (Klocker, this volume). Such approaches respond both to Robson's (2004a: 243) call for 'more child-centred radical approaches to research', and agendas for children's active participation in research (e.g. Alderson 2000a; Boyden and Ennew 1997; Christensen 2004). As already identified many researchers have made substantial shifts to conceptualize children as 'social actors' and 'active research subjects', helping to take young people's views more seriously. Despite progress towards recognizing children and young people as agents, few researchers have moved beyond the involvement of children as informants in *their* (adult-owned) research, towards the participation of children and young people as researchers in their own right (e.g. Clacherty and Kistner 2001; Kellett et al. 2004; Klocker, this volume; Mayo 2001; McIvor 2001; Nespor 1998; Schäfer, this volume).

It takes significant time and financial resources to support young people as researchers. Furthermore, working with young researchers presents many challenges and ethical concerns relating to power, confidentiality, consent, appropriate workloads, payment, and so on (Alderson 2000a). Despite these difficulties, existing efforts to include children and young people as researchers have been encouraging and the potential advantages to such an approach cannot be ignored. In Box 11.2 Natascha Klocker suggests, from her positive experience of engaging young people directly as investigators in research, that adult researchers should aim to enhance the agency of young people by engaging them as researchers to narrow the academia/activism divide and offer a point of entry into self-advocacy for young people.

Box 11.2 Young people as researchers: Child domestic workers in Tanzania—Natascha Klocker

Making space for Tanzanian girls to be key researchers and self-advocates in our (not my) investigation into child domestic work (CDW) is one practical channel for 'thickening' their agency (Klocker, 2006). The three former child domestic workers with whom I work have minimal formal education, yet, throughout this research process they have come to recognize that they can be researchers and have even begun to self-identify as such in casual conversations. In a questionnaire conducted with the young researchers, to ascertain their perceptions of (and feelings about) their participation in this project, all three of them identified a substantial increase in their self-confidence since the beginning of the project. One of the girls commented that since becoming a researcher 'I have seen that I am a person who has the ability to do bigger things' (Klocker, 2006). Another said that participation in the research will help her in her future life because if people come to ask her to help with different research, 'I won't have any obstacles because I will have the ability to do any research at all'.

All three girls indicated that being researchers is one area of their lives in which they are able to make everyday decisions. Some positive outcomes of their participation include new knowledge, being able to express their ideas, skills that will help them in their future, and a sense of pride that they are working on an important issue. Such findings indicate that although this child/youth-centred research project cannot eliminate the numerous factors that 'thin' the agency of rural Tanzanian girls and lead them into CDW, it can at least endeavour to provide a space within which a small number of former child domestic workers can exercise agency to a greater capacity (Klocker, 2005b).

If children and young people are facilitated to research both their peers and adult stakeholders, we might make important progress towards destabilizing uneven adult–child power relations and 'democratizing' our research relationships (Leyshon, 2002). As children and young people prove their ability to undertake research, perceptions of their abilities as actors in *other* areas of society may also begin to shift and they may gain skills which are beneficial to their futures. Furthermore, Nespor's (1998: 383) experiences demonstrate that children design their research to have a 'clear, pragmatic, political aim', so involving young researchers may lead towards a 'shallowing' of the academia/activism divide. In addition, young people may even gain an 'employable' skill by learning to be researchers. Indeed, in Clacherty and Kistner's (2001) participatory research project with 'hard-to-reach' boys in South Africa, the boys were later commissioned by various other organizations to undertake new research.

FUTURE DIRECTIONS

There are several further aspects of possible future academic agendas on rural young people's agency that we would like to highlight briefly. To begin with as already argued, within academic existing studies of rural childhood and youth there is a relative absence of attention to the actions and lives of particularly marginalized groups of young people living in rural areas of both the Majority and Minority worlds. More work is needed to identify and highlight the agency of disabled and other marginalized groups of rural young people, such as those associated with itinerant, nomadic or displaced populations.

While it is firmly established that young people tend to have less power than adults, there is also a need for more research to be focused on scaling up young people's agency, identifying where young people feel able to negotiate (equally) with adults. This links to agendas on children's rights and participation, particularly amongst practitioners and NGOs involved in helping young people to develop 'life skills' (including critical thinking, negotiation skills, rights awareness) with the goal of equal participation in decision-making that affects their lives (see Ansell 2005: 223–254; Auriat et al. 2001; Black 2004; J. Hart et al. 2004; R. Hart 1992). These strategies and their effects could be a fruitful area for further study. Better understandings of the constrained nature of the environments and contexts in which young people live and are (un)able to act is vital for these types of intervention and research to take place effectively. Furthermore, future research agendas could usefully explore the (dis)empowering nature of daily (un)equal peer-to-peer negotiations and relationships which rural children are embedded in, and the effects these have on encouraging young people to initiate such negotiations with adults.

There are a range of views in relation to participatory and action research with young people (e.g. Johnson et al. 1998. The justifications for increasing young people's agency via participation in the research process are already explored above. Some would promote more action research, and this may require extra training for researchers, or creating better links with agencies that carry out action research in a long term process, with young people being facilitated by researchers to implement changes themselves. There is an ethical debate about a researcher's ability to facilitate change on their own, without the support of an NGO or other organisation which can support change in the long term. The arguments about the moral and scientific imperative for researchers of rural children's lives to increase the agency of their subjects reflect wider debates about activism and the academy and the obligations of academics to conduct research in order to improve policy versus generation of knowledge (Spencer 2005). Many researchers would like their research to be useful to the children who contributed to it and such an approach is firmly advocated within children's geographies (Matthews 2005), although with a few dissenting voices (Horton and Kraftl 2005). While action/participatory research may resolve some problems it can also create new dilemmas and unequal power relations (see Cooke and Kothari 2001). Some argue that ethnography is just as effective a way of enabling young people to really participate in research, and that participatory and/ or action research is not always as bottom-up as intended (Gallagher and Gallacher forthcoming 2008).

In this chapter we started from the acknowledgement of 'children as competent agents' (Valentine 1996), albeit often constrained by adult expectations, authority figures, and institutions, and examined different approaches to conceptualising the agency of young people. Overall, we support furthering academic discourses of 'active' youth to fully embrace rural young people, while also advocating deeper recognition of young people's *agency and everyday actions* towards achieving a more integrated dialogue for studies of young rural lives in which young people are recognized as creative, knowledgeable, and competent members of their own Majority and Minority world societies. Finally, we emphasize that agency is inextricably linked to power whereby the exercise of power is dependent on agency. Without agency, there is no exercise of power. How rural young people negotiate power is addressed in the following chapters of Part III.

NOTES

1. We acknowledge this chapter represents collaborative efforts beyond that of the named authors and wish to thank those whose contributions to the 2005 conference session fruitfully stimulated our discussion of agency (especially Anne Sofie Laegran).
2. However, it is also important to recognize that some children are victims and others may choose to be passive at times.
3. The cultural turn has largely overshadowed earlier behavioural and humanist approaches which, with the central and active role given to human agency, had capacity to generate detailed material and hermeneutic patterns of daily life linked to local contexts and as such remain a valid trajectory for understanding everyday landscapes and rhythms of young lives through foci like rural children's mental maps, wayfinding, time geographies, and life worlds.
4. There are several other dimensions of agency which can also be acknowledged, e.g. living in the Majority or Minority world and socio-economic wealth/class affect young people's experience of rural living and the behaviours they choose with respect to household survival and prosperity.
5. Although some NGOs and other bodies pursuing agendas informed by notions of children's rights promote such interaction, e.g. school councils, youth forums, and the like.
6. This attention to emotion and agency also complements developments in youth geographies beyond the rural environment (e.g. Robinson et al. 2004; Thomas 2004).

Part III

Power relations and processes

12 Generational power relations in rural Bolivia

Samantha Punch

It can be argued that childhood is a relational concept which forms part of the generational order and that generational processes shape the nature of child–adult relations (Alanen 2001; Mayall 2002). When the social positions of 'children' and 'adults' are 'constituted, reproduced and transformed through relational activity' (Mayall 2002: 40), this can be referred to as practices of 'generationing' (Alanen 2001). Thus, as Alanen (2001: 21) argues, childhood and adulthood are connected and interdependent. However, children's structural position in society means that generally they have less power than adults. Thus, adults' generational location enables them to wield more power over children and this is an example of Lukes's (2005) relational definition of power as one social group exercises 'power over' another.

Power has different meanings in different contexts, and is linked to both agency and structure (Lukes 2005). Whilst there is some overlap between the concepts of power and agency (see Robson et al., this volume), at the level of individuals, power can be defined as having 'the will to effect changes in another actor's behaviour, context or view of the world' (Westwood 2002: 14). Thus, as Scott argues 'power is the capacity to influence others' (2001: 138).

Whilst it is generally recognized that children's power tends to be constrained as adults often use their generational power to regulate children's bodies and minds (Brannen et al. 2000: 178), it is also widely accepted that children have an ability (albeit often limited) to counteract adult power (Valentine 1999; Waksler 1996). However, as children are faced with unequal adult–child power relations, they may have to negotiate more than adults in order to assert their power and gain greater control over certain aspects of their lives.

Thus, practices of generationing involve a two-way flow of power where children and adults can significantly influence each other (Scott 2001). This coincides with the view of power as multi-dimensional and ubiquitous (Lukes 2005; Westwood 2002). Interpersonal power is also exercised within generations, as well as between them. This chapter explores both inter- and intra-generational power relations (see also Bell; Dunkley and Panelli, this volume) in everyday contexts of social interactions in rural Bolivia.

As there are different forms of power (Lukes 2005), this chapter recognizes that power also operates at a more macro level, encompassing wider economic and environmental factors (see Bushin et al., this volume). The power of place should not be underestimated in relation to the opportunities and constraints which shape the lives of residents in particular geographical locations. Rural communities in Bolivia do not hold a strong position of economic or political power compared with urban areas, and are often marginalized in terms of resources and basic services. Furthermore, on a global scale, Bolivia is in a relatively marginal, fragile position in relation to the global economy, having suffered from the ills of two decades of neo-liberalism and increased indebtedness (Green 2003). Thus, whilst this chapter focuses on the micro level, face-to-face interactions of generational power relations and the spatial power dynamics of the local contexts of home, school and work, it also recognizes that the rural environment of this economically poor country has a strong impact upon the extent to which young people can yield power and control over their daily lives.

RURAL CONTEXT

Bolivia is the poorest country in South America with approximately 60 per cent of the population living below the poverty line (Graham 1997). It faces a range of structural problems including 'low productivity, scarce investment, a weak capital market, and a precarious export economy' (Peirce 1997). In particular, Bolivia has experienced more than twenty years of neo-liberal economic restructuring (Gill 2000) which has resulted in increased unemployment, lower wages, and greater inequality (Green 2003).

Until relatively recently its population has always been predominantly rural, but the proportion of people living in urban areas increased from 39 per cent to 58 per cent during the period 1976 and 1992, mainly as a result of urbanisation and rural–urban migration (Preston 1994). There are marked differences in the quality of life between urban and rural areas. For example, the overall infant mortality rate is 73 deaths per thousand live births, but is twice as high in rural areas and life expectancy is 51 years in the countryside compared with 61 years in towns (Graham 1997). Urban areas have greater access to better health and educational facilities, as well as more opportunities in terms of employment. Rural areas suffer particularly from the lack of adequate medical, sanitation, and school services. For example, in 1996, 66 per cent of the total population had access to safe water, but 87 per cent of those living in urban areas have access compared to only 36 per cent who have access in the countryside (UNICEF 1997: 84).

The chapter draws on ethnographic research which I undertook in Churquiales, a rural community[1] in Tarija, southern Bolivia (see Fig-

Figure 12.1 Map of the study region, Tarija.

ure 12.1). Churquiales is an economically poor and relatively isolated agricultural community which lacks basic services such as electricity and safe drinking water. The opportunities for waged employment are limited, and schooling is only available for the first six years of primary education. The ethnographic fieldwork included participant observation and interviews with young people, parents, and grandparents from a sample of 18 households (Punch 2001b). At the community school I carried out a variety of task-based techniques including photographs, drawings, diaries, and worksheets (Punch 2002a). This chapter explores the extent to which power and place intersect by considering the ways in which young people's everyday experiences at home, school, and work take place within complex webs of power that are played out within and across generations.

HOME AND POWER

In rural Bolivia, many daily household tasks need to be carried out to ensure household survival and they have to be distributed among the different household members. However, the distribution and division of reproductive work is not clear-cut, but constantly negotiated between children and parents, and between siblings (Punch 2003). Parents depend on their children's help and need their co-operation, but it has to be negotiated. The following example taken from my ethnographic field notes illustrates parent–child and sibling negotiations surrounding the household division of labour:

> 'Go sons, and fetch water', said Felicia to her three sons, and off they went. Later, when she went out of the kitchen she saw the water containers still there. She went to find her sons but they were nowhere in sight: 'Lazy boys, they've escaped, I can't even see them.'
>
> Later, they came back, and one of her sons, Dionicio, was on a second-hand bicycle that his dad had recently bought.

> 'You lazy children, why didn't you go and fetch water? Put that bike away, Dionicio. Two of you go and fetch water and one of you sweep the storeroom'.

> Marco: 'I'm going to get water.'
> Dionicio: 'Me too.'
> Ramón: 'And me.'
> Felicia: 'And I'm going to sweep the kitchen, wash the cups, and cook.'

> In the end, Ramón swept the storeroom, Marco and Dionicio went to get water.

> 'And when you get back, you've got to feed the pigs.'[2]

The extract indicates that children do not always obey their parents, they also have their own agenda of activities which sometimes compete with their household responsibilities. After initially escaping from their assigned task, the brothers all showed a preference for fetching water rather than sweeping, most likely because two of them would go together to fetch water and the boredom of doing a particular job can be lessened with someone to chat to and play with along the way (Punch 2001c). Furthermore, collecting water can be more fun because it is away from the house and parental surveillance, thereby providing more opportunities to resist adult control and divert into non-work activities (see Figure 12.2). Exactly how the three children subsequently negotiated who was going to be the one to sweep the storeroom is not clear, but they managed to work it out amongst themselves. The boys' mother organizes the distribution of household tasks and attempts to control her children's division of labour. She emphasizes the importance of them sharing the work of the household, which is why she stresses that while her children are fetching water and sweeping, she will

Figure 12.2 Going on errands with siblings, away from the adult gaze, enables work to be combined with play.

be cleaning the kitchen and preparing their lunch. She also reminds them of the constant nature of domestic work, which is never complete, by telling them they must feed the pigs later.

The above example illustrates that in a subsistence-based, labour-intensive economy parents rely on children to work unpaid for the household and this results in children having more bargaining power to negotiate how their responsibilities will be fulfilled. Parents may enforce discipline, including physical punishment, but children have a range of strategies for job avoidance, including delegation to a younger sibling (and in this case, quietly escaping), or the lessening of job monotony by combining work and play (Punch 2000). Thus, as Foucault reminds us, 'Where there is power, there is resistance' (1979b: 95) and generational power relations within households are interdependent and negotiable. It is also worth bearing in mind that household power relationships do not always involve struggle, resistance, and contestation. When one household member strives to assert their power over others, their actions may be accepted and complied with in a co-operative manner with no attempts to compromise or negotiate (see also Kabeer 1994). Family expectations and obligations mean that most children have a strong sense of responsibility towards their household yet this has to be balanced with their own needs and desires.

SCHOOL AND POWER

Mayall's research in the UK found that the social setting of the home offered children more possibilities for negotiation compared with the school:[3]

> ... at home children are identified not merely as socialization objects but as participants in and negotiators of their social worlds, and thus as important family members. At school, they are essentially projects for adult work. (Mayall 1994: 125)

These findings have similar relevance in the arenas of home and school in rural Bolivia, despite the socio-economic and cultural differences between the two countries. As mentioned, in Churquiales, children's work enhances the negotiating power they have at home with their parents who depend to some extent on their unpaid work or economic contributions from their paid work. At school, children's potential for negotiation is more limited than at home because their relations of interdependence with teachers are weak (Punch 2004) and the classroom is much more the teachers' domain of control (Avalos 1986). For example, teachers use a series of punishments (often threats are enough) to enforce discipline: detention at break time, cleaning the toilets, rigorous physical exercises, leaving the classroom, and ear pulling.

Nevertheless, to some extent rural teachers depend on children's attendance at school because teaching is the main part of their livelihood. If all the children in the community are not registered at the start of the school year, the local government delays paying teacher's salaries and threatens to withdraw a teacher if not enough children attend. Although children's power in the classroom is limited, they can take advantage of the multigrade system as one teacher has to divide their time between several different year groups. Thus whilst the teacher is distracted, pupils may play at their desks instead of continuing with their assigned tasks (Punch 2004). The ways in which children create playspaces for themselves, often combined with school and work, indicates that they can assert some power and control over their use of time and space, despite being constrained by their work or school responsibilities and threats of adult discipline (Punch 2000).

WORK AND POWER

In Churquiales, once children reach about 12 years of age, their unpaid household work may be combined with paid work, depending on the opportunities and constraints which face them at home, work, and school. The following extract from my ethnographic field diary illustrates the work strategies of two siblings from a relatively poor household:

> When Antonio was 13 years old, he said to his father: 'Dad, I help you a lot but you don't help me. Perhaps you buy me some trousers, but if I don't ask, you don't buy me any'.[4] He said he now needed to start earning his own money to be able to buy clothes and save for a second-hand bicycle that he wanted. His father, Fulgencio, agreed to give him

a small plot of land in return for his help in the fields. Antonio chose to sow peanuts and he bought the seed by selling a goat that he had been given on his birthday a few years previously. His younger brother, Javier, helped him plant the seed and Antonio agreed to give him the harvested peanuts from five lines of the crop. Antonio not only took great pride in his work but it also gave him a sense of control, since he could choose how to spend his earnings and did not have to wait for his parents to buy him new clothes.

Victoria, Antonio's older sister, has worked as a domestic maid since she was 12 years old, at first for her godparents in a nearby rural community and later in the town of Tarija for the sister of a family friend. Antonio sometimes complains he is bored in the countryside while his sister is 'Taking it easy in Tarija without having to work very much'.[5] However, compared with Antonio, Victoria has no luck with raising animals, the only two goats she had both died. She does have a hen and seven chicks, but because her mum looks after them while she is working in Tarija, she will give her two of the chicks. She says she will either sell or eat the other ones. Antonio is lucky with animals and sold a goat to buy some clothes for school. He also bought some clothes for his younger siblings. They are allowed to buy what they want with their own money, but sometimes their parents tease them when Vicki buys makeup or Antonio buys toys: 'Eat what you've bought or put on what you've bought to wear to school!'[6]

Victoria and Antonio both actively contribute to the maintenance of their household which gives them a sense of satisfaction and pride. They balance responsibilities towards their parents and siblings with their own individual needs. Their example highlights the negotiation of interdependent relations between children and their parents, and between siblings. Antonio's unpaid work which he carries out for the household provides him with bargaining power to negotiate a small plot of land of his own from his father. His brother helps him and in return Antonio gives him some of the harvest. Household interdependent relations change over time, as can be seen when Victoria gives her mother two chicks in return for looking after them, even though originally she had been given the hen by her parents. This indicates that the nature of interdependencies between family members is renegotiated as individuals' situations and needs change over the life course.

The above example shows that children have different strategies for increasing their economic power even in a context of unpaid subsistence family labour. They make use of the limited but different economic opportunities that are available to them, such as negotiating the use of a small piece of their parents' land and sowing some crops for sale in the local market (see Figure 12.3). Another strategy that can be particularly effective

Figure 12.3 Young people cultivating their own crop on a small plot of their parents' land.

around their birthday or Christmas time is if they ask their parents to let them have an animal of their own in return for helping to look after all the household's animals. Sowing their own crops or raising their own animals not only increases young people's sense of control over their labour but also enables them to start becoming more economically independent as well as learning and developing useful skills.

Furthermore, in the above extract, Antonio complains that his unpaid rural work is more strenuous than his sister's paid urban work, although she did not agree (see Chapter 7 for a discussion of urban domestic work in Tanzania). He is sometimes jealous that her paid work gives her greater access to a cash income and his concern echoes the recognition that subsistence-based agriculture requires a high level of physical labour, as Griselda points out:

> In the countryside they [children] have to see to the animals, help feed them, give them water. In the town they come out of school, some have their obligations to fulfil but most in the town don't. In the countryside we always cultivate everything, the only thing we buy is meat. In the town they don't cultivate anything, it's the hand into the pocket for everything.[7] (Griselda, parent)

Some people perceive the labour-intensive work involved in subsistence production in the countryside to be harder manual labour compared with many urban jobs. This coincides with Johnson et al.'s research (1995) in Nepal when they found that some rural girls preferred their families to send them to work in carpet factories because they felt that the work was easier than at home. In contrast rural children from a different village reported that they would rather work at home as their factory work was relentless and the working conditions were poor. Similarly, some young people in rural Bolivia preferred to work in their home community rather than in rural Argentina because a day labourer in Churquiales works on average eight hours, but in Argentina they may have to work up to twelve hours, under a much hotter sun, at a faster pace (Punch 2007). Thus, in Bolivia, urban work was perceived by some people as lighter compared with rural subsistence production, but migrant work on agricultural plantations in Argentina tended to be perceived as tougher than rural work in Churquiales.

Consequently children's future aspirations depend to some extent on whether their imagined future (see Dunkley and Panelli, this volume) is rural or urban, in Bolivia or Argentina. Most are likely to end up working in agriculture or domestic labour (predominantly girls) whether that is at home, in the town of Tarija, or in rural Argentina. They have some choice, albeit greatly constrained by material conditions and family responsibilities (see Beazley; Bell; Klocker, this volume), and in some ways seasonal migration offers them an opportunity to try out possible pathways (Punch 2007). Their constrained choices impact upon the influence of collective imaginings of different types of work (rural/urban; at home/migratory), and they impact as well on children's actual place-based experiences of power.

MIGRATION AND POWER

In rural Bolivia, household livelihood strategies are diverse and dynamic, adapting mainly to the amount of land and labour which is available. Since most people own smallholdings of approximately two hectares there is not sufficient land to be divided up between all the children of a household. Consequently it is necessary that most young people migrate and search for work or land elsewhere, at least temporarily, either to the nearby town of Tarija or more traditionally to the agricultural plantations of neighbouring Argentina (Reboratti 1996). Whilst farming in Churquiales provides mainly for the household's subsistence needs, migration facilitates access to a cash income (see also Beazley; Carpena-Méndez, this volume).

Migration is a good illustration of the ambiguities of power, as rural young people can be both constrained and enabled by their experience of leaving the community. Migration can lead to young people feeling empowered and powerless in different ways at the same time which is an indication of the complex, multi-faceted nature of power (Lukes 2005). Initially it can be very difficult for young people to leave their relatively isolated rural community, particularly because they tend to have had very limited experience outside Churquiales. This is reflected in the following quotations by parents who were explaining the perceived differences between rural and urban childhoods:

There is a difference. In the town they are more talkative, not shy. In the countryside they are fearful even to talk. In the town they grow up with people. Here they just grow up with the family. I see it with my children when I take them to Tarija, they can't even eat because they are so embarrassed.[8] (Tomás, parent)

In the countryside the child is timid, bashful, doesn't go out.... In the town there's television, maybe they go for a walk at the weekend, to the park, walking along the avenues, or go to the cinema. Children in the countryside, how are they going to know what a cinema is?[9] (Felicia, parent)

Young people's limited access to a wider social network and communications such as television increases their relative powerlessness outside their community. Leaving the familiar zone of their home rural community can be very intimidating. Mónica describes her first trip to Argentina when she was 17: 'I didn't go out and I didn't know anybody there. I didn't dare go further away or anywhere on my own.'[10] Hence, migration can make the young person feel quite vulnerable, lonely, and relatively powerless, especially at first with the unfamiliarity of a new place. In addition, new migrants are commonly paid less until they have learnt the appropriate skills, and in Argentina they usually receive less pay than an Argentinian for the same job. Migrant work also tends to require working extremely long hours in often quite poor conditions (Punch 2007). Consequently, despite the economic opportunities which migration offers, some young people prefer to stay in their rural community where life is more relaxed:

It's more comfortable at home because you work when you want, and you can rest.[11] (Sebastián, 18 years)

We're from the countryside, we're used to this type of work, we're not going to live in the city.[12] (Edmundo, 24 years)

Nevertheless, most rural young people in Churquiales lack access to available land or permanent work, and this places them in a precarious economic position. It also means that they are vulnerable to fluctuations in the global economy because they are dependent on some form of migrant work. For example, the recent economic crisis in Argentina (López Levy 2004) will have impacted upon their agricultural or domestic work opportunities, perhaps resulting in much lower wages or no jobs at all for some migrants. Therefore, power is not only discursive or relational in the immediate circumstances of children's everyday lives, but is also 'material' in terms of global economic dynamics.

However, in another sense, migration can enhance young people's economic power and, when they are back home in their rural community, this in turn increases their social power (Punch 2007). By contributing eco-nomically to their household, they earn more decision-making power and more control over their use of time and space when in Churquiales. Having access to a cash income also increases their consumer power as they can buy material goods and clothes which they would not otherwise be able to afford. This also enhances their ability to engage in a more global culture and when they return to their community with 'symbols of modernity' (Sklair 1994) their status amongst their peers is increased. Having travelled to new places to work and returning with new goods and greater knowl-edge of life outside of the community, means that some young people feel more empowered because of the wider horizons they have experienced.

Thus, in terms of power, the migrant identity is an ambivalent one (see Ansell and van Blerk, this volume), often meaning relative powerlessness in the destination but resulting in increased power and status back home. Furthermore, the impact of migration on the rural community has both positive and negative effects. On the one hand, it may lead to increased ten-sions with non-migrants who resent the migrants showing off their newly acquired goods. In particular, it can cause rifts between the generations as many older people disapprove of the young migrants spending their earnings on alcoholic drink and festivities during their time back in the community. Migration can also end up creating conflicts between old and new knowledge (Katz 2004) and ultimately it may exacerbate inequalities between households within the community (see Carpena-Méndez, this vol-ume; Pribilsky 2001). On the other hand, migration benefits those who stay behind by reducing stress on limited resources and land, as well as decreas-ing competition for scarce work opportunities. Therefore, young people's lived migratory experiences illustrate not only a place-based and material link to power, but also demonstrate the fluidity and fluctuating nature of the relational aspects of power.

RURAL INTER-DEPENDENCIES

This chapter has shown that using a holistic approach, which considers the inter-connections between home, school, work, and migration, is a useful way to explore the limits, extent, and interplay of power and resistance. It has argued that, despite their inferior position in relation to more pow-erful adult social actors, children develop a variety of strategies to resist adult control and negotiate their role within rural households. Household power relationships may involve conflict, tension, and negotiation but they may also be co-operative and compliant (Punch 2001c). Negotiating gen-erational power relations may include compromises or balancing different interests, such as individual preferences and household needs. However, in the school arena children's agency is more limited than at home, but the spaces between home and school offer greater opportunities for asserting control over their use of time and space (Punch 2000). Despite the limited economic opportunities for paid work within the rural community, children negotiate ways to increase their economic power, such as taking full responsibility for planting their own crops or raising their own animals. In contrast, migrant work opportunities may be more extensive but can be both enabling and constraining for young people. On the one hand, many young people lack power in relation to migration as they are almost forced to seek migrant work with relatively harsh conditions, but, on the other hand, it can increase both their economic and social power when back in their rural community (Punch 2007).

Thus, this chapter has argued that young people can be both powerful and powerless simultaneously with respect to different aspects of their social worlds. Their everyday lives move back and forth along a continuum of diverse experiences in relation to changing degrees of power and powerlessness. Power relationships are negotiated and renegotiated with different people in different contexts at different times. Interdependent power relations within rural households are dynamic and evolve over the life course. As children acquire economic power, this tends to increase their social power, and relationships between children and parents are renegotiated accordingly. For example, through time children may contribute more financially and parents may give children land or animals as part of their inheritance to enable them to establish a more independent livelihood.

Intra-generational relations also influence the ways in which power is distributed within the household. The hierarchy of the birth order shapes siblings' opportunities and constraints regarding work, education, and migration. For example, younger siblings are more likely to spend longer at school as their older siblings may be contributing financially to the household. However, when parents get older and are less able to carry out physical labour, there may be more pressure on the youngest sibling to stay and care for them rather than migrating in search of more lucrative work elsewhere.

Nevertheless, in the same way that inter-generational power relations are not fixed, power relations between siblings are also negotiated and worked out in practice (Finch and Mason 1993). Thus, whilst birth order position impacts upon siblings' responsibilities and obligations, the sibling order is not rigid in determining the ways in which economic and social power is divided amongst household members. Caring for parents in older age is related more to birth order rather than gender, but it also depends on whether an older sibling prefers to stay in the community rather than migrate. So although it is likely that the youngest sibling, regardless of gender, is expected to care for their parents in old age, this may not necessarily happen, as another sibling may choose to stay to look after them, remittances may be sent home instead, or parents may join their children at the migrant destination.

Similarly, just as daily power relations and responsibilities are not set but worked out between family members, longer term generational power relations are also negotiated. Households renegotiate the ways in which power is played out in relation to family responsibilities, work, and education, according to the different constraints and opportunities which exist, including household wealth (usually determined by the amount of land and animals), household composition and available labour power, birth order, age and gender of siblings, and the competencies and preferences of individual household members. This chapter has argued that generational power relations are complex and reflect the interdependencies between and within generations as well as between the interconnecting arenas of home, school, work, and migration. Therefore, practices of generationing shape the ways in which the exercise of, and resistance to, forms of power are played out in everyday interactions in a range of rural contexts.

NOTES

1. The names of the community and the research participants have been changed in order to maintain anonymity and confidentiality. The community has a population of 351 residents and it is 55 km from Tarija, the regional capital.
2. *Vaya hijos a traer agua.*
   Chicos flojos, se han escapado. Ni se les ve.
   Hijos flojos porque no han ido a traer agua. Guarda esa bici Dionicio.
   Dos van a ir a traer agua y uno va a barrer la dispensa.
   Marco: *yo voy a traer agua*
   Dionicio: *yo también*
   Ramón: *y yo*
   Felicia: *Y yo voy a barrer la cocina, lavar las tazas y cocinar.*
   Y cuando vuelven tienen que dar de comer a los chanchos. (Dionicio's household)
3. To some extent this may be changing given the introduction of school councils, particularly in Minority world contexts, although as Alderson (2000b) points out they are sometimes ineffective or tokenistic, which can cause additional problems of disillusionment amongst pupils.
4. *Papi, yo les ayudo harto a ustedes pero ustedes no me ayudan a mí. Talvez me compran un pantalón pero si yo no pregunto, no me compran.* (Antonio, 13 years)
5. *Echada en Tarija, sin tener que trabajar mucho.* (Antonio, 13 years)
6. *Come lo que has comprado o ponerte lo que has comprado para ir al colegio!* (Fulgencio, parent)
7. *Del campo hay que ver los animalitos, hay que ayudar a dar de comer, hay que darles aguita. En la ciudad salen de los colegios, algunos tienen su obligación de que van a hacer, pero la mayoría del pueblo no tienen. En el campo siempre siembra todo, lo único que compra es la carne. En la ciudad no siembra nada, mano al bolsillo para todo.* (Ariselda, parent)
8. *Hay differencia. En la ciudad son más habladores, no timído. En el campo tienen miedo hasta para hablar. Se crían en la ciudad con gente, con el pueblo. Aquí se crían con la familia no más. Así veo con mis hijos cuando los llevo a Tarija, no pueden ni comer están con la verguenza.* (Tomás, parent)
9. *En el campo el niño es timido, vergonsoso, no sale.... En la ciudad hay televisión, talvez va de paseo el sábado o el domingo, yendo al parque,*

caminando por las avenidas, o va al cine. El chico del campo qué va a saber que es cine? (Felicia, parent)

10. *No salía y no conocía anadie allá. No me animaba ir más lejos u a otro lugar sola.* (Mónica, 23 years)

11. *Es más cómodo en casa porque así uno trabaja cuando quiere, y puede descansar.* (Sebastián, 18 years)

12. *Somos del campo, acostumbrado a este tipo de trabajo, no vamos a ir a la ciudad.* (Edmundo, 24 years)

13 'Preppy-jocks', 'rednecks', 'stoners', and 'scum'

Power and youth social groups in rural Vermont

Cheryl Morse Dunkley and Ruth Panelli

Vermont, a small state in northern New England, looms large in the North American geographical imagination as a rural place. For over a century, the state has billed itself as a wholesome and beautiful landscape; tourists come here to ski, view colourful fall foliage, buy local cheese and maple syrup, and stay in 'cosy' bed and breakfasts (Hinrichs 1996). In many respects, the rural idyll deployed here is very similar to notions of rurality in the United Kingdom, with its mix of pastoral landscapes, forests, small villages, and associated assumptions of healthy living, traditional lifestyles, and ideal childhoods (O. Jones 1997; Bunce 1994; Matthews, Taylor et al. 2000). Although any place in Vermont is located just a few hours drive from the major urban centres of Boston, New York, and Montreal, it is by one census measure the most rural state in the nation. Most of Vermont's residents (61.8 per cent) live in small towns and villages (Northeast Midwest Institute 2005). The population is predominately white, or Euro-American (98 per cent according to the Centre for Rural Studies and Vermont Centre for Geographic Information 2005). Browsing through the state's popular glossy magazine, *Vermont Life*, one might get the impression that this is one of the most cohesive and homogenous populations imaginable. However, research with young people living in rural Vermont unsettles any notion of uniform or stable geographies.

Young Vermonters living in rural areas face a lack of social, recreational, and built resources, and therefore assemble their social networks and produce their own places within a landscape that is mostly controlled by, and for, adults. As they assert their agency, they also wrestle with constraints placed on them by the physical landscape and climate, parental rules, and a lack of financial resources. Furthermore, young people negotiate and reproduce difference amongst their peers as they attempt to find places for themselves in the small towns and surrounding areas where they live. In particular, clique identities fracture young people into several disparate groups who operate different spatialisations (O. Jones 2000). These different geographies are expressions of power negotiations among rural youth.

YOUNG PEOPLE, POWER, AND RURAL LANDSCAPES

Foucault (1995: 26) contended that power is 'exercised rather than possessed' and is an effect of strategic positions. Rather than imagining power as a universal entity, power can instead be understood as the outcome of embodied relations in material places. Similarly, Latour (1993) insists that power is the ability of an actor to control a number of exchanges or relations within a network comprised of people as well as other nonhuman entities. A person who has access to a greater number of resources and relations, and the wherewithal to influence them, can generate powerful effects. Together these notions of power assist in explaining how young people exploit their socio-material environments to create social opportunities, and why some are better positioned than others to do so.

Rural researchers have shown that young people are not simply passive figures in a landscape of adult-dominated power relations. Smith and colleagues (2002) have shown how young people in New Zealand are capable of making their own meanings of rural life, and Childress (2000), Laegran (this volume), Panelli et al. (2002), and Skelton (2000) have documented how American, Norwegian, New Zealand, and Welsh youth use particular materials and spaces to express their identities and shape their lives. In these accounts, power is manifested through a group's ability to access, occupy, and lay claim to a particular space, even if only temporarily. In this chapter we emphasize that this involves two sets of manoeuvres. First, young people must negotiate with, or work around adults such as parents, landowners, and police officers, to access their preferred places and pastimes, and second, young people must compete or negotiate with other subgroups of young people who are also seeking space. In each case, power is exercised in dynamic relations and specific places.

NORTHERN VERMONT

The following discussion draws upon research conducted with young people in an area of northern Vermont we describe as 'St. Elizabeth'. The area includes two towns (of less than 2500 residents each) and several smaller villages, situated close to the Canadian border and surrounded by lakes, farmed fields, and mountains.[1] The region is criss-crossed by dirt roads, snowmobile trails, and a few paved (sealed) roads. The rolling countryside, forests, farm buildings, and 'quaint' villages of white clapboarded houses surrounding town greens fit Vermont's pastoral image (Hinrichs 1996, and see Figure 13.1). In contrast to this ideal are the boarded-up shop-fronts, economic decline, and geographic and service isolation found in the region (see Figure 13.2). This is a relatively impoverished area of the state and measures of youth well-being indicate a less than idyllic situation for young people. According to state of Vermont statistics, St. Elizabeth's

Figure 13.1 Farmed fields in 'St. Elizabeth', Vermont.

young people consume alcohol, marijuana, and cigarettes at higher rates than the state average. Rates of child abuse and aid to families also exceed the state average (Vermont Agency of Human Services 2003). The goal of the research was to understand how young people build their socio-spatial geographies in a place that contains few material and activity resources for them.

Fieldwork was conducted in the winter of 1999–2000 and involved the collection of 76 completed questionnaires (from 15 per cent of the high school student population attending the two district high schools), nine in-depth interviews with young people, informal conversations with local adults, and observation of public areas and key 'hang-outs' nominated by the participants. Subsequent field trips were taken in 2002, 2003, and 2005

Figure 13.2 Empty storefronts in a St. Elizabeth town.

to observe youth behaviour in the public areas of the region, including on the street, in parking lots, in parks, on the back roads, and at named popular places.

NEGOTIATING POWER IN THE 'ADULT' LANDSCAPE OF ST. ELIZABETH

The impact of adults on young people's rural lives is well documented. Valentine (1997a), O. Jones (2000), and Matthews, Taylor et al. (2000) have variously emphasized the 'adultist' nature of many rural settings in terms of the parental and other adult constraints that are placed on young people. These constraints stem from judgements and beliefs adults have concerning what are appropriate locations, uses of space, and behaviours for young people (see also Bell; Carpena-Méndez; Jones; Punch, this volume). While urban research has also explored these issues, it often focuses on young people's experiences of adult power relations in public, built environments (Van Vliet 1983; Owens 1994; Vanderbeck and Johnson 2000; Thomas 2005). In contrast, rural studies have combined both an interest in public spaces and other types of space that occur in rural settings (see for example Matthews, Taylor et al. 2000). Rural young people negotiate spaces that can variously (and sometimes simultaneously) be understood as (a) home *and* work sites, such as negotiating adult authority on farms (Leckie 1996; Wallace et al. 1994), or as (b) public-but-'wild' sites, such as common marginal land or isolated tracks and pathways. In the latter case, O. Jones (2000), and more recently Cloke and Jones (2005), have argued that young people's use of common but marginal, ramshackle or derelict places can challenge, or even fall outside, adult conceptions and expectations about the ordered management and use of space.

The young people in St. Elizabeth live in both small settlements and on widely dispersed farms and homes beyond the town centres. Some homes are located over ten miles (17 km) from a village or town centre, as well as the local high school. As for recreational sites, there are no movie theatres (cinemas), shopping malls, major fast-food chain stores, arcades, skate parks, or bowling alleys; nor are there community centres, sports centres, public swimming pools, or busy street corners in the area. The closest large town containing a few of these kinds of sites is located a 20- to 30-minute drive from St. Elizabeth; Burlington, Vermont's largest city with a population of approximately 39,000 (U.S. Census Bureau 2005) is an hour's drive away. Moreover, the likelihood of very cold and snowy weather between November and April means that the lack of public, indoor space for half the year further limits young people's options. In a very practical sense, the warmer periods enable young people to exercise more flexibility in the geography of their lives. For instance, popular sites for leisure and socialising in the summer months include swimming holes, hay fields, hunting camps, abandoned buildings, and gravel pit or construction sites, all located out-doors. These patterns illustrate the seasonal variations noted by Bushin et al. (this volume), suggesting that the social geographies of rural youth are necessarily more sensitive to season and weather conditions than are those of urban youth.

Even during the warmer time of year, power relations with adults are important in young people's lives. There is no surety about their social landscape for these places have both a physical character and socio-cultural qualities (Creed and Ching 1997) shaped by the tension between youthful and adult power relations. In St. Elizabeth young people must appropriate places from adults since nearly all of potential social sites are located on private land or are in some way associated with adults' work patterns or other uses of the sites. Thus, use of the sites is always temporary and the need to move on and avoid adult 'interference' is a constant part of life.

Furthermore, as seventeen-year-old John explained, both seasonal and social contingencies affect socializing—even in the warmer months:

> ... in wintertime, there aren't a lot of parties because the parties have to be at somebody's house...and then in the summertime, hanging out in a certain place, you just say, 'Oh let's have a party up there on that hill' and we go up there. So it's...but during the summertime when we're not in school there isn't hardly any parties cause the word don't get around and...usually everybody splits up, cause they're all work-ing and when you go back to school all the parties start again. But the summer's [vacation is] kinda dead.

Summer social events are also limited by the fact that many young peo-ple work during the summer;, for example, doing labour on dairy farms, working in convenience stores, and working with children at a day camp.

Securing access to gathering places, then, is contingent on several factors including: season, time of day, communication networks, and the unex-pected presence of adults or police. Jocelyn, a 16-year-old girl who lives in one of the smallest villages in the area, confirmed the fleeting nature of social sites when asked to identify her favourite hang-outs: 'I don't know, it all varies you know? I mean, you could be here one minute, and there the next, and there the next, you know? There's no necessarily, specific spot.'

Because St. Elizabeth's settlement pattern is diffuse, teenagers too young to drive (younger than 16) or those without access to their own or a family car, must rely on parents or friends to transport them to nearly any activity: school events, parties, visits to friends' homes, etc. Tucker and Matthews (this volume) find this same dependence on parental transport in the social lives of young people living in a rural region of southern England. There is no public transportation in St. Elizabeth. While some young people (those who live within a few miles of a town) may use a mountain bike for trans-portation, this is not a viable option when the narrow dirt roads are covered

Figure 13.3 Young people 'hanging out' in their cars, St. Elizabeth, Vermont.

with snow and ice in winter. The car, therefore, is of great importance to St. Elizabeth youth geographies. It is not only a means to get somewhere but it also provides a (mobile) space to hang out in its own right. Similar to findings from Laegran's research (this volume), key activities reported in this study included: parking in empty parking lots (car parks) to socialize with other youth, driving around the main streets of the towns, driving the dirt back roads of the region, or stopping to interact with peers seen out walking (see Figure 13.3). Julian (age 15), a relative newcomer to the area said:

> There's just hardly anything for a social life in Andrewsville [a town in St. Elizabeth]. You're either walkin' around all day, being a bum or you're in school or you're working. There's, like the most productive thing you see people doing in Andrewsville is turning their car around when they're drivin' up and down the [main street].

Highlighting both the temporary and mobile nature of gathering spots, and pointing to the 'cat and mouse' dynamic between teenagers and authority figures in St. Elizabeth, John explained why there are no 'classic' or permanent party spots in the area: 'The cops break them up'. John said that about one month after a new place has been in use for parties, the police discover it and force the young people to disperse. John complained, 'But what the cops don't realize is that every party place that we have, they end up finding it so they think they're doing their big deal about finding the party spot, but we'll just [go on] riding around drinking.'

A further way that power relations with adults texture the everyday geographies of young people in St. Elizabeth centres on the range of rules and curfews that are set by authority figures, especially parents. Some young people, especially girls and younger boys (see Dunkley [2004] for details), are prohibited by their parents from visiting certain places known as drinking party spots, or have an evening curfew, or are forbidden to drink alcohol, smoke cigarettes, or use drugs. These prohibitions reduce the number of places and activities available to some youth. In addition to these variations, identification with a social group or 'clique' also fractures youth geographies in quite powerful ways. Attention to the differing spatialities of cliques highlights how young people exercise power amongst themselves.

SOCIAL CLIQUES AND SPACE

Young people are neither passive, nor uniformly accepting of the power relations surrounding them. Indeed, increasing numbers of researchers are documenting the innovative and diverse ways young people negotiate their lives and the spatialities of the youth cultures they wish to support (Kraack and Kenway 2002; Panelli 2002; Tucker and Matthews 2001; Tucker 2003). In St. Elizabeth these capacities are also evident, but we argue that creativity should not be reified uncritically as positive dimensions of young lives. Instead, we suggest that the experiences of girls and boys in St. Elizabeth point to the complex and sobering ways that power relations differentially transect youthful possibilities.

Lacking public or dedicated built space (other than the schools), young people in St. Elizabeth appropriate a range of outdoor places, and in some cases, private homes, as well as the mobile space of the car to site their social activities (see Dunkley 2004). Some of the young people also frequented bars in Quebec, located just a few miles away across the border, because the drinking age there is 18 and not enforced, while the drinking age in Vermont is 21 years. In general, the places young people access can be understood as geographically marginal to the centres of social life. Cloke and Jones argue that marginal territories and disordered space both challenge and 'tear at' adult conceptions of space while also being crucial to young people's geographies:

> Disordered space is an important territory for childhood because it is the space where children can live out their otherness to adult ordering and adult expectations. (Cloke and Jones 2005: 330)

In a similar way, the back roads, wooded areas, and fields of St. Elizabeth's rural landscape provide opportunities for some young people to perform their youth culture outside the immediate view and control of adults (see also Jones, this volume). A closer look at the spatialities of the young people in St. Elizabeth shows that social groups have quite different engagements with space. In other words, they tend to occupy different places, and indeed, the use of particular spaces can identify an individual with a social group.

Stark differences amongst peer groups emerged in St. Elizabeth when participants were questioned about social cliques, and then asked to locate themselves socially.[2] When asked about 'cliques at your school' everyone named 'jocks' or 'jock-preps' or 'preppy-jocks,' describing them as the popular athletes and school leaders.[3] The second group identified was the 'rednecks,' young people who enjoyed stereotypically rural activities like snowmobiling, hunting, and fishing, listened to country music or rock and roll, or who came from farming families.[4] 'Partyers' were also referred to as 'stoners'. They are known for heavy drinking and smoking marijuana, laid-back attitudes, and frequent parties.[5] A final collection of young people was variously termed 'scrubs', 'scummies', and 'outcasts'. Young people said these people are 'lower income', 'don't have good hygiene', are 'on welfare', 'could work but don't', 'dirty', and 'keep to themselves'.

Power relations between the different cliques were most evident surrounding the marginalisation of the 'outcasts' and the privileging of the 'preps'. A geography of exclusion and abjection—drawing on notions of purity and pollution; order and ambiguity (Kristeva 1982; Sibley 1995b)—can be seen among the youth in St. Elizabeth. The 'preppy-jocks' are understood as a clean-cut, familiar group, operating within orderly spheres of sport and academic pursuits. In contrast, the 'outcasts' are aligned with dirt and live separate lives from other groups, not involving themselves with extra-curricular and other socially accepted activities and spaces.

While identification of these social cliques was common in St. Elizabeth, individual young people rarely named themselves in a specific grouping.[6] Likewise, no one labelled themselves as an 'outcast', nor could any interviewees identify someone they considered to be in that group, signalling the degree of social distance and exclusion operating among some of the cliques. The personal disassociation with the 'outcast' group even extended to young people who themselves experienced severe marginalization. For example, Julian had recently moved into the area and for several months during the winter was homeless because he had run away from his unsatisfactory foster home. He differentiated himself from the 'outcasts' and 'scum' in his recollection of his 16th birthday:

> It was like my first...seven months here in Andrewsville. It was the night before my 16th birthday and out of the blue, a couple of the kids that I had met...pulled me out behind the bank and they got me drunk. I was beyond drunk, I couldn't walk.... I hardly even knew 'em but the people everywhere were just...I dunno. I don't even know how they found out. But they did and...people I hardly even knew were walking up to me and you know, 'happy birthday' and all that. And, 'here, drink a beer'. It's just—you know that even though they are scum, they do have hearts, some of 'em.

Julian's description of life in St. Elizabeth contrasted sharply with the accounts of other young people (Dunkley 2004; Vanderbeck and Dunkley 2003). He described a violent culture in which physical fights, drug busts, and violent encounters with police occurred in the main street and in lower-income housing. Lacking access to independent transportation, Julian and his neighbours created places for themselves in outdoor, abandoned, and hidden spaces within the larger town of Andrewsville:

> There's never an indoor party in Andrewsville...they're either up at the [gravel] pits or they're just on the street...it's a movin' party. It's just a bunch of people goin' all over the place.. And you meet anywhere and you could have a party.... There's places like the Castle, which is out back of those buildings on the opposite side of the road. It's an old, abandoned building. It's all cement. It has no roof or anything. Just four walls, just basically all you need to have a party.

Young people belonging to other social groups identify spaces with different characteristics in their social geographies. Jocelyn, a self-professed 'partyer', valued places where she felt a high degree of freedom. Her favourite hang-out was a local swimming hole, and a reggae festival in a neighbouring rural town was the site of her 'funnest' day ever. She said, 'It's definitely a big thing, being able to do what I want and not having strings attached or anything like that.' Alternatively, young people whose activities fit into the 'preppy-jock' group cited private homes (where they hold 'house parties') as important social sites, in addition to Quebec bars, and the gravel pit, the site of large 'pit' parties where numerous young people from different social groups gather around a fire. They also described the importance of sports. The popular athletes and students spent much time in sports-related places like playing fields, basketball courts, and the school gymnasium.[7] It is important to note that membership on a travelling sports team also provides 'preppy-jocks' with the opportunity to visit places outside St. Elizabeth, and to create relationships with students from other schools. These friendships extend the preppy-jocks' personal networks beyond the local community.

John distanced himself from the 'preps', and his favourite activities of hunting, four-wheel driving on off-road terrain, working, and raising trouble with authority figures every once in a while, place him closer to the 'redneck' group. He reported that he would describe social life in St. Elizabeth as:

> ...running the back roads; either that, or every once in a while having a party at somebody's house. But it's usually just four or five cars riding around on the back roads and every once in a while [we] stop and get out and talk.

John's group of (male) friends, who all have their own vehicles, enjoyed moving through the area: up muddy logging roads, over snowy snowmobile trails, and long distance driving from one end of the county to the other. (The interview data indicated that it is much more likely for a boy to own his own car than a girl, see Dunkley [2004].)

THE PRODUCTION OF POWER AND
DIFFERENCE THROUGH SPACE

The activities and spaces of a group help shape a group's social identification, and can be read by other groups as exercises of power (Foucault 1995). Pick-up trucks with NASCAR (car racing) stickers, and the off-road trails accessed by the 'rednecks', for example, may be understood as signs of their identities as hard-playing, hard-working, practical people who enjoy the rural aspects of St. Elizabeth. In contrast, the 'preppy-jocks" occupation of an outdoor basketball court, or the dance floor of a Quebec bar, are spatial exercises of power that shore up their identities as athletic and perhaps more urbane than the other groups. Some informants suggested that members of the 'preppy-jocks' received preferential treatment from schoolteachers, hinting that social cliques have differential levels of power and influence in the community, and that feeling at home in school space is a symbol of more prestigious social positions. Conversation with young people revealed a perceived hierarchy of cliques, with 'preppy-jocks' at the top, 'rednecks' and 'partyers' in the middle, and 'outcasts' at the bottom. While social clique did not appear to map directly onto economic status, Latour's (1993) attention to resources and relations is pertinent in this study. Specifically, those young people with access to a greater number of resources—cars, friends with cars, part-time work that generated personal income, families that supported extra-curricular school activities, educational support—were better positioned to create desirable social opportunities, and reap the social status that comes with popularity.

Power was also expressed through the exclusions and boundary maintenance practices between social cliques. For instance, 'outcasts' are neither invited to, nor welcomed at, the parties of 'popular' youth. One way to maintain groups' distinctive identities is by using discrete spaces. Jenna indicated that problems can erupt when groups attempt to mix in tight spaces. She explained that there were frequent fights in the Quebec bars, not between Canadians and St. Elizabeth youth, but amongst St. Elizabeth teenagers.

Activities can also signal membership in one group or another, resulting in subsequent reactions from peers. For example, Jennifer described how she stopped spending time with a good friend who began to frequently smoke pot. This behaviour marked her friend as closer to the 'stoner' group and distanced the girl from the 'preppy-jock' group she belonged to as a member of varsity sports teams. Jennifer's exercise of power involved social distancing from this friend who had become in some ways 'ambiguous' and potentially 'abject' (Kristeva 1982).

This kind of boundary maintenance does not imply that social positions are fixed or that the exercise of power surrounding social cliques is consistent. Clique boundaries are ambiguous and permeable, evidenced by the many interviewees who positioned themselves between a number of groups. The small size of the local youth population limits the construction of rigidly defined social boundaries between groups. As the students from the smaller of the two high schools indicated, young people from many social groups mix together at large outdoor parties; navigating social power relations is part of the experience, and some individuals move between or hold multiple positions within different groupings. In these instances, cliques do not fade away but border crossings are more smoothly achieved.

Through inclusionary and exclusionary socio-spatial practices, young people reproduce social difference within their rural community, and these have implications for their future aspirations. The clearest illustration of this issue involves the distinctions between 'redneck' and 'preppy-jock' identities. While these differences are formulated through the meanings and practices of contrasting social cliques, they also are embedded in broader geographical imaginations. The use of the term *redneck* links St. Elizabeth young people with a national narrative of white, rural, working class people who are variously coded as obsolete and uneducated, or traditional and patriotic (Jarosz and Lawson 2002). While the 'redneck' narrative circulates at the national level, it implies allegiance to local rural places and is performed through activities such as hunting that rely on the local rural landscape. In contrast, the 'preppy-jock' identity is at least partially performed by drawing upon wider, 'urban' imaginaries.[8] Hip-hop and rap music, baggy jeans, and a voiced disdain for, or despair of, limited opportunities in the local region characterize this group; its symbols, interests, and imagined futures are located far from St. Elizabeth. The 'preppy-jocks' interviewed for this research said they believed they would need to leave the region to pursue their education and careers (Dunkley 2004; Vanderbeck and Dunkley 2003). Consequently, members of this group move through their present with an appreciation of their current (more prestigious) positions and with the expectation that they will leave the area to search for the different experiences that can provide the kinds of adult lives they desire.[9] The ability of this group to draw on a diverse set of resources while in secondary school positions them to have the kind of success in high school required to gain entry into post-secondary education and training programs in places far from home. Their futures will be elsewhere, while 'rednecks', particularly the young men who find satisfaction in the 'rural' outdoor activities, imagine lives deeply rooted in the St. Elizabeth landscape.

CONCLUSIONS

The young people of St. Elizabeth build their social lives upon a constantly shifting terrain. They are affected by adult spatial codes and controls that shape where they can be and how they should behave. Their ability to secure a place to 'hang out' is dependent on a host of physical and social contingencies: available sites, season, time of day, weather, parental rules, social group, distance from town centres, access to transportation, and gender. In their place-finding activities, young people of St. Elizabeth must not only contend with the 'adult community' (see Bell, this volume) but also with difference amongst their peers, expressed in the on-going formation, boundary maintenance, and specific socio-spatial practices of cliques. Spaces and practices come to be associated with the identities of those groups who lay claim to them, and the various degrees of 'ruralness' accorded to specific places and activities influence their desirability for differing groups. Furthermore, individual young people, as well as social groups are variously positioned within socio-material networks; those with access to a wider range of resources enjoy a greater number of recreational opportunities.

The young people of St. Elizabeth must navigate the 'entanglements of power' (Sharp et al. 2000) posed by adult geographies, but they also create their own tangles, composed of 'us' and 'them', trucks and soccer fields, hopes of distant lives and aspirations to stay at home. Indeed, working through such entanglements is the way that power is exercised. Processes of inclusion and exclusion are expressions of power worked out not only over young people by adults, but also amongst young people as they attempt to find their places in the world.

NOTES

1. All place names and research names are pseudonyms. We cannot provide a map of the area as the geographic knowledge could reveal the identities of the participants given the small population size of the region.
2. These questions were asked early in the research, during the interview recruitment phase. The 'snowball' method was employed to develop contacts for semi-structured interviews; teachers, a health professional, acquaintances, and young people suggested individual young people who might be willing to be interviewed. Potential interviewees were initially contacted by letter, and then by telephone several days later. During the phone call, the researcher asked questions from a screening tool that was designed to produce a pool of young adult interviewees of diverse backgrounds, ages, activity preferences, geographic locations (whether they lived in one of the large towns, small villages, or in the most rural places), and social cliques.
3. These young people (both girls and boys) could be distinguished as the sports focused 'jocks' or the scholastic focused 'preps', but were often grouped together by informants because of their popularity and high social status.
4. *Rednecks* is often a derogatory term distinguishing conservative and 'backward' perspectives. For a wider discussion see Jarosz and Lawson (2002).

5. Members of other social cliques also drink and use drugs but their involvement in other activities figures more highly in the descriptors of their group identities.
6. For example, Jake and Jeremy self-identified as 'jocks', and Jocelyn said she was a 'partyer'. The remaining young people either called themselves 'average' or located themselves as 'in between' a couple of the groups.
7. Jeremy (age 15) even imagined that the addition of a teen fitness or weight centre or a movie theatre could bring social cliques together: 'Weight rooms and then movies; I think that'd help bring people together more, like the different cliques. You know, you start talkin' to somebody, they like the same movies as you, you know, it would just build up on it'.
8. It is important to note, however, that the location of such an identity, as an '*urban*' one is also problematic. This highlights the binaries of status (simple: sophisticated and ordinary: elite) that are ascribed to homogenizing stereotypes about rural: urban societies, cultures, and people, see Vanderbeck and Dunkley (2003) for a discussion of this.
9. This is particularly the case for older girls. The questionnaire results showed that only 31 per cent of 16- to 18-year-old girls plan to live in the St. Elizabeth region when they are 20- to 30-year-olds compared to 86 per cent of boys (Dunkley 2004).

14 'The child drums and the elder dances'?

Girlfriends and boyfriends negotiating power relations in rural Uganda

Stephen Bell

The Ugandan proverb, 'the child drums and the elder dances',[1] is mentioned regularly when parents, community elders, and other adults who play important roles in the lives of young rural Ugandans discuss issues of young people's[2] agency and empowerment. At face value this proverb mirrors calls within academia and the NGO world for recognition that young people have an active role in (re)constituting their lives and those of people around them (Stephens 1995; Scheper-Hughes and Sargent 1998; Hart et al. 2004). A deeper analysis of young people's lives in rural areas of Uganda leads to several important questions interrogating this proverb and highlighting problems faced by young people when they try to negotiate established power relations and gain more control over their own lives. Are adults dancing to rhythms chosen independently by young people, or do they choose to dance only when young people drum rhythms taught to them by their elders? What are the consequences for young people when they choose to drum their own rhythms?

This chapter explores the circumstances of young people who choose to transgress behaviours expected of them and engage in (sexual) relationships with members of the opposite sex. The chapter begins by contextualizing the dominant socio-cultural expectations that dictate how young people should behave with regard to (sexual) relationships, and in terms of respecting their elders. Secondly, within the context of such expectations the conceptual framework is explored by linking theoretical notions of social norms and socialisation processes with those relating to power, empowerment, and subtle resistance strategies. Thirdly, case study material is presented in order to illustrate young people's negotiation of these dominant socio-cultural expectations. This includes young people's decision-making processes that lead to the initiation of forbidden relationships, strategies utilized to maintain such relationships, and potential and actual consequences arising from these decisions. Evidence highlights that young people are agents in their own lives, engaging in the negotiation and resistance of what I have called 'parenting power'. Furthermore, young people negotiate a varied and complicated range of relationships with boyfriends/ girlfriends, friends, and peers. The chapter concludes by outlining core messages to be taken from this case study, and highlighting avenues for further thought, research and action by academics and practitioners working with rural young people in the Majority world.

BACKGROUND TO THE STUDY

Case study data used in this chapter was collected during participatory and ethnographic research that explored processes of empowerment amongst male and female young people participating in HIV/AIDS prevention and sexual and reproductive health (SRH) programmes initiated by local and international non-governmental organizations (NGOs) and community-based organizations (CBOs). This research was carried out in three culturally distinct rural locations across Uganda with the Bagisu ethnic group in

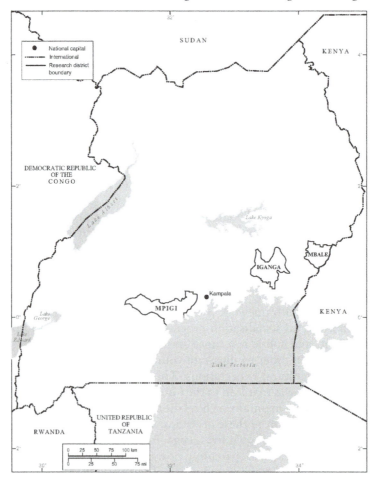

Figure 14.1 Study areas in Uganda.

Mbale District, the Basoga in Iganga District, and the Baganda in Mpigi District, highlighted in Figure 14.1 (based on UN map). With each cultural group, the prefix changes in a regular pattern to refer to the area (Buganda), the people (Baganda), an individual (Muganda), and their language (Luganda).

During an initial six-month research trip, 52 single-sex focus groups were carried out with young people in and out of school, of different ages and genders, to explore local problems they face, issues of power and powerlessness, and social difference. One hundred seventeen young people across the three areas were asked to participate in informal in-depth interviews exploring a range of differing life circumstances, sexual and reproductive health attitudes, and behaviours. Further in-depth ethnographic research was undertaken with 23 young people previously involved in interviews during a second five-month research trip to explore SRH-related themes in more detail. Parents, guardians, and other influential adults living within and outside their communities were also interviewed throughout the research trip.

An important goal of the research was to learn from boys and girls, as to how boys' sexual decision-making, attitudes, and behaviours affect girls, and vice versa, but it was inappropriate for me to spend time talking about sexually related issues with girls on my own. Consequently, I worked with male and female research assistants throughout the research to overcome this communication barrier in order to gain girls' experiences, and to address language difficulties encountered, particularly amongst elder generations and young people who were out of school, and more generally in Mpigi and Iganga Districts.

SOCIO-CULTURAL EXPECTATIONS
RELATING TO YOUNG PEOPLE

Discussion with young people, their parents, and other community members emphasized that boyfriend–girlfriend relationships are unacceptable, whether or not relationships are sexual. While most parents suggest that friendship between boys and girls is a positive experience because they learn from each other, other parents urge that friendship is destructive and leads to promiscuity. All parents agree that the stage when a friendship develops into a boyfriend–girlfriend relationship is forbidden until they have left school and are ready to marry.

This is a general trend across the rural areas in which I have worked, though exceptions and contradictions arise due to individual circumstances and local cultural practices. For example, one boy had been looked after by his grandmother since he lost both his parents by the age of four. She became too frail to support him, and at 17 years, with his grandmother's support, he found a girlfriend to marry and help him with the domestic chores his grandmother had once taken care of, including cooking, cleaning, and maintaining his subsistence crops.

The Bagisu celebrate boys' transition to manhood during circumcision ceremonies every even year, though there is no alternative public celebration of a girl's transition to womanhood. According to strict cultural beliefs, maintained today by older generations and clan leaders in particular, a boy cannot be considered a man until he has completed the circumcision process, after which he gains access to adult male privileges, including marriage, sexual relationships, and more public respect from community members. In the past circumcision was meant for boys aged 18 and above as they were considered strong enough to cope with 'manhood'. Currently, however, boys as young as 12, and regularly 15 and 16, are circumcised alongside those aged 18 and above, often because their parents believe circumcision at a younger age will prevent their children from being involved in celebrations involving alcoholic consumption and early sexual experiences. Interviews with young people and adults indicated that perceptions vary about the contemporary relevance of this cultural transition due to the circumcision of younger boys. The notion of 'manhood' becomes contentious when boys are circumcised young and try to behave like men, especially when some elders actively promote the cultural significance of this ritual.

Young people also emphasized the importance of 'behaving well'[3] in the home and wider community. 'Giving respect'[4] was mentioned by all young people when describing their relationship with elders (see Klocker, this volume). An important implication is that it is considered disrespectful for young people to debate or argue with their elders. Boys highlighted loving girls, acting irresponsibly, and failing to cooperate with other community members as bad behaviours. Girls listed activities such as loving men or boys, being seen talking or mixing with the opposite sex regularly in public, and wearing inappropriate clothing like miniskirts which bare too much flesh. These are associated with promiscuity and girls are supposed to act with self-restraint and social discipline. Despite an awareness of good behaviour amongst the younger generations, there is wide acknowledgement amongst community adults that young people are not abiding by these values, indicating inter-generational conflict, and a degree of resistance amongst younger generations with regard to expected behavioural norms.

YOUNG PEOPLE, POWER, AND EMPOWERMENT

The socio-cultural expectations presented above are examples of 'social norms' (Turner 1991). Interviews indicated that these are taught to young people by parents and other community adults, as they grow up, to ensure young people behave according to what is deemed socially acceptable for people of their age and sex by the wider community (see Dunkley and

Panelli, this volume). This draws on the concept of socialisation whereby an infant gradually becomes a self-aware knowledgeable person, skilled in the ways of the culture into which (s)he is born (Giddens 1989). It became evident that as young people grow up in the rural areas where I worked, they are influenced by their peers, observing other people's behaviours, and being influenced by popular national radio stations, for example. These all affect the values young people hold and the behaviours in which they choose to indulge, encouraging them to develop an individual sense of self-identity and the capacity for independent thought and action. This independent thought and action is a focus for the rest of this chapter.

Empowerment has been defined as a fluid, often unpredictable process leading ultimately to a fundamental social transformation of society that enables marginalized groups and individuals, including young rural Ugandans, to make decisions allowing them more control over their lives (Scheyvens 1998; Parpart et al. 2002). Exploring what is meant by processes of empowerment revolves around a nuanced understanding of 'power'. Orthodox conceptions of power tend to equate it with domination: as a dominating force to be exerted or wielded by the powerful to impose their will on others (Sharp et al. 2000). However, Foucault (1979a) rejected the idea that power can be possessed by somebody, arguing instead that power permeates throughout society, and exists in complex everyday social relationships.

Drawing on Foucault's interpretation of power, processes of empowerment amongst young people involve the *exercise* rather than the possession of power (Parpart et al. 2002). This occurs within the web of social power relations in which young people are situated with other community members of differing age, sex, religion, and financial status. As well as paying more attention to the controlling and facilitating aspects of broader political, economic, and cultural norms and contexts within which young people live (Parpart et al. 2002), it is crucial to understand the relationship between agency and power, because individuals entangled in this web are able to exercise power, and experience it, in different ways, with differential influence and impact, over time and space (see Klocker; Punch, this volume).

In the context of the controlling nature of adult influence on young people as they grow up, the following sections explore how power is exercised and experienced by young people and other influential individuals. Case study evidence illustrates that power is bound up in conformity and resistance, and differential freedoms of choice and agency. When exploring young people's resistance, I draw on work by Scheyvens (1998) and Desai (2002) that illustrates the 'subtle strategies' utilized by women to resist dominant everyday power relations.

> The term 'subtle strategies' refers to any strategies that attempt to achieve profound, positive changes in women's lives without stirring up wide-scale dissent. (Scheyvens 1998: 237)

Subtle strategies are a quiet, often invisible way in which marginalized individuals or groups attempt to (re)assert themselves in their homes and communities, and illustrate how groups, generally considered powerless, exercise power through informal strategies designed to quietly resist prevailing dominant power relations (see also Beazley 2000b; 2002; Hart 1991; Scott 1990). This chapter highlights a variety of subtle strategies utilized by young people to initiate and maintain forbidden relationships, which suggest that power is exercised in a range of private and public spheres (see Punch, this volume).

It is useful to explore young people's perceived abilities and strategies to exercise power to change their own situations for the better, and to understand empowerment as an unpredictable set of processes. It is therefore important to study the positive and negative consequences of young people's decision-making processes and actions. Young people's agency generates small but important positive changes in their personal lives, building self-esteem and happiness, and gaining access to financial and material needs, and demonstrating personal psychological and economic aspects of power. However, long-term consequences that occur as a result of young people's strategies becoming public knowledge can be hugely inhibitive. Case study material presented below illustrates that rejecting norms and expectations can lead to 'social exclusion',[5] loss of 'social capital',[6] and disciplinary action due to being considered as 'out-of-place' by parents, community members, and their peers (Cresswell 1996). This emphasizes the responsive, disciplinary, exclusionary, and controlling aspects of power exercised by other influential people, and a lack of sustainability in young people's agency, negotiation of power relations, and strategies of self-empowerment.

INITIATING AND MAINTAINING
FORBIDDEN RELATIONSHIPS

Choosing whether or not to engage in relationships represents an early stage in resisting and negotiating expectations and power relations. Figure 14.2 highlights some reasons and risks involved in young people's decision making that arose during interviews and focus groups.

One of the most prevalent reasons for girls becoming involved in relationships, for example, is that boyfriends act as a livelihood by providing basic financial and material needs for girls, young mothers, and their children. This is not unique to Uganda, and has also been documented extensively in other African contexts (Baylies and Bujra 2000; Amuyunzu-Myamongo et al. 2005). Relationships are perceived as necessary for some girls whose parents choose not to, or are unable to provide them with their basic day-to-day needs, and who decide that boyfriends are a more reliable option. While these decisions ensure that basic short-term needs are met,

REASONS SUPPORTING A (SEXUAL) RELATIONSHIP		REASONS AGAINST A (SEXUAL) RELATIONSHIP
Stability in one's life		Getting a girl pregnant
Understand girls when married		Imprisonment or/and fine for defilement
Peer pressure (want to fit in, and advised it is good)		Having to run away from home and community
Natural urges and sexual desires	**B O Y S**	Positive peer pressure
Idle out-of-school boys with nothing better to do		Observation of peers in bad circumstances
Encouraged independence for out-of-school boys		Financial burden - culture of regular financial support for girlfriend
Culturally encouraged (e.g. post circumcision for the Bagisu)		'Can't serve two masters at once' (education and girlfriend)
Companionship		Risk of disobeying parents
Increased self confidence and self-esteem		Parental punishment (caning, beaten, chased from home)
Someone to confide in and be with	**B O T H**	Bad community reputation
Happiness		Community surveillance and consequent parental discipline
		Sexual and reproductive health risks (STIs, HIV/AIDS)
Feelings of love		Dropout of school
A natural progression as you grow up		
Boyfriend as a livelihood (gain of basic needs and material benefits)		Increased burden of looking after child alone
Enjoy sex	**G I R L S**	Becoming pregnant
Necessary support for out-of-school girl and child		Increased poverty post-pregnancy
Feelings of increasing independence for out-of-school girl (with child)		Mistreatment in marriage
Encouraged by family as financial coping strategy for out-of-school girl		Previous negative experiences with men (rape, cheated, tricked)

Figure 14.2 Young people's decision-making processes to avoid or initiate (sexual) relationships.

they increase the likelihood that long-term consequences will occur, including unplanned pregnancy, early marriage, and SRH risks. For example, male dominance in society, lack of awareness of and access to contraception and family planning methods, and circumstances where girls lack control over decision making within the relationship in terms of when and how often they 'play sex'[7] (often without protection), can lead to increased risk of sexually transmitted infections (STIs) and pregnancy. As relationships proceed secretively young people lack the necessary support networks to draw upon should problems arise in the relationship.

Young people maintain relationships through a variety of 'subtle strategies' adopted to resist dominant expectations until parents and the wider community perceive relationships to be acceptable, or the relationship ends. Secret meetings at various places throughout the community are a frequently cited example of such strategies:

> We play [sex] every weekend. We hide and go to my boyfriend's hut at around 6–7 pm. I have to run back home early enough so that my parents do not notice that I have been out for a long time.[8] (16-year-old school girl, Mbale District)

> I have ever played [sex] because I wanted…. We play at night. In secret places where they cannot see me. In the bush'.[9] (17-year-old school boy, Mpigi District)

Secret meetings take place in 'safe' places, whether 'in the bush' amongst the dense banana plants or in a boy's individual home. Observations and conversations highlighted that in Bugisu and Busoga areas, boys aged 15 or 16 construct their own houses within or near their father's compound. According to interviewees it is culturally unacceptable for boys in these areas to live under their father's roof for a variety of reasons, including the importance of becoming more independent, as well as to avoid being tempted into sexual relationships as a result of hearing his parents 'playing' sex. Boys who live within their parent's home often make arrangements to meet their girlfriends in a friend's house. Meetings can also occur, unknown to the parents, when young people have been sent to do jobs, like fetching water or buying goods from trading centres.

Other subtle strategies are adopted to limit SRH risks and minimize the risk of the relationship becoming public knowledge. Accessing and using condoms is one example:

> It is maybe acceptable to play sex…. We got some condoms from the health centre. I felt shy getting them because the condoms, the parents do not want to see condoms. I went at night because I didn't want someone to see.[10] (17-year-old school boy, Mbale District)

Girls employ a broader range of perceived risk limitation strategies, though not all are safe. Some girls 'play' sex during the 'safe' days after menstruation, though there was some dispute as to when the safe days occurred. Others swallow 'panadol' immediately before they 'play' sex as a form of family planning, based on hearsay and 'good' advice from friends who have done the same and failed to become pregnant. The SRH implications of these strategies are numerous, including transmission of STIs and unexpected pregnancies.

These examples illustrate the subtle nature of young people's negotiation and resistance of expected behaviours. During relationships mistakes occur, potential risks actualize, subtle resistance becomes public, and negotiation and exercise of power becomes more overt and confrontational. By presenting three case study profiles, the following section illustrates some of the possible consequences of young people's agency, and the power struggles occurring in their everyday lives.

CONSEQUENCES OF RESISTANCE

Musa, a 17-year-old Mugisu, was 15 when I met him in 2003, married, living with his wife in his own home within the father's compound, and looking after a three-week-old baby. Initially the father had chased him from the home because he was angry about the unplanned pregnancy, but family members persuaded him to allow Musa back. When I met Musa in 2004 he had divorced his wife. This year I heard rumours he had been chased from home for getting another girl pregnant. When I found him living with his maternal grandparents 8 km from his parents' home, he explained he had been seeing a school girl, but one of his peers informed the girl's father because he disapproved of the relationship. When the girl's father confronted Musa's father, he called the local police. Musa's older brother overheard, found him before the police, and advised him to run to his grandparents' home. He is currently angry with his father for wanting to punish him, and is unhappy not to have seen his girlfriend since he ran away.

Scovia, an 18-year-old Muganda, gave birth to an unplanned baby girl 18 months ago after a mistake in a consensual relationship. She wanted to have an (illegal) abortion, but because the boyfriend would have to pay and because he did not want her to have one, she was unable to negotiate and continued the pregnancy with the promise of his financial support. Her parents were furious, immediately refused to pay her school fees, and demanded she stay at home to complete the household's domestic work. After five months, and once the boyfriend had spent two weeks in a local prison for defiling her and paid a USh500,000 (£160) fine,[11] the parents accepted the baby. Currently the boyfriend and his parents support Scovia financially, as her own family has stopped contributing and closed down income-generating opportunities with her brothers in Kampala because she is now the boyfriend's responsibility.

Nulu, a 15-year-old Mugisu, recently decided to leave school to marry her boyfriend against advice from friends, and eloped to the nearby town without telling her guardian and friends. When the relationship collapsed she moved back to the village where she was excluded from friendship groups and rejected from her guardian's house, who criticized her and spread rumours about her bad behaviour. She lacks any regular financial support from her guardian, but is supported by her brother in return for working in his shop and doing his domestic work. She does not have a good relationship with his wife, so she lives alone in a hut next door.

These case studies highlight a range of inter- and intra-generational power struggles in young people's lives. 'Parenting power', referring to the role of parents and other community adults in parenting young people who are not their children, conflicts most obviously with young people's agency, because parents influence or control their child's life if they disapprove of their behaviour (see Dunkley and Panelli; Klocker; Punch, this volume). Scovia and Nulu both experienced dramatic lifestyle changes in terms of school attendance, support networks, day-to-day activities, and use of time and space. Nulu's scenario highlights more significant repercussions of social exclusion due to her guardian's decision to punish her publicly rather than privately within the home. However, parenting power is not an all-encompassing force over young people, as young people react to it in different ways. Musa's example not only highlights a repetition of poorly perceived behaviour, but also illustrates continued resistance through anger directed at his father, and his decision to stay away from his father's home.

There is an interesting array of power-based relationships that exist between young people themselves (see Dunkley and Panelli; Laegran; Punch, this volume). Interviews indicate a 'culture' of boyfriends giving their girlfriends financial or material assistance during a relationship. Financial support ranged from US$3,000 (£0.85) per month to US$10,000 (£3) per week, whilst material benefits included small items such as knickers and powder. The amount of assistance depends on personal circumstance. Some boys explained that if they could not pay one week/month, the girlfriend would (have to) accept the assistance could not be made. Irregular and unpredictable support is, however, generally unacceptable on the girl's terms, even though she is not always able to determine the quantity of assistance, and if a boy wants to keep a girlfriend he must contribute in some way.

These power differentials within a relationship are complicated further by boyfriends' demands for sex. One girl explained this was called 'payback',[12] and that it normally occurs a month into the relationship. Some girls submit to the requests without question, because they love the boy and want to 'play' sex. Others accept it is part of the deal, and English phrases including 'pay as you go' and 'sweet for touch is fair game' were used frequently among girls in Mbale to indicate the informal contractual nature of the relationship. Use of contraception varies according to how willing the boy is to use condoms and listen to his girlfriend's demands, how well a girl can negotiate for the use of condoms in a relationship, and how available or accessible condoms are. Girls emphasized that if condoms are used, the boy will demand sex more regularly than if condoms are not used, in order to be 'paid back' satisfactorily.

Other girls resist sexual demands. One girl explained she was aware of 'payback' expectations, but chooses to hop from one boyfriend to another when each starts demanding sex (see also Amuyunzu-Myamongo et al. 2005; Nyanzi et al. 2001). Although appearing to be in control of her situation, she risks building herself a poor reputation or finding a boyfriend who forces sex when she denies the payback. Focus group discussions indicated this to be a regular event in rural communities.

Nulu's and Musa's case studies indicate further power differentials between young people when siblings, friends, and peers find out about and publicize a relationship. Those involved in relationships fear rumours spreading through the community, and conversations suggested that friendships break down as people are perceived as 'spoilt', meaning badly behaved or ill-mannered, because they love their peers.

CONCLUSIONS

Several important issues illustrated in this chapter help contribute to a conceptual understanding of young people's experiences and negotiation of power-based relationships within their communities. This chapter highlights how dominant socio-cultural norms and expectations, promoted through surveillance, socializing and controlling strategies by adults, encourage young people to behave in certain ways as they grow up. Additionally, young people exercise power through decision-making processes and a range of 'subtle strategies' (Scheyvens 1998; Desai 2002). This emphasizes important links between agency, power, and empowerment, as agency amongst young people is necessary for them to exercise power in ways they perceive to be empowering.

Changing dynamics of social power relations become evident by exploring the decision-making processes that lead to resistance, the variety of strategies employed by young people to actualize their decisions, and the positive and negative consequences of doing so. By actively negotiating and resisting expectations, young people find that new relationships evolve, and old ones become more complicated. Young people continually face, or are subjected to, a new range of consequences and opportunities for further decision-making and action, resulting from previous decisions and actions, and other influential individuals exercising power in response.

There are several avenues where further analytical and empirical work could be of value to deepen our understanding of the web of power relations young people find themselves in, and the agency they use to negotiate this. Underlying these, it is vital that research agendas pay attention to the vast diversity of life circumstances for young people aged 16, let alone from

12 to 25. Without this care and attention to detail, we will not explore the diverse rural experiences of young people around the world.

Firstly, it would be interesting to understand why young people tend to prioritize the short-term over the long-term in day-to-day decision making and strategies of negotiation and resistance, as well as exploring circumstances where young people do focus on long-term needs. Secondly, longitudinal explorations analysing how young people's decisions and actions lead to changes in the very structures and expectations they are resisting or negotiating would prove invaluable. This chapter has focused on subtle negotiations, but further documentation of the consequences of subtle, and more public, displays of resistance over time would contribute to understanding acceptable, sustainable, and transformational processes of social change and empowerment. Finally, I propose the importance of research analysing how young people can be assisted or facilitated in their attempts to take more control over their lives by other actors, such as CBOs/NGOs, and the challenges and successes of such assistance. This would have lasting consequences for both a conceptual understanding of the changing power dynamics that young people are involved in, and the effectiveness of practical interventions relating to their SRH.

Acknowledgements

I would like to thank the Economic and Social Research Council (ESRC) for funding this doctoral research, and David Simon, Vandana Desai, Samantha Punch, Elsbeth Robson, and other participants at the Rural Young Lives RGS-IBG conference session for their comments. Many thanks also to Claire Scrutton, Kisakye Lydia, and Wankya Tom for their invaluable support as research assistants.

NOTES

1. Translated from the Bagisu proverb, 'Umwana akuba ingoma, Umukhulu washina'.
2. The term *young people* is often met with blank facial expressions in Uganda. It becomes evident from interviews and government documents that the term encompasses several other definitions and categories. 'Children' are under 18 years of age, and 'Adolescents' are between 10 and 24 years. 'Youth' are generally understood as those between 18 and 30, though interviews with representatives at local and national levels of government indicate that government programming uses the term *youth* to refer to those aged between 12 and 24, while policy documents refer to those between 12 and 30 years. In line with the editorial decision, the case studies referred to in this chapter are young people under the age of 18. However, this research emphasizes that daily issues—including lack of school attendance, lack of voice, and respect in the wider community, parenthood, marriage, roles, and responsibilities that affect a 16-year-old can be just as diverse and complicated as those facing a 22-year-old.

3. 'Okweyisa obulungi' in Luganda.
4. 'Okuwa ekipipwa' in Luganda.
5. Social exclusion is a process through which individuals and groups are partially or wholly excluded from full participation in the society in which they live, and experience disadvantage, alienation, and lack of freedom (Bhalla and Lapeyre 1997; de Haan 1998).
6. This is known as 'social capital' and refers to 'features of social organisation such as networks, norms and social trust that facilitates co-ordination and cooperation for mutual benefit' (Putnam 1993, cited in Desai 2002: 232). McAslan (2002) develops this concept further with her distinction between 'horizontal' and 'vertical' social capital. Respectively, this is the distinction between uniting people across their social group, and connecting these people to others outside, or 'above' this immediate social grouping.
7. 'Okwegatta' in Luganda.
8. 'Bankola buli weekendi. Twekeka ne tugenda munyumba yo mulenzi wange kusawa kumi na bbiri oba sawa emu. Eya kawungenzi ku ntekwa okukumawo mangu ekka nga addazade te banaba oktegera' in Lugisu.
9. 'Negase nabawala bangi kubanga mbade negomba. Mbadde nkikola ekiro. Mubiffo ebyekufifu webatasabola kundaba. Munfiiko' in Luganda.
10. 'Kyinzika okwegatta... Tufuna obubiira obumu okuva kudwaliro. Nawulira ensonyi okufuna obubiira. Okuva dwaliro, abazadde bange tebadala kulaba bubira. Nagenda kirro nga sagal kundaba' in Lugisu.
11. The Penal Code in Uganda (Government of Uganda 2000) explains that 'defilement' is applied to all cases of sexual contact outside of marriage, involving girls younger than 18, regardless of consent or the age of the 'perpetrator'. Defilement carries a maximum sentence of death, or imprisonment for 18 years with or without corporal punishment. In the rural areas this is often dealt with informally, and boys are held within the local prison until a settlement fine is paid by him or his family.
12. 'Owakyolina okufuna kyotalia' in Luganda.

15 Rurality, power, and the otherness of childhood in British contexts

Owain Jones

Power is a critical aspect of child–adult relationships and the formation of children's geographies. It is tempting to see the adult world as all powerful and children's worlds as subjected to control and direction, but the picture is more complex than that. Children do have less power in many respects, but they also have agency, and child–adult relations have complex inter-plays of power; for example, children's skilful manipulation of parents and adults. One way in which power flows between adults' and children's worlds is through adult constructions of what childhood is and how it should be treated. Jenks (2005) shows that differing ideologies of childhood result in children's lives being shaped in markedly different ways.

One such ideology of childhood is the country childhood idyll. This is the idea that the countryside offers children a range of goods which includes, freedom, nature, space, fresh air, exercise, adventure, and so on. This powerful imagined geography can be found in various arenas of discourse, including literature (Bunce 2003), film/television (O. Jones 2006), toys, and advertising images. Importantly, discourse can become practice as parents and other actors (including organisations) try to bring children and country spaces together in a number of ways. This positive association between childhood and rural spaces tells us a lot about how each element, and other hidden elements such as the urban, are imaginatively constructed and the power relations between them (Williams 1985).

Ideas of country childhood idyll are driven by deeply embedded notions of childhood, nature, the country and the city shaped by romantic sensibilities (Macnaghten and Urry 1998; Jenks 2005). They are often dismissed as unrealistic, superficial, nostalgic views with no foundation in reality, and views that mask the problems faced by many rural children in everyday life (Davis and Ridge 1997). While not denying these concerns, I suggest that in some instances these constructions and their associated practices and spaces do offer children space/times which are less constrained and monitored by adult authority. Consequently, children's otherness and its related geographic expression can flourish in ways quite distant from adult imaginations and surveillance. In other words, these constructions of childhood and space can scramble the flows of power between adult and child worlds, and, in some instances, inadvertently empower children to be other.

The rural is imagined as a childhood idyll because it is seen as a natural, innocent space which brings the benefits already outlined. The child who exploits such space is the romantic child who, in the adult gaze, embodies naturalness, innocence, and purity. This is a quite culturally specific discourse in terms of certain imagined times and spaces of British childhood (although there are versions of the country childhood idyll in certain elements of North American and European culture). It casts shadows over the lives of the vast majority of children who now live in urban areas (Ward 1990), is quite specific in terms of class, ethnicity, and has gender imbalances too (O. Jones 1999).

However, where this ideology of childhood and its related practice does flourish, certain children have (though maybe less so today) high degrees of spatial and symbolic power/freedom which allows them to build their own geographies and becomings. This is not done without difficulties, conflicts, and traumas of various kinds, but it allows children freedom to be themselves (with all the developmental benefits this is supposed to bring).

Elsewhere I have argued that Romantic constructions of childhood, although problematic in some respects (see also Higonnet 1998) have served children well. Children, or the idea of childhood, became valued, cherished, even revered. This led to changes in child welfare, beneficial shifts in educational ideologies, and eventually the idea of children's rights. As Jenks (2005) points out, the Apollonian (romantic) view of childhood displaced, but did not eradicate, the Dionysian view of childhood which had previously 'necessitated' strict regimes of coercive upbringing and education.

Of course many individual children still suffer death, hardship, and poverty within the complexities, contradictions, and ruptures of these constructions of childhood, in what has been called 'The Century of Childhood' (i.e. the twentieth century; Humphries et al. 1988). But at least in principle, ideas of children as valued beings, and children's rights have been established. The trouble with the romantic legacy is that it thrusts onto children an agenda which is much more about adult desires and fears than it is about the condition, needs, and desires of children. Another problem is that the original notion of romantic childhood has become increasingly unsustainable in the era of urbanized, globalized, consumption, ICT based capitalism, and thus ideas of 'the end of childhood' (Postman 1982), and a series of moral panics (Valentine 1996) about childhood continue to unfold.

My argument is that romantic constructions of childhood can allow children at least some space (physical and symbolic) and the freedom to use it. I suggest that this reaches some kind of logical conclusion in the notion of the country childhood idyll. The space and freedom which is accessible to some children empowers them to express themselves (as other) under the cover of the notion of innocent childhood in the innocent countryside. They are able, to some extent at least, to build their own worlds. The discursive power of this idea of childhood, in effect, enhances children's ability to find/make spaces for themselves, thereby increasing their power to counteract adult control of their lives. This might offer wider lessons about how childhood is imagined and shaped by adulthood.

THE OTHERNESS OF CHILDHOOD

> In a sense every child 'dies' by becoming an adult. (Woodward 2005: 5)

> ...the abyss that separates the child from the adult. (McEwan 1988: 33)

> They had entered the thorny wilderness, and the golden gates of their childhood had forever closed behind them. (Eliot 1985: 270)

There are large differences and large distances between the experiences of childhood and adulthood. Once left, the precise nature of the landscapes of childhood, are, to great degree, unknowable or irretrievable by adults. Treacher (2000: 135–136) and Greenfield (2000) also discuss the inevitable distances between adulthood and childhood (see O. Jones 2003).

Children and adults live in parallel universes. This does not mean there are no connections between the two, these palpably are manifest, but those connections do not amount to knowability or reversibility. Often the connections between the adult and childhood world are those of unequal power relations riddled with misapprehensions, with adults attempting to control or coerce children's worlds (Mayall 2002).

If we are to take the body and scale seriously, to remember that the social is embedded in the material and physiological, if we are to take knowledge, memory, and experience seriously—if we are to take power seriously—then there have to be marked differences between the becomings of children and the becomings of adults. Age is critical in all this. One simple formula would be to suggest that the younger a child is, the more distant he or she is from adults and what can be known of their inner world. Growing up is about going through great changes. As Bachelard puts it, 'from the time a child reaches the "age of reason" [ ] he loses his (sic) absolute right to imagine the world. He is stuffed with sociability' (Bachelard 1971: 107). If the young child is pre-socialized, and to 'grow up' is to be subject to the technologies of subjectification (as Foucault shows), then the pre-social child must be truly other, and is thus a subject of desire for poststructuralists (Zourabichvili 1996) and romantics (Ferguson 2003) alike. But to see growing up as a steady move from the condition of the otherness of childhood to the sameness of adulthood might well be an over-simplification. Guattari (1996) points out that the traumas of adolescence are also very other to adultness, and are unrelivable in emotional terms by the adult who eventually emerges from them.

Some notion of the otherness of childhood is captured in the following analysis of Bataille's work on transgression.

> ...for Bataille childhood is a state that for him is beyond good and evil. His vision of childhood is a kind of—a bit like Freud, a state of polymorphous perversity—a state of welcoming experience as both innocent and strangely perverse, because it doesn't obey adult rules. [...] [B]ecoming a child would be becoming a kind of innocent that's not very innocent; it's not innocent in a Christian sense of not having any knowledge of sin. In a sense, a child doesn't care about sin. (Noyes 2001)

Bataille explored his notions of childhood, innocence, and otherness through a reading of Bronte's novel *Wuthering Heights* and how the sovereignty of childhood has to be sacrificed to the social order.

> The fundamental theme of Wuthering Heights is childhood [...] and that there is something fundamentally perverse about children and their orientation toward the world. For Bataille [...] children are inherently sovereign. Society is governed by its will to survive. It could not survive if these childish instincts, which bound children in a feeling of complicity, were allowed to triumph. Social constraint would have required the young savages to give up their innocent sovereignty; it would have required them to comply with those reasonable adult conventions which are advantageous to the community. [...] Heathcliff and Cathy are constantly poised between the sovereign instincts of childhood and the social constraints of rational adulthood [...] They are poised between what we usually call Good and the divine intoxication (usually called Evil) which society must suppress in order to survive into the future. (Everman undated ms: 11–12)

Pushing this notion about the 'otherness of childhood' is, in some senses, a high risk strategy in methodological, political, and ethical terms. But I am encouraged by the fact that Jenks (2005) finishes the second edition of *Childhood* with a new chapter entitled 'Childhood and Transgression'. He analyses the idea of transgression through the work of Nietzsche, Bataille, and the poststructuralist ideas of Foucault and Deleuze. Here, amongst other things, he explores further the idea that adult being and social order, are only sustainable through 'amnesia' which closes off the transgressive urges of childhood as we grow up. He suggests that we might 'employ their [children's] disruption as a source of critical examination of our dominant means of control', and finally concludes that, 'children explore the very limits of consciousness and highlight, once again, the indefatigable, inherent, and infinitely variable human capacity to transgress' (Jenks 2005: 150).

Studies of Romanticism also suggest that envisioning the child as other was a key manoeuvre in this fundamental reframing of childhood. Ferguson (2003) argues that the whole edifice that Romantics built around children depended upon childhood otherness—'the Romantics [ ] created a new economy of respect by seeing children as different from adults [...] one could value the traits of children only by establishing a way of singling out and separating them off from other, older people' (Ferguson 2003: 216). In other words, children were seen as other, but, importantly, as an other that was valued, cherished, and desired even. Ferguson adds that under such constructions, 'the time of childhood became a space, and children came to have their own institutions and *live in a world apart from adults*' (Ferguson 2003: 216, emphasis added).

Austin too suggests that the romantic construction of childhood was based on the notion of otherness. She suggests that Wordsworth had a 'belief in the unrecoverability of the condition of childhood' (2003: 4). This, she argues, is evident in Wordsworth's 'Ode: Intimations of Immortality', 'which evokes a shared sense among adults of inevitable forgetting, of the remoteness of the condition of childhood' (Austin 2003: 4). It is worth noting that these Romantic envisionings of childhood as other were often deeply embedded in nature and rural spaces. The vision of the country child, and the notion of the country childhood idyll is perhaps the most complete and rarefied vision of the romantic child.

This potent mix of childhood otherness, other space and rural/natural spaces can be found in much childhood literature. Honeyman (2001) suggests in relation to North American children's literature, that their constructions of country childhood idyll were often imagined as other spaces, haunted by a longing for an Edenic past, and by the shadowy dualism of modern urbanity. The urban is not only seen as an inappropriate space for modern childhood but as an inappropriate space for the romantic adult self as well. Thus an enormous weight of collective cultural longing has quietly settled onto (country) childhood throughout the last few centuries in the industrialized Minority world, an invidious, yet powerful shaper of children's lives.

If children are constructed as innocent, and 'natural creatures' (in need) of freedom, outdoor experiences, contact with nature, then parental and other adult surveillance has to be, by definition, relaxed. If the spaces of childhood are those of the countryside which are not imagined as a threat to childhood, but rather as a requirement of childhood, this reinforces the desire to let children be free. So, just as the cover of innocence gives some space to childhood identity, the cover of the innocent country child in innocent country spaces has, in some circumstances, allowed children freedom. But within this freedom they do not live out adult (romantic) assumptions about childhood, but rather begin to live out their lives and build to some extent at least, their own geographies.

My argument is that under the cover of the constructions of the innocent child in the idyllic countryside, some children, in some periods and some places, have had high degrees of freedom and thus the power to build their own worlds and to trace out their own geographies. This is not to say this is not possible in urban space, and indeed there are some remarkable accounts of children making the city their own in various ways (e.g. Thomas 1938), but here children's geographies are up against increasingly restrictive forces which range from parental fear of danger from traffic and strangers, to government and corporate mistrust of children in urban public open space. Children's lives are, in a messy, contested way, ordered/structured by adult power. The power of place and imagined spaces plays a part in this, but in the case of the countryside in Britain and elsewhere, it can enable children to have more opportunities for relative autonomy. As Jenkins (1998) points out in an essay, 'in the 19th century, children living along the frontier or on North America's farms enjoyed free range over a space which was ten square miles or more. Elliot West (1992) describes boys of nine or ten going camping alone for days on end'. This now contrasts with the constricted spaces of modern urban childhood for which the virtual space of computer games become at least some kind of alternative.

GLIMPSES OF THE OTHERNESS OF CHILDHOOD IN THE COUNTRYSIDE

The observations below stem from ongoing participant observation in my home village. I have researched childhood in the village quite intensively in the past (O. Jones 1997) and now continue to observe the movements and activities of children in the village, partly through my interaction with them as a parent of two boys. The village is quite small, being formed of approximately 80 households, and has had a series of cohorts of children growing up in it in the last 15 years or so.

From a very early age, say 5 or 6, our two children and some other village children, could be 'out and about' in certain parts of the village without us knowing exactly where they were, and sometimes we would not be able to find them instantly. (Not all children were granted such freedom and some were less inclined to join in the outdoor play than others.) The freedom that some children enjoyed was dependent on a number of factors, notably those following:

1. The micro-geographies of the village include arrangements of houses, paths, gardens, walls, a semi-disused farmyard, a green lane, and a cricket pitch, footpaths, and a stream, all in a critical relation to the main village road—i.e. away from it. The road itself is a quiet single

track lane, a key factor in the village's ruralness, but still a danger and worry.

2. Families with children of similar ages living in relatively close proximity to each other (thus unchaperoned movement between houses and gardens is an early outdoor geography).
3. The presence of older siblings or trusted older children who could 'keep an eye' on younger children.
4. Parental knowledge of the local environment.
5. Family/adult knowledge of/engagement with the wider community, including arrangements such as lift sharing. (There is no village school.)
6. Parental desire for their children to be outdoors and live a sort of middle class version of the country childhood.

Elsewhere (O. Jones 2002), I have discussed the extent to which this relative freedom has allowed some of the children to build their own geographies with the fabric of the adult(ist) material/symbolic geography of the village. Here I offer some observations of what could be termed 'practices of otherness', which can be witnessed, if not fully appreciated in terms of experience of being (other).

Chopping the tree stump

Near our house was a huge old tree stump, on its side, with the buttresses which once turned into spreading roots making a wild gothic form. Here for a number of years our own and other children played. The tree stump was a place to climb and hide (Figure 15.1)—classic activities of 'the country

Figure 15.1 The tree stump—now hacked away to nothing.

child'. But it was also the site of 'other' practices. One was chopping and bashing. Being a farm, and ours a household where DIY projects are often to the fore, tools such as hammers, hand axes, and bill hooks were often to hand. I still feel a small squirt of anxiety when I think about it, but our children, and others, determinedly commandeered these and, over the years, have hacked away at the tree stump, which was nicely rotten in places, until it is now no more. Sometimes, almost in a trance, one or two children would chop, chop, and chop away, scattering bits of wood all around. (The tools were also used for the more apparently constructive task of den and tree house building.)

Stingy bashing

Past the tree stump the track is fringed by piles of rubble around which a sea of vigorous nettles have grown. Another favourite pastime was, and still is to an extent, 'stingy bashing', which involves scything down ranks of stingies with a stick, or even better some sharp instrument (e.g. long or short handled hook). Stingies sting, they are enemies. (I can remember doing this on the farm I grew up on.) With smaller children the stingies might be taller than them, a strong sideways stroke may take out a dozen or more, they buckle and fall like felled bodies as the stick smashes the strength of their fibrous stems—they may fall on you.

Bonfire

Further round the track again, on the way to the barn, which was a place for play for a number of years, is the bonfire site. Garden waste, DIY waste, cardboard which the recycling will not take from a number of households is dumped here. A large pile builds up, looking unsightly sometimes, and then is burnt. Our children (and guests/neighbours) have always thought it great fun. They lean in, shielding their faces, and set sticks into the flames, and them pull them out and wave the smoking ends around trailing sparks. In the autumn tall cow parsley stalks with dying flower heads can be set fire and carried like torches; it is better in the evening when it is getting dark. When the fire has burnt right down and adults are long gone, a favourite pastime is gathering bits of dried grass and old bits of wood and trying to get a small fire going again.

Tree houses and dens

Behind the bonfire site is the tree house/den site, reached by a small bridge across a ditch, made by the children out of a domestic central heating radiator. Over the last 20 years or so, a series of groups of children have built tree houses in a stand of Leylandi (Figure 15.2). It is a craze for a while, with hammering and sawing and climbing, and the odd territorial dispute

Figure 15.2 The bridge over the ditch and the tree house (note: some children can just be seen in the tree).

and destruction of other's work, before the site is abandoned and the trees slowly shake off the old planks nailed to them through the winter storms. Below the tree house numerous dens have been made and unmade including one dug into the ground and covered with planks and junk from the barn (Figure 15.3). This is of course a classic country childhood activity, but it also speaks eloquently of children's desire to literally build their own worlds where the scales and logics of the adult world are left behind.

All these practices, and many others not described here, are more about the otherness of childhood than the innocence and purity of childhood. In terms of 'research' and study, I can record that children bash the stingies, or play with the embers of the bonfire. I could also study how some children are excluded from these activities by more careful or 'paranoid' parents. But I cannot fully reproduce the experience of smaller bodies, chopping into wood with a steel blade, twisting in exertion as they swing the stick, gazing intently as the fire flares up again, and the imaginative, affective, emotional becoming unfolding as the blade bites, the flame flares. What is the feeling of power? What is being mapped into the (developing) self? The children have marked and shaped the environment, including drawing on the road (Figure 15.4) these strange hieroglyphics speaking to very differing mappings of beings in space.

What I can say is that it seems that these children have been able to perform these desires because of the physical and symbolic contexts of their

Figure 15.3 The underground den.

Figure 15.4 Drawing on the road.

home life and the context of discourses of country childhood which sanction them. Some parents at least want the children to be out in the fresh air, being active, forming gangs, and not quite knowing where they are. The space is trusted, the practices sanctioned by a powerful ideology of childhood, the children get some space and some freedom.

IDYLLS OF CHILDHOOD OTHERNESS IN THE CITY?

Amanda, a neighbour who had moved to the village from a major inner city with her husband John and two young children, said, 'well, you see, he (Jack) couldn't be a wild thing in St. Andrews Road [their old address] without people telling him off and whatever, whereas out here he can, can't he?'

Children being wild in the city can be seen as feral, dangerous, and out of control, whereas in the country wildness can become innocent (natural), or at least harmless to the adult gaze. Amanda also said 'they can't do wild things in the city can they without, without sort of damaging things...Jack running around with a huge stick (here) sort of, it looks funny rather than menacing doesn't it'.

Children's presences in urban space seem more problematic, particularly if, say, they were running round with axes, chopping things. Cities can offer derelict, other spaces to children (Cloke and Jones 2005), but these are often considered corrupt and threatening (maybe with good reason). Other, more ordered spaces such as parks will be a lot less amenable to children reshaping them (e.g. building dens, using axes, and building fires) due to the prevailing power of adult surveillance and control. The intimate childhood geographies of the village might be replicated in city streets and cul-de-sacs (perhaps especially so in the suburbs) but equally it might be constrained by fear of traffic and fear of danger.

CONCLUSION

I think children everywhere find ways of expressing their otherness and building geographical expressions of it; for example, in the virtual worlds of ICT (worlds where the village children also go) into which parents might find it difficult to enter; in the unofficial moral economies of school life; in their daydreams and nightdreams and daymares and nightmares; in their drawings and games; by finding and making their own spaces wherever they can. It would seem right they have the chance to do this, and important in terms of development. What is childhood if it is not other to adulthood?

There are, however, marked differences in the means by which, and the extent to which children can do this. Within all the complexities and intensities of the adult woven world, the chances different children have to be themselves and to make their own worlds will vary. Some children will have to fight all kinds of oppression and obstacles, including poverty, war, child labour, and gender and race inequality to make their own worlds. They might have little time and space outside the patterns imposed on them by adult power (for example see Beazley; Bell; Carpena-Méndez; Klocker; Punch, this volume). They might also be up against power expressed as spaces hostile to childhood, and as adult ideologies hostile to the otherness of childhood.

Some circumstances will allow some children greater degrees of power and autonomy. Perversely, poverty might be one such circumstance and also various disruptions to the pattern of life, even war. Do not forget that many classic children's stories begin with the loss of or separation from parents and guardians. Adult power has to be removed, or at least reduced, for the adventure to begin. The country childhood idyll, although an adult discourse, I suggest can be one such circumstance. As recorded in literature and film, and as observed in my home village, (some) children have a greater degree of power to define their own worlds in ways which are condoned by the prevailing currents of adult discourse about childhood, nature and landscape. This empowers children to make their own worlds. I further argue that these are very other worlds to those of adults and sometimes can be quite dark and scary (from the inside and the outside). The wider lessons to be drawn from this is that, firstly, children should be given more power and space to be themselves and that the adult world should not try to micromanage children's lives, and that, secondly, for this to occur, the world in all its material and symbolic forms should be more amenable to the free, unaccounted for movement of children, as the countryside has sometimes been.

16 Power and place for rural young people

Samantha Punch, Stephen Bell, Lauren Costello, and Ruth Panelli

CONCEPTUALISING POWER

This chapter provides an overview of how power affects, and is mobilized by, young people in rural settings. It also reflects on the theoretical frameworks operationalized in the preceding four chapters. In this process we recognize that each of the authors has very different ways of deploying notions of power in relation to young rural lives. This is a fruitful situation since the most problematic aspect of defining power is that it has no essential materiality (though it achieves material and social effects). Consequently, different approaches to power enable different emphases to be made and a fuller picture to emerge concerning the way power weaves through young rural lives.

We cannot see power; it is invisible, and it takes no constant form. We do, however, spend enormous amounts of time tracing the pathways and effects of power, asking: who did what to whom and what happened? The intangible nature of power creates a dilemma, especially considering Foucault's claim that 'power is everywhere' (1990: 93). Within human geography, power has become a key focus of analysis and contemporary thought; it seems to be everywhere. But this apparent ubiquity of power in the works of geographers has stimulated debates regarding definitions of power, how it is understood and how it is analysed in individual cases. Low (2005) wonders whether the ubiquity of power, and its unspecified use by human geographers, means that any in-depth exploration of the different theoretical manifestations is required. Simply put, Low's argument questions whether we need to ask ourselves what power means, especially since it is a term primarily used to augment explanations of social difference. The ramifications of this position are that it reinforces the unmediated ubiquity of power. It also does not recognize the spatially and culturally divergent ways in which power is manifest across the globe (Taylor 2004). In contrast, Allen (2003) argues that understanding power and its spatial manifestations is a core task. He reminds us that the relationship between people, place, and power creates very real lived experiences that should not be simply characterized as the effect of power—a ubiquitous, yet generalized, mediating force 'out there'. Consequently, as well as providing an overview of dominant under-standings of power in geography, this chapter considers the relationships between power, as a mediating force, on conceptions of young people, rural spaces, and socially negotiated relations.

There are many ways to conceptualize power, and for the purpose of this discussion, frameworks for thinking about power have been divided into two main groups. First, power is seen as an object or possession; some-thing that institutions, groups, and individuals hold, harness, and direct towards others—including young people. In this framework, agency in a realist sense, is placed at the centre of conceptualising the working of power; operated by the haves (e.g. adults or schools) and inflicted upon the have-nots (e.g. young people). As such, power is primarily conceptualized as a negative and dominating process where it disempowers, oppresses, or creates disadvantage. Second, rejecting power as an object, a further approach theorises power as relational. As such power cannot operate inde-pendently, but has the capacity to constitute identities. The justification behind this simple division is that much recent debate in geography about which version of power is 'right' has unintentionally utilized this division as a starting point. The following discussion is not intended to be in any-way comprehensive, but rather to be an illustration of the main themes in these perspectives (for a detailed analysis see Allen [2003]).

CONTRASTING APPROACHES TO POWER

Power as an object

In this understanding, power is seen to 'belong' to, or be held by, the pow-erful and dispensed upon the less powerful. Its effects are observed in the actions of individuals or institutions. This book shows the ways that flows of power between adult/youth or parent/child can operate at the individual level (e.g. within families) or at wider social and institutional levels, where adults act in ways to control and mediate the lived experiences of younger people. We can see the immediate attractiveness of this understanding of power. We can identify the unequal forces and indeed we often note those who wield power to the disadvantage of others. However, this conceptuali-sation of power does not always readily distinguish between authority and influence, nor explain where these come from.

Recently, the work of Bruno Latour (2004) and Actor Network Theory has been adopted in order to more fully understand the operational aspects of authority, influence, and the workings of power. For Latour the social world is made up of a network of actors, including individuals, institu-tions, and technologies that produce a base or centre from which power is dispersed. Latour sees power as moving amongst a range of actors in these networks, but also that actors, both human and non-human, can do things

(Allen 2003). The network and the actors are mutually constitutive, but the power of one actor over another is dependent upon an actor's position in the network (Latour 2004). It also depends upon the scale of the network. For example, the ability to have children comply with adults' demands can operate differently according to the network in which the actors are operating. In a family network, the positioning of actors and the operation of power will differ from a community network that would include institutions such as the police and schools.

Conceptualising *power as an object* becomes tenuous because at times it, power, is simplistically turned into an object that is wielded by the powerful. The effects of such thinking gives power materiality and can ignore the crucial, yet micro-scale, manifestations and negotiations between actors.

Power as relational

The second conceptualisation of power focuses upon it as relational phenomena. Undeniably the most influential thinker of 'power as relational' is Foucault (1990: 98) who contends that power cannot be held or bought as if it were a commodity.[1] Likewise Halperin (1995: 16) adds: '[p]ower should not be conceptualized as the property of someone who can be identified and confronted, nor should it be thought of (at least in the first instance) as embedded in particular agents or institutions'. For example, power embedded in adulthood does not give individual agents (i.e. adults) definable power, but the capacity to harness the privilege that operates around adulthood.

Employing a relational perspective, Mouffe (1996: 247) contends that power is not external to subjects and, '...we should conceptualize power not as an *external* relation taking place between two preconstituted identities but rather as constituting identities themselves'. As such, understandings of childhood can be thought of as embedded in the mechanisms of power and privilege; where certain subjects (e.g. children and youth) are constituted via powerful relations and discourses.

Foucault contends that power requires knowledge to have a disciplining effect over subjects (Campbell and Carlson 2002). The disciplining of bodies is not regarded in this relational framework as repressive, but productive (English 2005) where the relationship between power and knowledge is fundamental. Foucault could not envisage a time or point where either power or knowledge operated without the production of the other: 'It is not possible for power to be exercised without knowledge, it is impossible for knowledge not to engender power' (Foucault 1980: 52).

It is also worth noting that knowledge can be produced via other nonpowerful routes and processes, and utilized by the 'subjects' both in secret and in public displays of them exercising their own power (see Beazley 2002; Scott 1990). 'Knowledge is power' is the basis of many grassroots status quo movements that aim to disrupt the status quo and raise awareness of inequality and marginalisation. Thus, knowledge has more than a disciplinary effect, and is fundamental to many resistance movements.

From this relational perspective, power operates in the circulation of discourses that construct sets of 'truth'. Discourse becomes a fundamental instrument of a relational understanding of power (Grosz 1990) as well as a link between language and the production of meanings (see Jones, this volume). For instance, discourses of adulthood speak of—and for—child/ren and also have the power to silence. In this way discourse does not just refer to thoughts or words but to an amalgam of silent regulations and codes that are privileged and unconsciously accepted.

Power and empowerment

Beyond the binary conceptualisation of power discussed thus far, recent empowerment literature (Parpart et al. 2002; Rowlands 1997) calls for a more nuanced understanding of power which recognizes that individuals or groups of people generally considered powerless exercise power in their own ways, individually and in groups (Rahnema 1992). An 'enabling' definition of power is not simply the ability to gain *power over* something but is a process which includes the development of *power within*, as well as the ability to enhance one's *power with* others who find themselves in a similarly marginalized situation (Rowlands 1997). This *power with* others may provide the collective *power to* bring about beneficial change and challenge existing discourses (Parpart et al. 2002). Rowlands argues that empowerment is personal, relational, and collective whereby marginalized people 'come to see themselves as having the capacity and the right to act and have influence' (Rowlands 1995: 103).

This work on empowerment has been explored primarily in relation to gender relations but we consider it as also pertinent to the study of generational relations. The challenge that the authors in this edited collection demonstrate, particularly in Part III, are the diverse ways that children and young people negotiate their daily lives in rural locales, with instances of both empowerment and disempowerment. These negotiations or operations of power, as illustrated in the following section, are not simply occurring between subjects but are mediated by a range of other factors such as hegemonic notions of rurality, and global inequalities between the Majority and Minority worlds.

POWER OF PLACE

To appreciate the ways in which rural young people are affected by, and participate in, layers of unequal power relations, it is also necessary to consider how power circulates through, or is associated in the rural environments and contexts in which they live (see Chapters 2–6, this volume). At a micro level, the power of place involves the everyday arenas in which young people move through a variety of spaces engaging with a range of inter- and intra-generational power relationships (see the following section on 'Social Relations and Power'). At the macro level, the power of place is partially dependent on a country's global position in the world economy and may also concern the nature of rural versus urban locations, both of which are discussed below in turn.

Global power relations

Simplistic distinctions between Majority world and Minority world rural areas are problematic because both children's and adults' experiences of rurality vary according to a range of factors such as culture, class, gender, sexuality, age, ethnicity, disability, religion, and birth order. Furthermore, the contrasting nature of different rural environments (discussed in detail by Bushin et al., this volume) also differs, both within and between countries (see Schäfer, this volume) as well as within and between continents. Nevertheless, whilst recognising the heterogeneity of rural living, it is still important to acknowledge some basic general differences of socio-economic power between the Majority and Minority worlds.

Despite the great diversity of lifestyles, it is hard to ignore that much of the Majority world is economically poorer than most of the Minority world, something which is reflected in a range of social and economic indicators (see Table 16.1). Whilst being cautious about over-generalising and recognising that there are major inequalities between the rich and poor in both the Majority and Minority worlds, there is no denying that the overall levels of income and standards of living are very unequal. Thus, what it means to be poor in a rural area of the Minority world is different from being poor in a rural community of the Majority world, particularly regarding access to education, health, basic services, communication networks, and infrastructure. In addition, the urban–rural disparities in wealth and

Table 16.1 Social and economic indicators of poverty by world regions

Indicator	Sub-Saharan Africa	South Asia	Latin America	Minority World
GNP per capita ($US)	$611	$600	$3,649	$32,232
Under-5 mortality rate (2004)	171	92	31	6
Infant mortality rate (2004)	102	67	26	5
Life expectancy (2004)	46 yrs	63 yrs	72 yrs	79 yrs
Adult literacy rate (2000–2004)	60%	58%	90%	98%
No of TVs per 1000 pop (1996)	33	50	204	638

Source: Adapted from State of the World's Children (UNICEF 2006)
<http://www.unicef.org/sowc06/index.php>

services tend to be much greater in the Majority world compared with the Minority world (Drakakis-Smith 2000).

There is no scope here to discuss in detail the reasons for the imbalance of socio-economic power between Majority and Minority worlds. However, it is significant to note that nearly all the economically poor countries of the Majority world were once colonies of many of the economically richer Minority world countries. Dependency theorists and more recently post-development theorists argue that the economic and social development of the Majority world has been shaped to a large extent by its colonial past and continues to be dominated by the Minority world in a system of neo-colonialism (Potter et al. 2004). These authors point out that much of the Majority world remains, to some extent, reliant and dependent on richer, capitalist Minority world countries through transnational corporations, the disadvantages of world trade, loans, and debt (Murray 2006).

In addition, the impacts of globalisation are also uneven and diverse (Hoogvelt 2001). Not everyone benefits from international capitalism nor has the same access to new technologies and forms of communication, such as the Internet and e-mail. Goods, ideas, information, capital, and people can be linked up at ever increasing speed nowadays, but this global interconnectedness is not quite as 'global' for all rural areas, particularly in the Majority world (see for example Beazley; Carpena-Méndez; Klocker; Punch, this volume). Murray argues that the 'relative distance between some places and some people has become greater' (2006: 6) as those who do not have access to new technologies become relatively more isolated (Drakakis-Smith 2000). Hence, we should bear in mind that global economic restructuring shapes people's rural lives to different degrees, especially in Majority world contexts of poverty or HIV/AIDS compared with the more resource-rich environments of the Minority world (Klocker 2005a).

Making a spatial interrogation of power enables us to observe the dynamic ways in which power and place intersect at both macro and micro levels. For example, in the case study of rural Bolivia, Punch (this volume) shows that at the macro level young people are constrained by living in a relatively isolated rural community in an economically poor Majority world country which suffers from a lack of communications as well as limited work and education opportunities. Thus, power imbalances between rural and urban areas, as well as between Majority and Minority world countries, impact upon young people's everyday lives. Furthermore, at the micro level, Punch illustrates how the diverse spatial contexts of home, work, school, and migration can be both enabling and constraining for young people (see also Carpena-Méndez, this volume).

The power of the rural? Idylls, performances, and geometries

Beyond global considerations, attention to issues of power also need to address the *power of place* and *power in place* that young people experience while living in—or originating from—specific rural settings. Cultural geography encourages recognition of powerful (arguably hegemonic) notions of rurality. These are place and time specific within different societies and are instrumental in framing how rural life occurs—and how young people fit into that life. As Cresswell (1996) has shown for other populations in rural areas (New Age Travellers), spatial hegemonies can be produced in societies which subsequently involve the reproduction and naturalization of certain sets of meanings and relations while positing others as disruptive and transgressive. The work of O. Jones (1999) illustrates how powerful notions of Minority world rural idylls produce meanings of rural life as peaceful, safe, and appropriate for children, although children themselves have the capacity to disrupt some of the orderly, functional scripting of the countryside with their play and 'disorder' (O. Jones 2000; and this volume). Adriensen's analysis of Egyptian desert reclamation (summarized in Bushin et al. this volume) also shows powerful imaginations about rurality motivating young families to aspire to a rural setting for their families as superior to an urban one.

In contrast, in the Majority world there can be an over-idealising of urban areas. Cities can be perceived as magnets for rural migrants, offering a disproportionate share of economic opportunities and social services (Drakakis-Smith 2000). Additionally, within the context of global neoliberalism, some rural areas of the Majority world find it increasingly difficult to compete effectively in agricultural production, resulting in decreasing opportunities in the countryside (see Beazley; Carpena-Méndez, this volume). Nevertheless, despite poor prospects, not everyone chooses to leave their rural community and many migrants return after temporary periods away (Ansell and van Blerk; Punch, this volume). Furthermore, there is a recognition that the reality of migrant work and urban living often does not match existing rosy urban myths (Klocker, this volume). Similarly, rural lifestyles in the Minority world do not always match the rural idyll, particularly for older young people (Matthews and Tucker, this volume).

Thus, the power of rural imaginaries is not simply a discursive or ephemeral phenomenon. Using Foucault's (1990) perspectives, we can also observe that power circulates through rural societies in relational dynamics that are constantly producing, and reproducing rural places and rural subjects (youthful or otherwise). Rural places and people are constructed and contested via circuits of discourse and material relations where dominant meanings and conditions are reproduced, but opportunities for resistance also occur. Taking dominant truths and subjects first, we can see in the case of Cusco, Peru (Box 16.1) that both material conditions and narratives of rurality are entwined in young people's lives. To have rural origins in this setting is to experience a form of shame and inferiority. So too, Punch's (2000; and this volume) analysis of Bolivian rural life indicates how young people navigate parental power relations and expectations of obedience and work diligence while also contesting some demands and securing time and space to play or pursue other interests.

Box 16.1 When rural origins mean shame: Perspectives from child traders in Cusco, Peru—Peter K. Mackie

Recent research on child traders in Cusco, Peru, illustrates some of the "power of the rural". Rural–urban migration has resulted in many rural children trading on the streets (Boyden 1991). In the Cusco study, approximately 42 per cent of ambulant child traders in the historic centre of Cusco are originally from rural areas but now work in the city selling their goods to tourists. During the study, when children were often surveyed in pairs, the problematic nature of rural origins emerged. On several occasions a child of rural origin stated that they were from the city. The child only admitted their true origins when corrected by a city friend. But, the question was not misunderstood. The child was not unsure of their origin, nor were they joking. Rather, they overtly chose to state an urban origin because they felt uncomfortable with rural origins. Subsequent, in-depth interviews with 30 child traders explored issues that had been raised in the surveys. Rural–urban differences became more apparent and further understandings of rural origins were framed in their narratives. For instance, when exploring the survey result that had shown children from the city tended to be more likely to sell postcards, clear views of educational differences and implications were identified. Approximately 93 per cent of children commented, or implied, that children from rural areas receive an inadequate education. They suggested that below-standard teaching, and a lack of schooling in general, resulted in rural traders' inability to work with tourists and to buy and sell goods such as postcards. Furthermore, child traders were asked why city children were able to speak English far more fluently, and the responses also focused on the superior education received in the cities. The following quotations illustrate some of the views expressed by the child traders:

They don't learn much in the country	(boy, 12, city)
Those (children) from the city are better	(girl, 10, city)
There are no schools in the country	(girl, 12, city)
Those from the city are more advanced than those from the country	(boy, 15, rural)
Teachers are better in the city	(boy, 15, rural)

Interviews with education officials confirmed children's views (Mackie 2007).

Few teachers are willing to move to work in rural areas, so the state is reliant on local teachers, many of whom have no professional qualification and often only completed primary education themselves. The idea that one origin is 'better' than another is a serious issue in Cusco. The fact that children feel the need to deny their rural background has potentially significant implications; influencing the future choices they make in terms of where they live, work, and bring up their own children. Little is known about how the sense of 'rural shame' is reproduced. Much of the literature suggests that the media are at least partially to blame for shaping children's attitudes (Holloway and Valentine 2000a) and this is certainly possible in Cusco, with a proliferation of satellite television and children's preoccupation with the Internet. However, this study indicates that the notion that city life is 'better' is also being conveyed to many of these child traders through their peers. Children's own lay discourses can perpetuate the powerful classification of rural and urban settings, leading to further denial of rural origins.

But Foucauldian perspectives also emphasize that where power is exercised, so too is resistance. Chapters in this third section of the book are already demonstrating these possibilities. Young people's constructions of their own knowledge, their own 'fun', even their own sexual lives, suggest diverse examples of contestation (see also McCormack 2002; Panelli et al. 2002).

A contrasting resource exists in Butler's (1990; 1993) work on performativity. It is possible to employ her critique of identity (and gender and sexuality) to appreciate how young people's lives might also be understood as reproducing both normative patterns (e.g. of heterosexuality and gender identities), but also strategically choosing and reconstructing opportunities for themselves within their (albeit confined) range of options. These types of possibilities are available for future work of the genre Bell (this volume) achieves where sexuality and the cultural and spatial power relations involved may in fact be both simultaneously reproduced and adapted in various settings (compare also Thomas's [2004] reading of urban teenagers' explorations and performance of sexuality).

A further device for conceptualizing the *power of the rural* rests with the notion of 'geometries of power' (Massey 1993a; 1993b). This supports ideas of rural lives as lived in *places* that will be contingent and relational. Massey's (1991) progressive sense of place enables young people's rural settings to be analysed as an intersection of relations, flows, and interdependences. Here then, we have a strategy for recognizing that rural lives are lived not only within rural places and power relations, but also that these are interdependent with the wider processes noted above. And the geometries of these conditions provide a conceptual device to acknowledging this complexity, for as Martin explains:

> A power-geometry implies that what is important is not just one's loca-
> tion within a set of spatial relationships but also one's ability to con-
> trol or construct the sites, flows, scales, and spaces that comprise that
> geometry. Such geometries are political and related to economic, politi-
> cal and cultural relations.... Such geometries shape and are shaped by
> multiple, differentiated, and unequal subjectivities. (Martin 2004: 27)

This perspective points to further directions in which we can appreciate
young rural lives as dynamic, heterogeneous encounters; where power is
negotiated in myriad social, economic, and political ways. Some of these
are explored in the following section.

SOCIAL RELATIONS AND POWER

The four preceding chapters, and several previous sections, illustrate the
complex, multiple dynamics of how power operates and is experienced by
young people in diverse relationships and settings. Throughout this volume, it is evident that inter- and intra-generational power relations are not
static. They are fluid and ever changing; evolving over a variety of public
and private locations within rural communities.

Inter-generational power relations

Inter-generational relationships are explored in detail throughout the chapters in this book. Young people are 'entangled' (Sharp et al. 2000) in a
range of relationships with adults, including their own parents (most chapters); relatives and neighbours (Beazley); friends' parents (Jones; Matthews
and Tucker); teachers (Punch); employers (Klocker); the police (Dunkley
and Panelli); landowners (Matthews and Tucker); and other community
members (Bell). The influence of adults in determining the behaviours and
'rules' that are expected of rural young people is clearly evident: they may
be supportive and offer spaces for opportunity, as well as being disciplinary and controlling. For example, Jones argues that at the heart of the
'rural idyll' in the Minority world lies parental expectations and perceptions that a rural lifestyle is healthier and offers more freedom without the
risks associated with urban spaces. Thus, parental desires for their children
to be outdoors, facilitates children's ability to create their own rural worlds
beyond the adult gaze. In contrast other chapters indicate the controlling
nature of adult influence on the lives of young people, revolving around
what adults perceive as appropriate. Bell highlights adult perceptions with
regard to (in)appropriate sexual behaviours between young people in rural
areas of Uganda, whilst Dunkley and Panelli note the regulating nature
of the police in reaction to young people's attempts to socialize in public
spaces and on private land in rural Vermont, USA. These examples illus-

trate the controlling and disciplinarian nature of adult *power over* young people (Lukes 2005; Parpart et al. 2002; Rowlands 1997) in both Majority and Minority world contexts.

Whilst power can be oppressive and constraining, it can also be enabling, whereby young people manage to exercise power, on their own and with other young people, in their daily lives in order to balance adult demands with their own needs and desires. For example, Punch illustrates that some children decide to collect water with siblings because, not only is it more fun, but it also gives them more opportunity to divert to non-work activities. Thus, whilst fulfilling parental expectations, young people also find time and space to engage in their own activities. This may occur beyond adult surveillance, or may lead to contestation with adults over the appropriate use of space (see Bell; Dunkley and Panelli; Jones, this volume).

Negotiation and bargaining emerge as key features of inter-generational power relationships. Matthews and Tucker, and Dunkley and Panelli illustrate how some young people agree to parental curfews and rules framing their lives, and Punch refers to children's negotiations with parents in order to gain more financial autonomy. Young people also engage in a range of subtle and overt strategies in order to resist adult expectations. For example, Bell describes how girls and boys maintain forbidden relationships in secret, and Dunkley and Panelli illustrate the 'cat and mouse' nature of young people's continued evasion of local police. These case studies illustrate that young people's management of their power relations with adults fluctuates between acceptance, cooperation, and compliance on the one hand, and resistance, struggle, and contestation on the other.

Intra-generational power relations

A key attribute of Chapters 12 to15 is that they recognize and further analyse the power relations and power differentials that exist between young people themselves, such as siblings (Punch), boyfriends and girlfriends (Bell), cliques (Dunkley and Panelli), and peer groups (Jones). These relationships can be supportive, where young people develop *power with* (Parpart et al. 2002; Rowlands 1997) each other for social purposes whilst playing and completing household tasks. This indicates the development of horizontal or bonding social capital to fulfil adult requirements as well as to resist adult expectations (Bell, this volume). At the same time, young people develop *power within* themselves through feelings of increased self-esteem and happiness from these relationships, finding people to confide in and trust, and to share their experiences of constraint or hardship. Peer networks are an important source of both *power with and within*, indicated in Laegran's accounts of råners teaching each other mechanical skills to support their identity and perform better, and Schäfer's description of boys and girls helping each other train for future job interviews.

However, intra-generational relationships are not always positive and harmonious. The preceding four chapters also highlight the divisive, conflicting, and hierarchical nature of power relations between young people. Dunkley and Panelli's account of the 'preppy-jocks', 'rednecks', 'stoners', and 'scum' illustrates how young people 'create their own tangles' based on perceptions of identity-based differences. Despite having fluid boundaries, the creation of social cliques leads to some groups being privileged and others marginalized, resulting in varying degrees of social inclusion/exclusion, whilst also inhibiting or encouraging the potential to develop social capital and access opportunities (see also Laegran). Birth order and age (see Punch, this volume), and financial status and consumer power (see Dunkley and Panelli; Matthews and Tucker; Laegran, this volume) are also illustrated to have a similarly divisive influence amongst young people.

Another important theme illustrated throughout this book is the dynamic nature of power relations between young people: the temporality and flexibility according to who they are interacting with, and the environment in which they are situated. For example, Punch explains the changing nature of the migrant identity. When working away from home a young person may experience decreasing confidence (power within), limited social support networks and friendships (power with), and may also be paid less than other employees (economic disempowerment). Yet, when a migrant returns home with cash, he or she may benefit from improved respect from peers and broaden his or her support networks (see also Beazley; Carpena-Méndez, this volume). Migration illustrates the importance of understanding the material, spatial, and relational aspects of power.

The empirical chapters also emphasize the dynamic nature of relationships between peer groups and individuals as a result of changing behaviours, and perceptions of what is good and bad, right or wrong. Dunkley and Panelli illustrate how a girl stopped spending time with a good friend who started smoking pot frequently. This exercise of 'social distancing' illustrates that peer relationships can fluctuate between those of support and inclusion to those which are divisive and exclusionary (see also Bell, this volume).

Gendered power relations

Power relations are negotiated across gender as well as age, birth order, and generation. This is particularly explicit in accounts from patriarchal Majority world societies where socio-cultural norms and practices promote male dominance in the creation of identities and in peer relationships (see Klocker; Bell, this volume). Young people's geographies of opportunity are also gendered. For example, Dunkley and Panelli explain that some parents prohibit their daughters from utilising certain spaces which are known as drinking party spots, and they set evening curfews. Likewise, Bell illustrates that boys in certain areas of rural Uganda are encouraged to build their own houses, and gain greater independence from their parents than girls, who are more closely controlled and observed. Indeed, it is this house building that increases both boys' and girls' opportunities to develop *power with* each other to resist parental demands and engage in sexual relations, albeit in a male space and on male terms. In contrast, however, Punch illustrates how a brother noted his sister's opportunities to engage in urban work away from the hard grind of rural subsistence labour, thereby increasing her access to a cash income and a higher status as a result of her contribution to the household income.

These scenarios indicate differing perceived and actual abilities to articulate and exercise power in various relationships for boys and girls. However, it is important to emphasize that relationships between boys and girls can be supportive, building *power with* or creating social capital as mentioned in the previous section. While certain relations are gendered and divisive, affecting young people's inclusion in society, others are mutually supportive.

NEGOTIATING POWER

This chapter and the four preceding ones have shown that interpersonal power is exercised both between and within generations in a variety of ways. Power has multiple and diverse meanings, and as Lukes points out: 'we use the vocabulary of power in countless different ways in different contexts and for different purposes' (2005: 62). The chapters in this book have discussed material, discursive, relational, and spatial aspects of power for rural young people, coinciding with Lukes's view that:

> ...social life can only properly be understood as an interplay of power and structure, a web of possibilities for agents, whose nature is both active and structured, to make choices and pursue strategies within given limits, which in consequence expand and contract over time. (Lukes 2005: 68–69)

The ways in which children respond to unequal power relations varies not only in different contexts and spaces, in response to different individuals, but also according to young people's actual and perceived competencies. To some extent, the way young people manage and negotiate the power relations surrounding their everyday lives depends on the opportunities and constraints of the rural environment. This includes physical, socio-cultural, economic, and political factors in relation to both global and local conditions. Hence, there is a continuum of power relations where the balance of power between young people, or between young people and adults, moves back and forth according to multiple factors. The dynamics of power which young people experience are not static, but change over time, ranging from shifting balances of power during daily encounters through to more gradual changes over the life course.

It is worth remembering that exercising power may not always be positive and there can be negative consequences to power (for example, see Bell, this volume). Similarly, young people do not always want to exert their power and are sometimes willing to accept a more powerless position or choose not to resist (see Klocker, this volume). Furthermore, the chapters in this section have shown that young people can be powerful and powerless at the same time (Punch, this volume), or in fluctuating cycles according to their shifting geographies of the different arenas of their everyday lives (Dunkley and Panelli; Jones, this volume).

Thus, there are undoubtedly a diverse range of ways that young people experience the mechanisms of power, yet it could also be argued that despite the multiplicity and fluidity of power, one universal characteristic is shared: the social positioning of children is more disempowering compared with the greater capacity of adulthood to maintain its position of privilege (see also Klocker 2005a). Mayall (2002) argues that ideologies, social policies, and institutional practices structure the way that childhood and adulthood are understood, and that these discourses and social practices are mediated through adults, thus enhancing an adult-based power in society. Thus, she calls for greater exploration of childhood as a relational category:

> Study of generationing is essential because childhood is essentially relational with adulthood, not least because the power to define it lies with adults, who define it as different from adulthood. Children are in no doubt that childhood differs from adulthood. (Mayall 2002: 40)

The chapters in this book provide many examples of the complex and multiple ways in which rural young people's everyday lives are enmeshed in different layers of unequal power relations. They experience *power over, power with,* and *power within* but their structural positioning constrains their ability to exert *power to* challenge and transform generational hierarchies (see also Parpart et al. 2002; Rowlands 1997).

NOTES

1. But note Rufo's (2003: 68) cautions about providing discourse with such power and agency. He asks: 'If a discourse can be called 'powerful', where then does that power reside'? Opponents of this conceptualisation of power argue that it withdraws the possibility that the action of the individual or groups can produce social change, where any shift in the relations of power can work in favour of the social order.

17 Conclusions and future directions for studying young rural lives

Elsbeth Robson, Ruth Panelli, and Samantha Punch

In closing this volume we aim to draw together the analytical concepts of identity, agency and power, whilst also considering the major theme of Majority-Minority world binaries. In addition, we finish by suggesting where global perspectives on young rural lives might lead in future. Thus we provide a selection of recommendations for future research that may extend this field and make connections with wider contemporary debates in geography, sociology, rural, youth, and childhood studies and related disciplines. We firmly contend that continued dialogue between disciplines and between different global contexts is necessary to further enhance research agendas on young rural lives.

MAJORITY AND MINORITY WORLD CONTEXTS: BINARIES AND BEYOND

Our book stemmed from an interest in speaking across contrasting research settings. As rural youth researchers we recognized the need to acknowledge vast differences between previously labeled 'west' and 'developed' countries and those 'less developed' or 'developing'. Seeking both to explore contrasts and commonalities, this volume has purposely constructed *Global Perspectives* by considering how a Majority–Minority world classification might inform our studies of specific places and the diverse contexts involved. While a Majority–Minority world division often helped in selecting and structuring this collection, it is timely to consider the limits, strengths, and alternatives to such a binary.

Differences and similarities between Majority and Minority worlds

This section summarizes some of the key differences and similarities that have emerged across the chapters according to world region. An attempt is made to tease out some of the main comparisons and contrasts, whilst also recognising the difficulty of homogenising world regions when the preceding chapters illustrate a vast range of diversity, even within small rural areas in their specific case studies.

There are noticeable differences in the material realities of rural areas across different parts of the globe. Rural regions in the Majority world represent some of the most impoverished places on the planet. Within the Majority world there are frequently considerable inequalities between rural and urban areas in terms of the services, communications, goods available, access to technologies, work and education opportunities. In contrast, in the Minority world, rural differences from urban areas are not so pronounced although we have seen that there is often less public transport and limited leisure facilities for young people living in rural locales (Matthews and Tucker; Dunkley and Panelli, this volume).

Cultural expectations of children's intergenerational responsibilities seem to be stronger, or more marked, in Majority world contexts (Bell, Klocker, Punch, this volume) as compared to their counterparts in the Minority world. Although Minority world children tend to remain economically dependent on their parents longer than in the Majority world, independence and self-sufficiency are also encouraged. In contrast, in the Majority world, children may achieve economic independence sooner, but long-term family interdependence tends to be maintained throughout the life course (Punch 2002b). In the absence of effective state welfare systems, prolonged family ties and the care of parents in old age is encouraged. This highlights how concepts of childhood and the expectations of children are defined differently in distinct Majority-Minority world social and cultural contexts. However, it should be noted that patterns of intergenerational caring can change in the context of migration (Ansell and van Blerk; Beazley, this volume).

Besides these differences, the chapters collected in this book document several important common themes in the lives of young people across the two world contexts. First, in both Majority and Minority worlds there appear to be restrictive forces limiting the agency of young people in urban areas including traffic congestion and pollution (Box 6.1), parental fears, government mistrust of youth (Jones, this volume), social stresses and spatial constraints in urban areas, which contrast with rural open spaces and relative freedom for young people living in the countryside.

Second, inadequate access to transport and lack of mobility is a key issue for young people in rural areas of both the Majority and Minority worlds (e.g. Matthews and Tucker; and Punch this volume). Not only is transport limited for young people in rural areas across the globe but they also generally complain about lack of services, leisure, educational, and work opportunities (Beazley; Carpena-Méndez; Dunkley and Panelli; Klocker; Matthews and Tucker; Punch, this volume). Third, in response to the insufficient opportunities in rural areas, migration for work or education is often necessary for young people in both Majority and Minority worlds (as identified by Robson et al., this volume).

Fourth, emotional aspects of belonging to a place and experiencing rural life are important to rural young people in both Minority and Majority worlds (Ansell and van Blerk; Jones this volume); but emotional issues are often overlooked in childhood/youth studies. Often it is the social relationships that take place in specific spaces which are important to young people's sense of identity and attachment to place rather than the place itself (Robson et al.; Bushin et al., this volume).

Thus, there are both limitations and benefits of adopting the terms Majority and Minority worlds. While providing useful conceptual tools, their potential drawback is that they divide global regions in an exclusive binary manner, when the world is not so neatly separated into clear cut and mutually exclusive categories. For example, within the Minority world there are relatively small numbers of extremely poor and socially excluded rural young people (such as itinerant traveller children) who enjoy fewer benefits of living in the privileged Minority world than their peers (see Bradbury et al. 2001; Ridge 2002). Similarly, there are wealthy children of elite families in the Majority world who live materially comfortable lives akin to their contemporaries in the economically richer countries of the globe (see Hecht 1998).

Beyond Majority/Minority binaries...

It is also important to recognize the liminality or blurring of conceptual categories as we look beyond a simple Majority–Minority world dichotomy. By pursuing more studies with young people who straddle the Minority–Majority world boundaries there are opportunities to challenge the clear-cut distinctions (see Carpena-Méndez and Schäfer, this volume). Similarly, it is also important to recognize the diversity of young people's experiences within the so-called Minority and Majority worlds. For example, within Majority world settings like Northeast Brazil there are vast differences in the life experiences of 'nurtured' and 'nurturing' children (Hecht 1998). Furthermore, the Majority–Minority world categorisation is one that speaks to the world today but also gestures towards temporal dynamics. Time-sensitive analyses are demonstrated in this volume—a century or more ago the nineteenth century world was a different place and even the children of new settlers, albeit belonging to the colonial classes, had to work long hours (Hunter and Riney-Kehrberg, this volume).

Finally, there is also significant potential in exploring conceptual options faced in other binary debates beyond youth studies. For instance, the work of Grosz (2005) includes the potential to consider how (in her case nature–culture) binaries may be reconfigured. Moving beyond a classification of privileged/marginalized or dominant/subordinate states, Grosz (2005: 47) suggests the traditionally 'subordinate term needs to be reconsidered as both the condition of the dominant term and as occupying its heart or centre'. We suggest this type of thinking opens up possibilities of more widely acknowledging the conditions and co-relations that are sustained at both global and regional levels. Thus the macro arrangements of Majority and Minority worlds and the incidence of Majority–Minority conditions across a Minority–Majority continuum, point to the power relations and cultural systems that sustain and reproduce complex configurations of livelihood, well-being, poverty, and opportunity. Some of these possibilities are considered further in the closing section of this chapter.

INTERROGATING GLOBAL PERSPECTIVES USING IDENTITY, ACTIONS, AND POWER

Having recognized differences and similarities across Majority and Minority worlds, a second goal of this book has been to support dialogue across these disparate contexts. Demonstrated in the three-part structure of this volume, we contend that generic conceptualisations are necessary if scholars are to move beyond the specificity of individual cases and engage one another in debate about how young rural lives are shaped and experienced across different settings. Thus, questions of identity, agency and action, and power have exercised our thinking both within and across the three sections of this book. These have been separately elaborated upon in Chapters 6, 11, and 16, but here we turn to synthesize the resources we offer for such dialogue.

Initially, and reflecting diverse rural contexts, authors in Chapters 2 to 6 focused on issues of identity. As with other groups, identities prescribed for —or elected by—young people act as both social frames and resources through which they can live their lives and find meaning about them. Part I of this book illustrated that, within and across Majority–Minority world divides, identities for children and young people are socio-culturally, economically, and even politically derived. For instance, Hunter and Riney-Kehrberg showed how historically modernizing societies developed maidenly and domestic constructions of farm girls' work and positions in Australia, New Zealand, and the United States. Similarly, Carpena-Méndez demonstrated how contemporary Mexican conditions under NAFTA draw young people into tensions between traditional support roles as family workers and carers, and new possibilities surrounding consumption of modern, technologically advanced, youth cultures. Other chapters that consider everyday actions and power relations (e.g. Ansell and van Blerk; Beazley; Bell; Dunkley and Panelli; Jones; Punch; Schäfer, this volume) also highlight how young people's identities are intimately woven from both traditions and cultures that position them in relation to kinship, systems of authority, and appropriate behaviour, as well as varying opportunities to pursue lives as play makers, risk takers, and even relatively autonomous workers, migrants, and sexual beings.

In sum, conceptualisations of identity provide a rich avenue for engaging with the complexity of young people's rural lives. On the one hand, both historic and cultural roots structure some of their opportunities. On the other hand, changing contemporary processes result in their senses of self and place in rural and wider worlds being ones that are often shifting, forward looking and responsive to local and external processes. In the former instances of continuity, identity can be critiqued for the way young people's lives and opportunities are prescribed by existing social contexts in which they live. Whereas in the latter cases of change, opportunities exist for teasing out how the wider processes affecting rural lives are also navigated to an extent by young people as they juggle, choose, subvert, and reinvent identities and ways of life for themselves. Of equal importance, a complex appreciation of identity also encourages scholars to better recognize the fluidity and dynamics of rural conditions and available life courses. One of the most striking observations from reading across the case studies collated here rests on the simultaneous here-now and there-future weavings young people make of their coincident present realities and possible imaginaries of later life. From Mexico, Tanzania, Bolivia, and Indonesia to Norway, eastern Germany, and the northern United States young people undertake both present configurations and future imaginations about their lives. Identity, together with notions of agency and action provide potent concepts for exploring these multiple tactics further.

Agency and action have constituted the second set of concepts we have tried to explore as currency for cross-world dialogue on young rural lives. Chapter 11 examines the premise that children are active agents in their everyday rural lifeworlds, although constrained by many different structures and circumstances; but their agency has not always been recognized. Indeed in some situations it is hard to identify the agency of young people in what appear to be especially oppressive or exploitative circumstances, such as instances of child labour or slavery, but we have argued that children everywhere resist power and authority in creative, challenging, and subtle ways. The chapters of this volume show that across Majority and Minority worlds young people create their own safe spaces and find strategies to play, work, and learn (often in overlapping ways) while situated along a continuum of agency. There are accounts of the startling competence of young migrant workers (Carpena-Méndez, Beazley), farmers (Punch) and career planners (Schäfer). Conceptualising children as active agents opens up possibilities for working with children as researchers and foregrounding previously invisible and marginalized groups of rural young people. At different times in the life course; in the different spaces of childhood (including work, leisure, and school); and in their various intra- and inter-generational relations (as noted in this volume by Bell in Uganda and Punch in Bolivia) young people experience moments of 'thicker' or 'thinner' agency (see Klocker, this volume). If we view both 'sets' of childhoods (Majority and Minority world) as consisting of dynamic and constantly shifting agency, we open up possibilities for a much more fluid and productive dialogue across these worlds (Klocker 2005a).

Finally, conceptualisations of power have provided a third lens through which to pursue Majority–Minority and other critiques of young rural lives. As Chapter 16 has illustrated, power (whether theorized as an object, as relational, or as suggestive of empowerment) textures all types of rural society in which young people live. The power of place can help register the complex locations in which rural communities and economies find themselves situated—which in turn shape the range of contentment, pleasure, dissatisfaction, or shame young people can feel as rural dwellers. Research presented in Part III illustrated the diversity of young people's engagement with power and experiences of autonomy; ranging from the bodily enactment of games or sexual activities, through to the navigation of adult authority and value systems that frame many of their options and environment. While also alluded to in some earlier chapters, this section demonstrated the multitude of material and intangible forms of power that shape young people's experiences of rural life and the negotiations they consequently conduct; whether, for instance, these be focused on different spaces (and distances), activities, genders, or peer and generational dynamics. Similarly, these writings encourage further understandings of young people as, not only subjected to diverse unequal power relations, but also active navigators of power *within* various social dynamics, which can even afford opportunities to transform existing conditions and relations.

In summary, studies that further extend our understanding of power may:

- Continue to record the often challenging realities that young people face when positioned as subordinate to powerful adult and institutional expressions of control (whether this be over young people themselves, or over the conditions, activities, or opportunities in their lives).
- Contrast young people's subordinate experiences of power with their ability to negotiate, mobilize, or resist power relations to their advantage (whether this is a transitory moment of opportunistic activity or rebellion, or a longer term experience of increased capacity and power to shape their own experiences and futures).
- Recognize and further analyse the power relations and power differentials that exist *between* young people themselves (where within families or schools or peer groups different experiences and opportunities exist for various young people as a result of their gender, age, ethnicity, class, physical capacities, birth order, and so forth).

Cumulatively, consideration of identity, agency, and power provides numerous possibilities for better appreciating the commonalities and contrasts in young rural lives. While structurally this book has been organized to spotlight each concept separately, the documented research and conceptual reflections across the chapters demonstrate that these notions are not mutually exclusive. Rather, they intersect or have a reciprocal impact on the expression of each other. Some sense of this is depicted in Figure 17.1 which shows how rural young people live within multiple and power-infused contexts. These dynamic and multi-layered worlds include many local socio-culturally specific practices and expectations, as well as diverse exogenous processes (originating from different scales) that affect the character and future configuration of rural areas. Within these settings, young people are positioned in relation to—and are actively electing from—a range of identities. The 'balloons' represent the constructed and shifting nature of these identities, some of which are prescribed for young people (with little room for choice) while others are more consciously selected. The engagement with these 'balloons' highlights the active practice and performance of identities (emphasized in Chapters 2 through 6) and points to how identity, agency, and everyday actions are intimately interconnected in individual lives. The choices made by Tanzanian domestic workers, English teenagers, and 'Malaysian orphans' (in Part II) illustrated some of the diversity of these connections, while the future imaginations of East German young people remind us that identities and actions are not only about immediate conditions and concerns but also point to young people's hopes and abilities to conceive their futures (e.g. Bell; Dunkley and Panelli; and Punch, this volume). Thus, the arrowed actions to the right of Figure 17.1 point to a selection of immediate and wider undertakings young people make in their lives. These undertakings could fruitfully bear more nuanced future research to show how they intersect with—and change—existing rural conditions as well as lead young people beyond rural settings (whether in terms of future migration-based lives elsewhere or wider understandings of how their rural societies intersect with other places, processes, and values, e.g. via the Internet or access to globally circulating cultures). Some of these possibilities motivate our thinking about future research agendas.

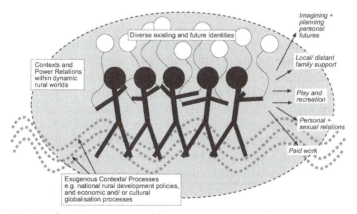

Figure 17.1 Synthesizing contexts, identities, actions, and power.

FUTURE PERSPECTIVES ON YOUNG RURAL LIVES

In drawing this book to a close, we take inspiration from a variety of sub-themes in this collection and point to the ways this volume can intersect with wider debates. Returning to the possibility of rethinking binaries, noted above, after Grosz (2005), we suggest that a continuation of dialogue across Majority–Minority worlds might fruitfully investigate the ways contrasting concepts (or worlds) invoke each other and stretch to include other composite forms (as Carpena-Méndez and Schäfer have reminded us). In particular, future studies might consider how young rural lives in Majority, or Minority, or mixed worlds intersect (implicitly or explicitly) with these other worlds and lives in reiterative and provocative ways (e.g. how do consumption opportunities for young people in the United States or Germany intersect with labour relations or migration processes framing young people's lives in Central America or Africa?). In addition, specific foci in wider social and rural studies could frame or complement these considerations, and we suggest five possible directions.

Hearing diverse young voices and other key accounts

Important arguments in the 'new social studies of childhood' (James et al. 1998: 184–191) have emphasized the importance of acknowledging the diverse voices of young people as active subjects of their own lives, capable of articulating meaning and participating in detailed research processes. The impact of this call has been widespread in the plethora of youth and childhood studies, and this book joins that endeavour. However, further work is needed to adequately recognize the complexity of some sub-groups who either by circumstance or choice are currently least visible. In rural research, this includes those young people who live transient, displaced, or strategically mobile lives, those who are homeless, those who do not use increasingly widespread technology, and those who are least easily reached because of especially difficult or restrictive circumstances (e.g. young refugees, disabled young people, young carers, institutionalized youth, children who are victims of abuse or powerful coercion). While there is much to be celebrated in the burgeoning studies of young rural lives, we cannot omit to acknowledge the gaps and silences in the youthful worlds thus far documented. Equally important, as a balancing of the discovery of young people's own voices, it is crucial to recognize that due diligence towards young voices will not in itself provide a 'whole' picture. Indeed, scholars pointing to the importance of 'generationing' (Alanen 2001; Mayall 2002) remind us that critical relational approaches to young people's lives are important for assessing conditions in relation to wider adult and institutional worlds that so strongly influence their experiences. Further work critiquing how young lives intersect with wider power relations and cultural systems will be significant in this regard.

Emotions, values, and morals

A second direction for future work, illustrated by several accounts in this book, centres on the complex ways affective and moral considerations permeate young rural lives. Studies such as Ansell and van Blerk, Dunkley and Panelli, and Jones (this volume) illustrate how young lives are not only physical or social experiences, but are also ones infused with diverse emotions from grief to pleasure and from ostracism to belonging. As wider geographies of emotion have become established, rich opportunities now exist for further detailed accounts of how affective relations shape the emotional landscapes of rural young people's daily lives (Anderson and Smith 2001).

Equally, wider critiques of morality and cultural values (e.g. Cloke 2002; Hubbard 2005) open up new avenues for rural youth studies. Following some accounts of how young people are judged and sometimes vilified (e.g. Kraack and Kenway 2002; Panelli et al. 2002), further questions surrounding young people's adoption and adaptation of value systems, and subversion or reshaping of moral codes, could be pursued in a variety of material, relational, and political senses (e.g. within rural exchange systems, schools, peer groups, sexual relations, public spaces, or the negotiation of community and place attachment).

Rematerialized and multi-scaled analyses

After the 'cultural turn' across the social sciences, including the intense reading of cultural constructions of childhood and youth, a third direction for rural youth studies resonates with increasing calls to rematerialize social and cultural studies (Anderson and Tolia-Kelly 2004). Specifically, the cross-world dialogue presented in this volume suggests the merit in further resources and research being devoted to the tangible textures and toil, and the socially valued, yet bio-physically structured environments in which young people work, play, learn, relate, and imagine their futures. Recognizing the mundane and the symbolic elements that are registered in both differentiated socio-economic conditions and changing technologies will also be important in future rural studies. Chapters such as Laegran's and Carpena-Méndez, Schäfer, Jones (this volume) suggest the fertile ground to be explored if the physical conditions and opportunities of young lives are to be read alongside the multi-scaled processes that affect rural areas (e.g. growth of the Internet, spread of hi-tech consumption goods, increase in migration patterns, or global fears mythologising cities with terror and countrysides with tranquility).

Embodied and performed childhood and youth

Associated with interests in rematerialized rural studies, many chapters in this book also inspire a heightened interrogation of the embodied and performed character of young lives. In part, works such as Ansell and van Blerk, Laegran and Jones (this volume) point to the active bodies, experiences of toil, speed, or vigour that might be further interpreted. Likewise, the carefully performed cliques narrated by Dunkley and Panelli, and the distinctions between migrant and non-migrant youth reported by Carpena-Méndez, and Punch (this volume) provide some further lines of enquiry. These possibilities connect with wider attention to the physicality and scripting of bodies as a site of identity formation and contestation, as well as pointing to the ways performance of identity and difference blurs with analysis of social actions and even subversions (e.g. Dwyer 1999; Hetherington 1998; 2000).

Questions of ethics and practice

Finally, while the scope of this book has precluded detailed attention to research methodologies, this collection stems from a diverse range of studies and stimulates several key ethical questions. Having embraced the call to increase recognition of young rural lives, authors such as those in this book can pause to consider the 'so what?' and 'where next?' questions that follow. The purposes and implications associated with our research encourage further reflection on the ethics of youth studies, especially those where rural populations are frequently marginalized or ignored. The merit of many fine words may be questioned by enduring rural challenges, and the nature of much rural fieldwork is transitory in the light of relatively long-term realities shaping many young lives. Resources from wider participatory, action, and collaborative methodologies may provide additional inspiration for researchers interested in furthering efforts to involve, consult, research, and collaborate with young people in rural areas (e.g. Johnson et al. 1998, Kelley 2006, Smith et al. 2002). One goal might be to work more actively for research programmes where, akin to some indigenous research approaches, young people and their communities have the recognition, resources, and opportunity to collaborate with academics and relevant agencies in prioritising research agendas, selecting appropriate data, choosing the interpretive lens, and circulating research in meaningful ways. Thus, following young people's own example of looking to the future, we might imagine a sequel to this book at some time that demonstrates collaborations in voice, critique, and agenda setting while continuing to document and review the contexts, creativity, and hopes of young people as they grapple with, value, or move on from complex rural worlds.

Contributors

Ruth Panelli (Reader, University College London) studied at the University of Melbourne after an urban childhood punctuated by frequent visits to a family property in rural Victoria, Australia where afternoon walks past grazing kangaroos to collect fresh Jersey milk in 'the billy' were an enduring highlight. She first developed a professional interest in young rural lives after broader research on social difference in rural Australia and New Zealand, and supervising Jaleh McCormack (2002) on her postgraduate research. While at the University of Otago, Ruth more recently completed studies on urban and rural contrasts (with Karen Nairn) and children's catchment-specific experiences (with Gretchen Robertson and the Taieri Trust). She recently joined UCL and plans to continue youth research while watching her own children incorporate, or move on from, rural experiences in their emerging adult lives.

Samantha Punch (Lecturer in Sociology, Stirling University) studied at Leeds University after an urban childhood in Kent, UK. Her initial interests in rural childhoods began in Bolivia with ethnographic doctoral research and ten years later she is conducting a follow-up study with the same children in order to explore their changing rural livelihoods. In between she has carried out research on young people's problems (with Roger Fuller, Christine Hallett, and Cathy Murray), household livelihoods in peri-urban Calcutta (with Stuart Bunting and David Little), children's experiences of sibling relationships and birth order in central Scotland, and young people's food practices in residential care homes (with Ruth Emond and Ian McIntosh). She currently lives in Stirling which enables her to escape to the Scottish hills at weekends.

Elsbeth Robson (Honorary Research Associate, Department of Anthropology, Durham University and Research Fellow, Centre for Social Research, University of Malawi) studied at the Universities of Durham, Oxford, and Tübingen following a suburban childhood in the English Midlands. She first developed an interest in the lives of African young people when working as a teenage gap year volunteer in an orphanage in Kenya. Her PhD work was conducted while a research associate at Ahmadu Bello University, Nigeria and included documenting the work of young people in a Hausa village. While a lecturer at Keele University, Elsbeth carried out research with young carers in Zimbabwe and orphans and young displacees in Kenya. She currently lives in Malawi researching young people's use of transport (with Gina Porter and team) while trying to give her son and step-son rich African childhood experiences.

Hanne Kirstine Adriansen (Senior Researcher, Danish Institute for International Studies) studied at the Universities of Copenhagen and of New South Wales, Sydney. During her suburban childhood in southern Denmark, she enjoyed frequent visits to her grandparents' farms. Her rural interest began when travelling in New Zealand and developed through her studies in human geography where she specialized in rural livelihoods in arid areas. Her fascination with life in desert regions led to a PhD on pastoralists in Senegal. Hanne's interest in young rural lives began with her post-doctoral work on the settlement of young Egyptians in new desert communities. This work gives her the opportunity to combine living in Copenhagen with visits to the desert in Egypt.

Nicola Ansell (Senior Lecturer in Human Geography, Brunel University) studied at Cambridge University after a childhood in the town of Bedford. She developed an interest in the lives of young people while teaching on the edge of London and, after a year spent travelling and working in Africa and South America, was inspired to do a PhD at Keele University which investigated the impacts of secondary schooling on the lives of rural young people in Lesotho and Zimbabwe. More recently she has undertaken research with AIDS-affected young people in Lesotho and Malawi and on the ways in which Lesotho's education sector is responding to AIDS. After a few years' sojourn in rural Shropshire, she has returned to live on the outskirts of London.

Harriot Beazley (Lecturer, University of Queensland) experienced a range of different childhoods: suburban, rural, and urban. She first developed a fascination with the lives of children in the Majority world—both rural and urban—when she travelled for over two years through Asia and Latin America. On her return she studied at the School of Oriental and African Studies (SOAS), and then at the Australian National University, conducting PhD research with street children in the city of Yogyakarta, Indonesia. On completion of her PhD she worked in rural Indonesia on an AusAid funded maternal and infant health project. More recently she has been working with Judith Ennew, Sharon Bessel, and Roxana Waterson as a technical advisor on a SAVE (Sweden) comparative research project on rural and urban children's experiences of corporal punishment in nine countries in the Asia-Pacific, and a UNICEF program to combat child labour and the commercial sexual exploitation of children in Java. Her daughter was born in Martinique, French West Indies, before the family moved to Australia, where they now enjoy a healthy mix of city, bush, and beach.

Stephen Bell (PhD student, Royal Holloway, University of London) is currently writing up his PhD thesis after an urban childhood split between Dorset, Cheshire, and Kent in Southern England following parental job moves. He first developed an interest in the lives of rural African young people, their sexual health and experiences of HIV/AIDS whilst working as a voluntary health educator for a small international NGO called Students Partnership Worldwide (SPW) in Zimbabwe during 2001. His PhD research explores how processes of empowerment occur amongst rural young people in relation to their sexual and reproductive health, and analyses the role of NGOs/CBOs in facilitating these processes at community level. He currently lives in south London enjoying city life, whilst planning postdoctoral research and an inevitable return to rural Africa in the near future.

Naomi Bushin (Postdoctoral Researcher, University College, Cork) studied at the University of Wales Swansea after experiencing childhood in Surrey. Her own experiences of both family migration and working with highly mobile children inspired her PhD research that focused on the counter-urban migrations of children within the UK. Having briefly worked for a commercial research company, carrying out assessments of the housing needs of Gypsies and Travellers, Naomi has recently moved to Cork to join a new Marie Curie Excellence Grant research team. This three-and-a-half year project explores children's migrations to Ireland and Naomi's research strand focuses on the migration experiences of children from Eastern Europe.

Fina Carpena-Méndez (PhD Candidate, University of California, Berkeley) has studied at the Universitat Autònoma de Barcelona and the University of California, Berkeley after a rural childhood in Catalonia (Spain). Surrounded by wheat fields, her native village is situated on the banks of a river where nineteenth century-built textile factories employed many rural youth until the end of this industry in the 1990s. This rural–industrial experience has been an enduring motivation in her research interests. First, Fina studied national and immigrant children learning food practices in rural and urban contexts in Catalonia. Later, she conducted doctoral ethnographic research on Nahua children and youth's experiences growing up in rural Mexico in the context of massive migration to the U.S. She currently lives in San Diego, where she is a research fellow at the Center for U.S.-Mexican Studies and the Center for Comparative Immigration Studies, University of California, San Diego.

Lauren Costello (Lecturer, Monash University) has lived a completely urban life in Australia moving to Melbourne from Sydney in the early 1990s to undertake a PhD. She has, along with her brother, spent the last 20-odd years avoiding the heat and flies of her parents' farm. The desire to avoid aspects of rural living was cemented after watching the 'hanging' of pig intestines as a child. Recent, but discrete interests in children, bodies, and identity (with Duane Duncan) and urban–rural migration has seen Lauren's research move in unexpected directions. While her research might have unintentionally shifted, she has no short or longer term plans for a tree-change.

Cheryl Morse Dunkley (Lecturer, Department of Geography, University of Vermont) is firmly rooted in rural Vermont. She grew up in the Upper Valley region of the Connecticut River and now lives in northern Vermont, between Lake Champlain and the spine of the Green Mountains. She received her BA Honors in Environmental Studies from the University of Vermont where she later earned a Master's in Geography. She and her family then travelled to Vancouver where she completed her PhD in Geography at the University of British Columbia. She is now back in Vermont teaching geography at her alma mater. Before she became an academic, Cheryl worked in sustainable agriculture, outdoor education, and special education. These days, she pursues these interests in research on nature–culture theory, youth geographies, therapeutic landscapes, and rural place making. When schoolwork is done she coaches youth lacrosse, serves as a town official, and tries to keep up with three (rather muddy) children.

Kathryn Hunter (Senior Lecturer, Victoria University Wellington) went to the city to study at Melbourne University after a childhood in a provincial town. Stories of her farming grandparents' childhoods, especially those of her grandmother (one of seven daughters) were part of the family lore and listening to her brother head off in the dark for morning milking was a part of family holidays. The family lore provided an impetus for her PhD dissertation that examines the lives of single, white girls and women on farms in Victoria, Australia (subsequently published as *Father's Right-hand Man: Women in Australia's Family Farms in the Age of Federation, 1880s–1920s*). Kate has lived and taught in Wellington, New Zealand for eleven years. She lives out of the city in the utopian hope that her children, currently two and three years old, will always have gumboots, love their chooks, and continue to eat peas out of pods and wild venison.

Owain Jones (Research Fellow, Department of Geography, University of Exeter) completed his Master's degree and PhD at the University of Bristol. His PhD focused on the linkages between childhood and the countryside in adult imaginations, discourses, and parenting practices. He has written extensively on various aspects of the geographies of childhood, including imaginations of urban childhood, and associations between children and disordered spaces. Some of this work has been undertaken with Professor Cloke and has been funded by the Arts and Humanities Research Council. He lives in a small English rural(ish) village where he compares academic accounts of rural childhood with that of his own children and their friends as they grow up there. He is associate editor of the journal *Children's Geographies*.

Natascha Klocker (PhD student, University of New South Wales) is currently conducting PhD research in rural Tanzania following a completely suburban childhood in Sydney. She had her first taste of rural living when, like Stephen, she worked as a Students Partnership Worldwide (SPW) volunteer in Tanzania in 2003. Although she very much enjoyed her time living in a rural village she decided, after returning to Tanzania in early 2005 for her PhD fieldwork, that it would be better to settle in a small town which (sometimes) has electricity. Her PhD research involves working with a team of young researchers to investigate (and hopefully improve the conditions of) Child Domestic Work in the Iringa Region of Tanzania. While these young researchers very competently conduct the fun parts of the research, she is mostly stuck behind a desk putting her Kiswahili to the test with a growing pile of interview translations.

Anne Sofie Laegran (Research Fellow, Norwegian University of Science and Technology [NTNU] and the University of Edinburgh) studied at NTNU in Trondheim following a childhood in the semi-urban fringe, next to grazing cows yet within walking distance of town. Inspired by her supervisor Anders Lofgren, she developed an academic interest in young people, in particular their use of technologies. Her PhD on Internet cafés and cars brought her to Edinburgh in 2002, a city that welcomed her so much that she settled, continuing her research on technologies in everyday life.

Jaana Lähteenmaa (Researcher, D.Soc.Sci,) studied sociology and philosophy in the University of Helsinki in the 1980s after a childhood and youth spent mainly in Helsinki. She investigated girls' relationship to rock music (1988) and her dissertation topic was late-modern youth culture (2000). In the 1990s, she worked in the Urban Studies Centre of Helsinki City. Jaana was born in the countryside, in northwest Finland, where her kin have been living and farming since the 1700s—her family name being derived from that farm: *Lähteenmaa* meaning "land of the spring". She spent all her summers there as a child, helping in the fields with her sisters and cousins. After her doctorate, Jaana turned to rural studies. First, she studied youth work in remote areas of eastern Finland. Since 2004 she has been investigating "Regional inequalities and its experience and cultural aspects in the lives of young people", in the Finnish Youth Research Network. Jaana lives in north Helsinki with her man and a big dog—in a house with a garden, apple trees, and a small potato field.

Hugh Matthews (Professor of Geography, The University of Northampton) can barely remember his suburban childhood in Kent, but seems to recall moving around parks, playgrounds, and open spaces within his neighbourhood in a carefree and happy manner. Since then Hugh has studied at Swansea University, gaining a PhD, and worked at Bournemouth University, Coventry University, and most recently at The University of Northampton, where he is Director of Research and Knowledge Transfer and Director of the Centre for Children and Youth. Hugh's research focuses on the outdoor behaviours of children and upon the ways in which their "voices" are often obfuscated by the structures that surround them.

Pamela Riney-Kehrberg (Professor, Iowa State University) studied at the University of Wisconsin-Madison after an urban childhood in Littleton, Colorado. She did, however, like to pretend that the irrigation canal across the street was somewhere on the far western frontier. She became interested in the history of farm youth while working on projects in family, community, and women's history. She turned that interest into a book length study, *Childhood on the Farm: Work, Play and Coming of Age in the Midwest, 1870–1920* (University Press of Kansas, 2005). She is thinking about writing a non-fiction book for children about farm children. She currently lives in Ames, Iowa, and spends a lot of time reading books about farms to her pre-school aged son.

Nadine Schäfer (PhD Researcher, University of Plymouth) studied sociology at the Universities of Potsdam and Dublin after an urban childhood in North Rhine-Westphalia (Germany). She developed a professional interest in young people's lives when working as a research assistant on an ESRC funded project on "Globalisation, Cultural Practice and Youth Identities in the Former East Germany" in the Saxon city of Leipzig (supervised by Kathrin Hörschelmann). In reference to this project, Nadine developed her doctoral research on rural young people's daily lives and future prospects in East Germany using participatory research methods (supervised by Richard Yarwood and Geoff Wilson). Nadine currently lives in Plymouth, UK and enjoys spending her free time in the countryside which enables her to gain an insight into rural life in Devon and Cornwall.

Faith Tucker (Lecturer in Human Geography, University of Northampton) spent her childhood in rural Wiltshire, moving to rural Northamptonshire in her teens. Following a brief period of urban living during completion of her undergraduate studies at the University of Reading, Faith returned to the countryside to carry out her doctoral research. This work, based at the Centre for Children and Youth, University of Northampton, focused on the lifestyles of teenage girls growing up in rural South Northamptonshire. Faith is Reviews Editor of the *Children's Geographies* journal and Secretary of the Royal Geographical Society (with the Institute of British Geographers) working group on the Geographies of Children, Youth and Families.

Lorraine van Blerk (Lecturer, University of Reading) has studied at the Universities of Strathclyde, London (Royal Holloway), and Coventry following a rural childhood in the West of Scotland. Her interests in young people's lives began with a research visit to Pakistan. Following this she undertook doctoral research exploring the social and spatial lives of Ugandan street children. Since completing her PhD, Lorraine's research has continued to focus on young African lives. She has worked with street children and their families in South Africa, young commercial sex workers in Ethiopia, and children affected by AIDS in southern Africa (with Nicola Ansell). She currently lives in Buckinghamshire with visits to South Africa, which enables her children to enjoy a diversity of British and South African childhood experiences.

References

Ackroyd, J. and Pilkington, A. (1999) 'Childhood and the construction of ethnic identities in a global age: a dramatic encounter', *Childhood*, 6: 443–454.

Adams, D. Little ghosts in a little ghost town, MS8769, National Library of Australia.

Admassie, A. (2003) 'Child labour and schooling in the context of a subsistence rural economy: can they be compatible?' *International Journal of Educational Development*, 23: 167–185.

Adriansen, H.K. (2003) Egypt's desert lands: new spaces or opportunity or new spaces of poverty? *DIIS/CDR Working Paper* 03.9.

Adriansen, H.K. and Madsen, L.M. (2004) 'Constructing multiple ruralities: practices and values of rural dwellers' in Holloway, L. and Kneafsey, M. (eds) *Geographies of Rural Cultures and Societies*, Ashgate: London: 79–99.

Aguirre Beltran, G. (1979) *Regions of Refuge*. Washington, DC: Society for Applied Anthropology.

Aitken, S. (1994) *Putting Children in their Place*. Washington, DC: Association of American Geographers.

Alanen, L. (2001) 'Explorations in generational analysis', in Alanen, L. and Mayall, B. (eds) *Conceptualising Child-Adult Relations*. London: Routledge Falmer.

Albornoz, O. (1993) *Education and Society in Latin America*. London: Macmillan.

Alderson, P. (2000a) 'Children as researcher: the effects of participation rights on research methodology', in P. Christensen and A. James (eds) *Research with Children: Perspectives and Practices*. London: Falmer Press.

Alderson, P. (2000b) 'School students' views on school councils and daily life at school', *Children and Society*, 14: 121–134.

Allen, J. (2003) *Lost Geographies of Power*. Oxford: Blackwell.

American Young Folks, 1875–1882.

Amuyunzu-Myamongo, M., Biddlecom, A.E., Ouedraogo, C., and Woog, V. (2005) 'Qualitative evidence on adolescents' views of sexual and reproductive health in Sub-Saharan Africa', *Occasional Report No. 16*. Online. Available at: <http://www.gutmacher.org/pubs/2005/03/01/or16.pdf> (accessed 20 July 2005).

Anderson, B. and Tolia-Kelly, D. (2004) 'Matter(s) in social and cultural geography', *Geoforum*, 35: 669–674.

Anderson, K. and Smith, S.J. (2001) 'Editorial: Emotional geographies', *Transactions of the Institute of British Geographers*, 26: 7–10.

Andrews, H.F. (1985) 'The ecology of risk and the geography of intervention: from research to practice for the health and well-being of urban children', *Annals of the Association of American Geographers*, 75: 370–382.

Ansell, N. (2004) Secondary schooling and rural youth transitions in Lesotho and Zimbabwe. *Youth & Society*, 36: 183–202.

Ansell, N. (2005) *Children, Youth and Development*. London: Routledge.

Ansell, N. and van Blerk, L. (2004) 'Children's migration as a household/family strategy: coping with AIDS in Malawi and Lesotho', *Journal of Southern African Studies*, 30: 673–690.

Auriat, N., Miljeteig, P., and Chawla, L. (2001) 'Overview—identifying best practices in children's participation', *Participatory Learning and Action (PLA) Notes*, 42: 5–8.

Austin, L. M. (2003) 'Children of childhood: nostalgia and the romantic legacy,' *Studies in Romanticism*. Online. Available at: <http://www.highbeam.com> (accessed 22 March 2003).

Avalos, B. (1986) *Teaching Children of the Poor: An Ethnographic Study in Latin America*. Ottawa: International Development Research Centre.

Bachelard, G. (1971) *The Poetics of Reveries: Childhood, Language, and the Cosmos*. Boston: Beacon Press.

Bagnoli, A. (2003) 'Imagining the lost other: the experience of loss and the process of identity construction in young people', *Journal of Youth Studies*, 6: 203–217.

Bandiyono, S., Raharto, A., and Romdiati, H. (1999) 'Legal or illegal? The choice facing migrants from Flores to Malaysia', *Development Bulletin*, No. 48: 37–40.

Barker, R. and Wright, H. (1955) *Midwest and its Children*, New York: Row, Peterson.

Baur, J. and Burrmann, U. (2000) *Unerforschtes Land: Jugendsport in ländlichen Regionen*. Aachen: Meyer und Meyer.

Baylies, C. and Bujra, J. (2000) *AIDS, Sexuality and Gender in Africa—Collective Strategies and Struggles in Tanzania and Zambia*, London: Routledge.

Beazley, H. (2000a) 'Home sweet home?: Street children's sites of belonging', in Holloway, S. and Valentine, G. (eds) *Children's Geographies: Living, Playing, Learning and Transforming Everyday Worlds*. London: Routledge.

Beazley, H. (2000b) 'Street boys in Yogyakarta: social and spatial exclusion in the public spaces of the city', in Bridge, G. and Watson, S. (eds) *A Companion to the City*. London: Blackwell.

Beazley, H. (2002) '"Vagrants wearing make-up": negotiating spaces on the streets of Yogyakarta, Indonesia', *Urban Studies*, 39: 1665–1683.

Beazley, H. (2003) 'The construction and protection of individual and collective identities by street children and youth in Indonesia', *Children, Youth and Environments* 13: Spring Online. Available at: <http://colorado.edu/journals/cye> (accessed 1 March 2006).

Beazley, H. and Ennew, J. (2006) 'Participatory methods and approaches: tackling the two tyrannies', in Desai, V. and Potter, R. (eds) *Doing Development Research*. London: Sage.

Beck, U. (1992) *Risk Society: Towards a New Modernity*. London: Sage.

Beck, U. (1994) 'The reinvention of politics: towards a theory of reflexive modernization', in Beck, U., Giddens, A., and Lash, S. (eds) *Reflexive Modernization*. Cambridge: Polity Press

Beck, U. (2000) 'Living your own life in a runaway world: individualisation, globalisation and politics', in Hutton, W. and Giddens, A. (eds) *On the Edge. Living with Global Capitalism*. London: Jonathan Cape.

Beck, U. and Beck-Gernsheim, E. (2002) *Individualization. Institutionalized Individualism and Its Social and Political Consequences*. London and New Dehli: Sage.

Beetz, S. (2004) *Dörfer in Bewegung. Ein Jahrhundert sozialer Wandel und räumliche Mobilitaet in einer ostdeutschen ländlichen Region.* Hamburg: Krämer.

Bendle, M.F. (2002) 'The crisis of "identity" in high modernity', *British Journal of Sociology*, 53: 1–18.

Bennett, L.R. (2005) *Maidenhood, Islam and Modernity: Single Women, Sexuality and Reproductive Health in Contemporary Indonesia.* London: Routledge.

Bequele, A. and Myers, W.E. (1995) *First Things First in Child Labour: Eliminating Work Detrimental to Children.* Geneva: International Labour Office.

Bhabha, H. (1994) *The Location of Culture.* London: Routledge.

Bhalla, A.S. and Lapeyre, F. (1997) 'Social exclusion: towards an analytical and operational framework', *Development and Change*, 28: 413–434.

Bingham, N. (1999) 'Unthinkable complexity? Cyberspace otherwise', in Crang, M., Crang, P. and May, J. (eds) *Virtual Geographies. Bodies Spaces and Relations.* London: Routledge.

Bjaarstad, S. (2001) 'Osloungdommers forestillinger om bygda. En studie av unges stedsforståelser, tilhørighet og identitet', unpublished master's thesis, University of Oslo.

Bjurström, E. (1990) 'Raggare. En tolkning av en stils uppkomst och utveckling', in Dahlen, P. and Rönnberg, M. (eds) *Spelrum.* Uppsala: Filmförlaget.

Black, M. (2004) *Opening Minds, Opening up Opportunities: Children's Participation in Action for Working Children.* London: Save the Children.

Blaut, J. and Stea, D. (1971) 'Studies of geographic learning', *Annals of the Association of American Geographers*, 61: 387–393.

Bonnet, M. (1993) 'Child labour in Africa', *International Labour Review*, 132: 371–391.

Bourdieu, P. (1990) *The Logic of Practice.* Stanford, CA: Stanford University Press.

Boyden, J. (1988) 'National policies and programmes for child workers: Peru', in Bequele, A. and Boyden, J. (eds) *Combating Child Labour.* Geneva: International Labour Organisation.

Boyden, J. (1990) 'Childhood and the policy makers: a comparative perspective on the globalization of childhood', in James, A. and Prout, A. (eds) *Constructing and reconstructing childhood.* London: Falmer.

Boyden, J. (1991) *Children of the Cities*, London: Zed.

Boyden, J. and de Berry, J. (eds) (2004) *Children and Youth on the Front Line: Ethnography, Armed Conflict and Displacement.* Oxford: Berghahn Books.

Boyden, J. and Ennew, J. (1997) *Children in Focus: A Manual for Participatory Research with Children.* Stockholm: Rädda Barnen.

Boyden, J., Ling, B., and Myers, W. (1998) *What Works for Working Children.* Stockholm: Rädda Barnen and UNICEF.

Bradbury, B., Jenkins, S., and Micklewright, J. (eds) (2001) *The Dynamics of Child Poverty in Industrialised Countries.* Cambridge: Cambridge University Press.

Brake, A. (1996) 'Wertorientierung und (Zukunfts-)Perspektiven von Kindern und jungen Jugendlichen. Über Selbstbilder und Weltsichten in Ost- und Westdeutschland', in Büchner, P. Fuhs, B. and Krüger, H.-H. (eds) *Vom Teddybär zum ersten Kuß. Wege aus der Kindheit in Ost- und Westdeutschland.* Opladen: Leske & Budrich.

Brake, A. and Büchner, P. (1996) 'Kindsein in Ost- und Westdeutschland. Allgemeine Rahmenbedingungen des Lebens von Kindern und jungen Jugendlichen', in Büchner, P., Fuhs, B. and Krüger, H.-H. (eds) *Vom Teddybär zum ersten Kuß. Wege aus der Kindheit in Ost- und Westdeutschland.* Opladen: Leske & Budrich.

Brandes, S. (1988) *Power and Persuasion. Fiestas and Social Control in Rural Mexico*. Philadelphia: University of Pennsylvania Press.

Brannen, J., Heptinstall, E., and Bhopal, K. (2000) *Connecting Children: Care and Family Life in Later Childhood*. London: Routledge Falmer.

Briggs, J. (1990) 'Playwork as a tool in the socialisation of the Inuit child', *Arctic Medical Research*, 49: 34–38.

Brooker, P. (2002) *A Glossary of Cultural Theory*. London: Arnold.

Brooking, T. (1992) 'Economic transformation', in Rice, G. (ed) The Oxford History of New Zealand. Auckland: Oxford University Press.

Bryant, J. (2005) 'Children of international migrants in Indonesia, Thailand and the Philippines: a review of evidence and policies', *Innocenti Working Paper No. 2005-05*. Florence: UNICEF Innocenti Research Centre.

Bunce, M. (1994) *The Countryside Ideal: Anglo-American Images of Landscape*. London: Routledge.

Bunce, M. (2003) 'Reproducing the idyll', in Cloke, P. (ed) *Country Visions*. London: Pearson Education.

Bundesamt für Bauwesen und Raumordnung (2000) *Raumordnungsbericht 2000*. Bonn: Selbstverlag des Bundesamtes für Bauwesen und Raumordnung.

Burawoy, M. and Verdery, K. (1999) *Uncertain Transition. Ethnographies of Change in the Postsocialist World*. Oxford: Rowman & Littlefield.

Butler, J. (1990) *Gender Trouble: Feminism and the Subversion of Identity*. New York: Routledge.

Butler, J. (1993) *Bodies that Matter: On the Discursive Limits of 'Sex'*. New York: Routledge.

Butler, R. (1998) 'Rehabilitating the images of disabled youth', in Skelton, T. and Valentine, G. (eds) *Cool Places: Geographies of Youth Cultures*. London/ New York: Routledge.

Bye, L. (2003) 'Masculinity and rurality at play in stories about hunting', *Norwegian Journal of Geography*, 57: 145–153.

Camacho, A.Z.V. (1999) 'Family, child labour and migration: child domestic workers in Metro Manila', *Childhood*, 6: 57–73.

Campbell, H. and Bell, M. (2000) 'Introduction to rural masculinities special issue', *Rural Sociology*, 65: 532–546.

Campbell, J.E. and Calson, M. (2002) 'Panoptican.com: Online surveillance and the commodification of privacy', *Journal of Broadcasting and Electronic Media*, 46: 586–606.

Carpena-Méndez, F. (2006a) 'Educación e Identidades Culturales en un Mundo Globalizado. Niños, Jóvenes y Escuelas Rurales en España y México', in A. Franzé et al. (eds) *Etnografía y Educación. Actas de la Reunión Internacional*. Valencia: Editorial Germania.

Carpena-Méndez, F. (2006b) *Growing Up Across Trenches, Letters and Borders. An Ethnography of Childhood, Youth and the Everyday in Neoliberal Rural Mexico*. Unpublished Ph.D. dissertation, University of California, Berkeley.

Center for Rural Studies and Vermont Center for Geographic Information (2005) *Vermont Indicators Online*. Available at: <http://maps.vcgi.org/indicators> (accessed 18 November 2005).

Chambers, R. (1990) *Rural Development: Putting the Last First*. Harlow: Longman.

Chambers, R. (1994) 'The origins and practice of participatory rural appraisal', *World Development Report*, 22: 953–969.

Chambers, R. (1997) 'Whose reality counts? Putting the first last', *Children's Rights Monitor*, 13: 13–15.

Chawla, L. (2002) 'The effects of political and economic transformations on children: the environment', in Kaufman, N.H. and Rizzini, I. (eds) *Globalization and Children: Exploring potentials for enhancing opportunities in the lives of children and youth*. London: Kluwer Academic/Plenum Publishers.

Childress, H. (2000) *Landscapes of Betrayal, Landscapes of Joy*. Albany, NY: State University of New York Press.

Christensen, P. (2003) 'Place, space and knowledge: children in the village and the city', in Christensen, P. and O'Brien, M. (eds) *Children in the City*. London: Routledge Falmer.

Christensen, P.H. (2004) 'Children's participation in ethnographic research: issues of power and representation', *Children & Society*, 18: 165–76.

Clacherty, G. and Kistner, J. (2001) 'Evaluating the Zimizeleni researchers' project: participatory research as intervention with 'hard-to-reach' boys', *Participatory Learning and Action (PLA) Notes*, 42: 29–34.

Cloke, P. (2002) 'Deliver us from evil? Prospects for living ethically and caring politically in human geography', *Progress in Human Geography*, 26: 587–604.

Cloke, P. and Jones, O. (2005) '"Unclaimed territory": childhood and disordered space(s)', *Social and Cultural Geography*, 6: 311–333.

Cohen, J. (1999) *Cooperation and Community. Economy and Society in Oaxaca*. Austin: University of Texas Press.

Cohen, M. (2000) 'Indonesia wants to send more workers abroad', *Far Eastern Economic Review*, 16 March. Online. Available at: <http://www.Malaysia.net/lists/sangkancil/2000-03/msg00378.html> (accessed 23 January 2006).

Cohen, P. and Ainley, P. (2000) 'In the country of the blind: youth studies and cultural studies in Britain', *Journal of Youth Studies*, 3: 79–96.

Connell, R. (1995) *Masculinities*, Cambridge: Polity Press.

Cooke, B. and Kothari, U. (eds) (2001) *Participation: The New Tyranny?* London: Zed Books.

Cornwall, A. (2003) 'Whose voices, whose choices?: Reflections on gender and participatory development', *World Development*, 31: 1325–1342.

Cornwall, A. and Pratt, G. (eds). (2003) *Pathways to Participation: Reflections on PRA*. London: ITDG Publishing.

Corrigan, P. (1979) *Schooling the Smash Street Kids*. London: Macmillan.

Côté, J.E. (2002) 'The role of identity capital in the transition to adulthood: the individualization thesis examined', *Journal of Youth Studies*, 5: 117–134.

Cotterell, J. (1996) *Social Networks and Social Influences in Adolescence*. London: Routledge.

Creed, G. and Ching, B. (1997) 'Recognizing rusticity: identity and the power of place', in Ching, B. and Creed, G. (eds) *Knowing Your Place: Rural Identity and Cultural Hierarchy*. London: Routledge.

Cresswell, T. (1996) *In Place/Out of Place: Geography, Ideology and Transgression*. Minneapolis: University of Minnesota Press.

Currie, C. Diary. MS19886, State Library of Victoria.

Davidoff, L., L'Esperance, J., and Newby, H. (1976) 'Landscape with figures: home and community in English society', in Mitchell, J. and Oakley A. (eds) *The Rights and Wrongs of Women*. Harmondsworth: Penguin.

Davis, J. and Ridge, T. (1997) *Same Scenery, Different Lifestyle: Rural Children on a Low Income*. London: The Children's Society.

Davis, J., Watson, N., and Cunningham-Burley, S. (2000) 'Learning the lives of disabled children: developing a reflexive approach', in Christensen, P. and James, A. (eds) *Research with Children: Perspectives and Practices*. London: Falmer Press.

Debord, G. (1970) *Society of the Spectacle*. Detroit: Black and Red.

de Bruijn, M. and van Dijk, H. (1995) *Arid Ways: Cultural Understandings of Insecurity in Fulbe Society, Central Mali*. Amsterdam: Thela Publishers.

De Certeau, M. (1984) *The Practice of Everyday Life*. Berkeley: University of California Press.

de Haan, A. (1998) 'Social exclusion: an alternative concept for the study of deprivation?', *IDS Bulletin*, 29: 10–19.

Debord, G. (1998) *Comments on the Society of the Spectacle*. London: Verso.

Department of Local Government and Regional Development (2001) *Om Distrikts og Regionalpolitikken*. Oslo: Department of local government and regional development. Online. Available at: <http://odin.dep.no/krd/norsk/dok/regpubl/stmeld/016001-040006/dok-bn.html> (accessed 16 January 2006).

Desai, V. (2002) 'Informal politics, grassroots NGOs and women's empowerment in the slums of Bombay', in Parpart, J.L., Rai, S.M., and Staudt, K. (eds) *Rethinking Empowerment in a Global/Local World*. London: Routledge.

Desforges, L. (1998) 'Checking out the planet': global representations/local identities and youth travel', in Skelton, T. and Valentine, G. (eds) *Cool Places: Geographies of Youth Cultures*. London: Routledge.

Dewsbury, J.-D. (2000) 'Performativity and the event: enacting a philosophy of difference', *Environment and Planning D: Society and Space*, 18: 473–497.

Dickinson, D. (2003) 'Tanzania 'housegirls' face sexual abuse': BBC News UK Edition. Online. Available at: <http://www.news.bbc.co.uk/1/hi/world/africa/3015223.stm> (accessed November 15 2005)

Dixon, J. and Durrheim, K. (2000) 'Displacing place-identity: a discursive approach to locating self and other', *British Journal of Social Psychology*, 39: 27–44

Dodman, D.R. (2004) 'Feelings of belonging? Young people's views of their surroundings in Kingston, Jamaica', *Children's Geographies*, 2: 185–198.

Drakakis-Smith, D. (2000) *Third World Cities*. London: Routledge.

Dunkley, C.M. (2004) 'Risky geographies: teens, gender and rural landscape in North America', *Gender, Place and Culture*, 11: 559–579.

Dunne, F. (1980) 'Occupational sex-stereotyping among rural young women and men', *Rural Sociology*, 45: 396–415.

Dwyer, C. (1999) 'Veiled meanings: young British Muslim women and the negotiation of difference', *Gender Place and Culture*, 6: 5–16.

Elder, G.H. and Conger, R.D. (2000) *Children of the Land: Adversity and Success in Rural America*. Chicago: University of Chicago Press.

Eliot, G. (1985) *The Mill on the Floss*. London: Penguin Books

Elkamel, F. (2005) 'Dialogue with the future: findings of a study on adolescents in three Egyptian governorates', paper presented at the conference *Changing Values Among the Youth*, Goethe Institute Cairo and Centre for Modern Oriental Studies Berlin, Cairo 20–21 June.

English, L.M. (2005) 'Foucault, feminists and funders: a study of power and policy in feminist organisations', *Studies in the Education of Adults*, 32: 137–150.

Englund, H. (1999) 'The self in self-interest: land, labour and temporalities in Malawi's agrarian change', *Africa*, 69: 139–156.

Englund, H. (2002a) 'Ethnography after globalism: migration and emplacement in Malawi', *American Ethnologist*, 29: 261–286.

Englund, H. (2002b) 'The village in the city, the city in the village: migrants in Lilongwe', *Journal of Southern African Studies*, 28: 137–154.

Epstein, J.S. (1998) 'Introduction: Generation X, youth, culture and identity', in J.S. Epstein (ed) *Youth Culture: Identity in a Postmodern World*. Malden, MA: Blackwell.

Escobar, A. (1996): 'Welcome to Cyberia: Notes on the anthropology of cyberculture', in Sardar, Z. and Ravetz, J. (eds) *Cyberfutures: Culture and Politics on the Information Highway*. London: Pluto Press.

Everman, W. (undated) *ABAB: Acker, Bataille, Argento, Bront*. Online. Available at: <http://www.calarts.edu/~acker/ackademy/everman.html> (accessed 24 February 2006).

Farmers' Advocate (1922–1926).

Faulkner, W. (2001) 'The technology question in feminism: a view from feminist technology studies', *Women's Studies International Forum*, 24: 79–95.

Fauske, H. (1993) 'Lokal forankring og global orientering? Holdningar til heimstaden blant unge i Oppland', in Heggen, K., Myklebust, J. O., and T. Øya (eds) *Ungdom i lokalmiljø*. Oslo: Samlaget.

Ferguson, F. (2003) 'The afterlife of the romantic child: Rousseau and Kant meet Deleuze and Guattari', *The South Atlantic Quarterly*, 102: 216–234.

Fetter, C. (2006a) 'Street children in Indonesia', e-mail. Lombok: Foundation Peduli Anak (8 June).

Fetter, C. (2006b) *The Research Study of Street Children, 2006, Lombok, Indonesia*. Lombok: Foundation Peduli Anak.

Field, R. Diary. MS11629, MF382, 383, LaTrobe Collection, State Library of Victoria.

Finch, J. and Mason, J. (1993) *Negotiating Family Responsibilities*. London: Routledge.

Fink, D. (1992) *Agrarian Women: Wives and Mothers in Rural Nebraska 1880–1940*. Chapel Hill: University of North Carolina Press.

Fischer, H., Karpinski, J., and Kück, U. (2002) 'Bevölkerungsentwicklung in Mecklenburg-Vorpommern seit der Wende-Bilanz und Ausblick', *Statistische Monatshefte Mecklenburg-Vorpommern*, 10: 249–262.

Forrester-Kibuga, K. (2000) *The Situation of Child Domestic Workers in Tanzania: A rapid assessment*. Tanzania: UNICEF.

Fosso, E.J. (1997) 'Industristeders arbeidstilbud og generasjoners forhold til utdanning, arbeid og sted—eksemplet Årdal', unpublished Ph.D. thesis, Norwegian School of Economics and Business Administration and the University of Bergen.

Foucault, M. (1979a) *Discipline and Punish: The Birth of the Prison*. Harmondsworth: Penguin.

Foucault, M. (1979b) *The History of Sexuality*, vol. 1. London: Allen Lane.

Foucault, M. (1980) *Power/Knowledge: Selected Interviews and Other Writing 1972–1977*, edited by C. Gordon. New York: Pantheon Books.

Foucault, M. (1982) 'The subject and power', in Dreyfus, H. and Rabinow, P. (eds) *Michel Foucault: Beyond Structuralism and Hermeneutics*. Harvester: Brighton, 208–226.

Foucault, M. (1990) *The History of Sexuality*, vol.1. London: Penguin.

Foucault, M. (1995) *Discipline and Punish*, translated by A. Sheridan. New York: Vintage Books.

Frost, L. (2003) 'Doing bodies differently? Gender, youth, appearance and damage', *Journal of Youth Studies*, 6: 53–70.

Fry, R. (1985) *It's Different for Daughters: A History of Curriculum for Girls in New Zealand Schools, 1900–1975*. Wellington: New Zealand Council for Educational Research.

Furlong, A. and Cartmel, F. (1997) *Young People and Social Change. Individualization and risk in late modernity*. Buckingham: Open University Press.

Fyfe, A. (1989) *Child Labour*. Cambridge: Polity Press.

Fyfe, A. (1993) *Child Labour: A Guide to Project Design*. Geneva: International Labour Office.

Gallagher, L. and Gallacher, M. (forthcoming 2007) 'Rethinking participatory methods in research involving children', *Childhood*.

Gallagher, L. and Gallacher, M. (forthcoming 2008) 'Methodological immaturity in childhood research? Thinking through "participatory methods",' *Childhood*.

Geertz, C. (1973), 'Thick description: toward an interpretative theory of culture' in Geertz, C. (ed) *The Interpretation of Cultures*. Essex, UK: Hutchinson.

Genette, G. (1982) *Figures of Literary Discourse*. Oxford: Blackwell.

Gibson, J. (1979) *The Ecological Approach to Visual Perception*. Boston: Houghton Mifflin.

Giddens, A. (1984) *The Constitution of Society: Outline of Theory of Structuration*. Berkeley: University of California Press.

Giddens, A. (1989) *Sociology*. Oxford: Polity Press.

Giddens, A. (1991) *Modernity and Self-identity: Self and Society in the Late Modern Age*. Stanford, CA: Stanford University Press.

Giddings, R. and Yarwood, R. (2005) 'Growing up, going out and growing out of the countryside: childhood experiences in rural England', *Children's Geographies*, 3: 101–114.

Gill, L. (2000) *Teetering on the Rim: Global Restructuring, Daily Life, and the Armed Retreat of the Bolivian State*. New York: Columbia University Press.

Goddard, V. and White, B. (1982) 'Child workers and capitalist development', *Development and Change*, 13: 465–477.

Government of Tanzania (2002) *Population and Housing Census*. Online. Available at: <http://www.tanzania.go.tz/census> (accessed 1 November 2005)

Government of Uganda (2000) *Laws of Uganda*. Kampala: Law Development Centre.

Graham, C. (1997) 'Building support for market reforms in Bolivia,' in Peirce, M.H. (ed) *Capitalization: A Bolivian Model of Social and Economic Reform*. Washington, DC: Woodrow Wilson Center.

Green, D. (2003) *Silent Revolution: The Rise and Crisis of Market Economics in Latin America*. London: Latin America Bureau.

Greenfield (2000) *The Private Life of the Brain*. Harmondsworth: Penguin.

Grosz, E. (1990) 'Contemporary theories of power and subjectivity,' in Gunew, S. (ed) *Feminist Knowledge: Critique and Construct*. London: Routledge.

Grosz, E. (2005) *Time Travels: Feminism, Nature, Power*. Durham, NC: Duke University Press.

Guattari, F. (1996) *Soft Subversions*.New York: Semiotext(e).

Guest, E. (2001) *Children of AIDS: Africa's Orphan Crisis*. London: Pluto Press.

Gutting, D. (1996) 'Narrative identity and residential history', *Area*, 28: 482–490.

Hadi, A.S. (2000) 'Regional labor circulation: Indonesian workers in Malaysia'. *Populasi*, 11: 61–76.

Hall, T., Coffey, A., and Williamson, H. (1999) 'Self, space and place: youth identities and citizenship', *British Journal of Sociology of Education*, 20: 501–513.

Halliday, J. (1997) 'Children's services and care: a rural view', *Geoforum*, 28: 103–119.

Halperin, D. (1995) *Saint Foucault: Towards a Gay Historiography*. New York: Oxford University Press.

Hart, G. (1991) 'Engendering everyday resistance: gender, patronage and production politics in rural Malaysia', *The Journal of Peasant Studies*, 19: 93–121.

Hart, J., Newman, J., and Ackermann, L. with Feeny, T. (2004) *Children Changing Their World—Understanding and Evaluating Children's Participation in Development*. Online. Available at: <http://www.plan-uk.org/pdfs/children-changingtheirworld.pdf> (accessed 4 October 2005).

Hart, R. (1979) *Children's Experience of Place*. New York: Irvington Publishers.

Hart, R. (1992) 'Children's participation: from tokenism to citizenship', *Innocenti Essays*, No. 4. Florence: International Child Development Centre, UNICEF.

Hart, R. (1997) *Children's Participation: The Theory and Practice of Involving Young Citizens in Community Development and Environmental Care*. New York: UNICEF/Earthscan Publications.

Haug, S.W. (2002) 'Ethnicity and multi-ethnicity in the lives of Belizean rural youth', *Journal of Rural Studies*, 18: 219–223.

Hebdige, D. (1979) *Subculture the Meaning of Style*. London: Methuen & Co.

Hecht, T. (1998) *At Home on the Street: Street Children of Northeast Brazil*. Cambridge: Cambridge University Press.

Helve, H. (ed) (2000) *Rural Young People in Changing Europe: Comparative Study of Living Conditions and Participation of Rural Young People in Estonia, Finland, Germany, Italy and Sweden*. Helsinki: Hakapaino Oy.

Hengst, H. (1997) 'Negotiating 'us' and 'them': children's constructions of collective identity', *Childhood*, 4: 43– 62.

Hetherington, K. (1998) *Expressions of Identity: Space, Performance, Politics*. London: Sage.

Hetherington, K. (2000) *New Age Travellers: Vanloads of Uproarious Humanity*. London and New York: Cassell.

Higonnet, A. (1998) *Pictures of Innocence: The History and Crisis of Ideal Childhood*. London: Thames and Hudson Ltd.

Hill, F. and Michelson, W. (1981) 'Towards a geography of urban children and youth', in Herbert, D.T. and R.J. Johnston (eds) *Geography and the Urban Environment: Progress in Research and Applications*, vol. 4. Chichester, UK: John Wiley.

Hinrichs, C. (1996) 'Consuming images: making and marketing Vermont as distinctive rural place,' in Dupuis, E. and Vandergeest, E. (eds) *Creating the Countryside*. Philadelphia: Temple University Press.

Hoggart, K. and Buller, H. (1987) *Rural Development: A Geographical Perspective*. London: Croom Helm.

Hollos, M. (2002) 'The cultural construction of childhood: changing conceptions among the Pare of northern Tanzania', *Childhood*, 9: 67–189.

Holloway, S. and Valentine, G. (2000a) 'Children's geographies and the new social studies of childhood. Introduction', in Holloway, S. L. and Valentine, G. (eds) *Children's Geographies. Playing, Living, Learning*. London, New York: Routledge.

Holloway, S. and Valentine, G. (eds) (2000b) *Children's Geographies: Playing, Living, Learning*. London: Routledge.

Holloway, S. and Valentine, G. (2000c) 'Corked hats and Coronation Street: British and New Zealand children's imaginative geographies of the other', *Childhood*, 7: 335–357.

Holloway, S. and Valentine, G. (2000d) 'Spatiality and the new social studies of childhood', *Sociology*, 34:763–783.

Holloway, S.L., Valentine, G., and Bingham, N. (2000) 'Institutionalising technologies: masculinities, femininities and the heterosexual economy of the IT classroom', *Environment and Planning A*, 32: 617–633.

Holt, L. (2004) 'Children with mind-body differences: performing (dis)ability in primary schools classrooms', *Children's Geographies*, 2: 219–236.

Holt, L. (forthcoming 2007) 'Children's sociospatial (re)production of (dis)ability in primary school playgrounds', *Environment and Planning D: Society and Space*.

Honeyman, S.E. (2001) 'Childhood bound: in maps and pictures, *Mosaic: A Journal for the Interdisciplinary Study of Literature*, 34: 117–132.

Hoogvelt, A. (2001) *Globalization and the Postcolonial World: The New Political Economy of Development*. Basingstoke: Palgrave.

hooks, b. (1991) *Yearning: Race, Gender and Cultural Politics*. Boston, MA: South End Press.

Hörschelmann, K. (2002) 'History after the end: post-socialist difference in a (post)modern world', *Transactions of the Institute of British Geographers*, 27: 52–66.

Hörschelmann, K. and Schäfer, N. (2005) 'Performing the global through the local-globalisation and individualisation in the spatial practices of young East Germans', *Children's Geographies*, 3: 219–242.

Horton, J. and Kraftl, P. (2005) 'For more-than-usefulness: six overlapping points about children's geographies', *Children's Geographies*, 3: 131–143.

Hubbard, P. (2005) 'Accommodating otherness: anti-asylum centre protest and the maintenance of white privilege', *Transactions of the Institute of British Geographers* NS, 30: 52–65.

Hugo, G. (1995) 'International labour migration and the family, some observations from Indonesia', *Asian and Pacific Migration Journal*, 42: 126–142.

Hugo, G. (2002) 'Women's international labour migration' in Robinson, K. and Bessell (eds) *Women in Indonesia: Gender Equity and Development*. Singapore: ISEAS: 158–178.

Hull, T., Rusman, R., and Djonan, E. (1999) 'They simply die: searching for the causes of high infant mortality in Lombok', *Development Bulletin*, 48: 21–24.

Humphries, S., Mack, J., and Perks R. (1988) *A Century of Childhood*. London: Sidgwick & Jackson.

Hunt, E. and Nash, J. (1967) 'Local and territorial units' in M. Nash (ed), *Handbook of Middle American Indians*, vol. 6, *Social Anthropology*. Austin: University of Texas Press.

Jabry, A., (ed.) (2002) *Children in Disasters: After the Cameras Have Gone*. London: Plan UK. Online. Available at: < http://www.plan-uk.org/newsroom/publications/childrenindisasters> (accessed 4 August 2006).

Jackson, P. (2000) 'Rematerializing social and cultural geography', *Social and cultural geography*, 1: 9–14.

Jacquemin, M.Y. (2004) 'Children's domestic work in Abidjan, Cote D'Ivoire: The *petites bonnes* have the floor', *Childhood*, 11: 383–397.

James, A. (1986) 'Learning to belong: the boundaries of adolescence', in Cohen, A. (ed), *Symbolising Boundaries: Identity and Diversity in British Cultures*. Manchester: Manchester University Press.

James, A. and Prout, A. (1990) *Constructing and Reconstructing Childhood*. London: Falmer Press.

James, A., Jenks, C., and Prout, A. (1998) *Theorising Childhood*. New York: Teachers College Press.

Jarosz, L. and Lawson, V. (2002) '"Sophisticated people versus rednecks": economic restructuring and class difference in American's west', *Antipode*, 34: 8–27.

Jeffrey, C. and McDowell, L. (2004) 'Youth in comparative perspective: global change, local lives', *Youth & Society*, 36: 131–142.

Jeffrey, C., Jeffery, R., and Jeffery, P. (2004) 'Degrees without freedom: the impact of formal education on Dalit young men in North India', *Development and Change*, 35: 963–986.

Jenkins, H. (1998) '*Complete Freedom of Movement*': *Video Games as Gendered Play Spaces*. Online. Available at: <http://web.mit.edu/cms/People/henry3/complete.html> (accessed 7 August 2006).

Jenks, C. (1996) *Childhood*. London: Routledge.

Jenks, C. (2005) *Childhood*, 2nd ed. London: Routledge.

Jensen, J. (1990) 'Native American women and agriculture' in DuBois, C. and Ruiz, V. (eds) *Unequal Sisters: A Multicultural Reader in US Women's History*. New York: Routledge.

Jensen, J. (1991) *Promise to the Land: Essays on Rural Women*. Albuquerque: University of New Mexico Press.

Jentsch, B. (2004) 'Experience of rural youth in the 'risk society': transitions from education to the labour market', in Jentsch, B. and Shucksmith, M. (eds) *Young People in Rural Areas of Europe*. Aldershot: Ashgate.

Jentsch, B. and Shucksmith, M. (2004) *Young People in Rural Areas of Europe*. Aldershot: Ashgate.

Johnson, V. (ed) (1996a) 'Children's Participation: Special Issue' *Participatory Learning and Action (PLA) Notes*, 25.

Johnson, V. (1996b) 'Introduction: starting a dialogue with children's participation', *Participatory Learning and Action (PLA) Notes*, 25: 30–37.

Johnson, V., Hill, J., and Ivan-Smith, E. (1995) *Listening to Smaller Voices: Children in an Environment of Change*. Somerset, UK: ACTIONAID.

Johnson, V., Ivan-Smith, E., Gordon, G., Pridmore, P., and Scott, P. (eds) (1998) *Stepping Forward: Children and Young People's Participation in the Development Process*. London: Intermediate Technology Publications.

Jones, G. (1997) 'Population dynamics and their impact on adolescents in the ESCAP region', in Economic and Social Commission for Asia and the Pacific, *Report and Recommendation of the Expert Group Meeting on Adolescents: Implications of Population Trends, Environment and Development* , Asian Population Study Series No.149. New York: United Nations.

Jones, G. (1999) '"The same people in the same places?" Socio-spatial identities and migration in youth', *Sociology*, 33: 1–22.

Jones, G. and Nagib, L. (1999) 'Education and labour market issues in East Nusatenggarra', *Development Bulletin*, 48: 13–16.

Jones, G. and Raharjo, Y. (1999) 'Introduction', *Development Bulletin*, 48: 7–8.

Jones, G. and Wallace, C. (1992) *Youth, Family and Citizenship*. Buckingham, UK: Open University Press.

Jones, O. (1997) 'Little figures, big shadows: country childhood stories', in Cloke, P. and Little, J. (eds), *Contested Countryside Cultures Cultures: Otherness, Marginalisation and Rurality*. London: Routledge.

Jones, O. (1999) 'Tomboy tales: the rural, nature and the gender of childhood', *Gender, Place and Culture*, 6: 117–136.

Jones, O. (2000) 'Melting geography: purity, disorder childhood and space', in S. Holloway and G. Valentine (eds) *Children's Geography: Living, Playing Learning*. London: Routledge.

Jones, O. (2002) 'Naturally not! Childhood, the urban and romanticism', *Human Ecology Review*, 9: 17–30.

Jones, O. (2003) '"Endlessly revisited and forever gone": on memory and emotional imaginations in doing children's geographies. An 'addendum' to '"To go back up the side hill": memories, imaginations and reveries of childhood' by Chris Philo, *Children's Geographies*, 1: 25–36.

Jones, O. (2006) 'Idylls and othernesses: childhood and rurality in film', in R. Fish (ed) *Cinematic Countrysides*. Manchester: Manchester University Press.

Jørgensen, G. (1994) *To Ungdomskulturer*, report no 1/1994. Sogndal: Vestlandsforskning.

Juckes Maxey, J. (2004) 'The participation of younger people within intentional communities: evidence from two case studies', *Children's Geographies*, 2: 29–48.

Kabeer, N. (1994) *Reversed Realities: Gender Hierarchies in Development Thought*. London: Verso.

Kaiser, F.G. and Fuhrer, U. (1996) 'Dwelling: speaking of an unnoticed universal language', *New Ideas in Psychology* 14: 225–236.

Kannangara, N., de Silva, H., and Parndigamage, N. (2003) *Sri Lanka Child Domestic Labour: A rapid assessment*. Geneva: ILO-IPEC.

Kansas Farmer (1872).

Karney, M. (1991) *No Rugged Landscape.* Dromana: Loch Haven Books.

Katz, C. (1991) 'Sow what you know: the struggle for social reproduction in rural Sudan', *Annals of the Association of American Geographers,* 81: 488–514.

Katz, C. (1993) Growing girls/circles: limits on the spaces of knowing in rural Sudan and US cities, in Katz, C. and Monk, J. (eds), *Full Circles: Geographies of Women Over the Life Course.* London: Routledge.

Katz, C. (2004) *Growing Up Global: Economic Restructuring and Children's Everyday Lives.* Minneapolis: University of Minnesota.

Kaufman, N.H. and Rizzini, I. (2002) *Globalization and Children: Exploring Potentials for Enhancing Opportunities in the Lives of Children and Youth.* London: Kluwer Academic/ Plenum Publishers.

Kaufmann, V. (2002) *Re-Thinking Mobility: Contemporary Sociology.* Aldershot: Sage.

Kellett, M., Forrest, R., Dent, N., and Ward, S. (2004) '"Just teach us the skills please, we'll do the rest": empowering ten-year-olds as active researchers', *Children & Society,* 18: 329–343.

Kelley, N. (2006) 'Children's involvement in policy formation', *Children's Geographies,* 4(1): 37–44.

Kifle, A. (2002) *Ethiopia. Child Domestic Workers in Addis Ababa: A Rapid Assessment.* Geneva: ILO/IPEC.

Kingdom of Lesotho (2003) Poverty reduction strategy paper (draft), Maseru.

Kitchin, R. (1998) 'Out of place, knowing one's place: space, power and the exclusion of disabled people', *Disability and Society,* 13: 343–356.

Klocker, N. (2005a) 'Connections and contrasts between the papers on global perspectives of rural childhood and youth', paper presented at the Royal Geographical Society—Institute of British Geographers Annual Conference, London, 30 August–2 September.

Klocker, N. (2005b) '"Get over it" or 'give up': the dilemmas of ethical postgraduate research in a cross-cultural setting', paper presented at the Royal Geographical Society–Institute of British Geographers Annual Conference, London, 30 August–2 September.

Klocker, N. (2006) '"I can see that I am a person who has the ability to do many bigger things": Participatory youth-led research with former child domestic workers in Tanzania', paper presented at the International Geographical Union Conference 2006, Brisbane, 3–7 July.

Knabb, K. (ed) (1981) *Situationist International Anthology.* Berkeley, CA: Bureau of Public Secrets.

Kollmorgen, R. (2003), 'Das Ende Ostdeutschlands? Zeiten und Perspektiven eines Forschungsgegenstandes', *Berliner Debatte Initial.Ostdeutschlandforschung Wende oder Ende,* 14: 4–18.

Kong, L. (2000) 'Nature's dangers, nature's pleasures: urban children and the natural world', in Holloway, S. and Valentine, G. (eds), *Children's Geographies: Playing, Living, Learning.* London: Routledge.

Kong, L., Yuen, B., Sodhi, N., and Briffett, C. (1999) 'The construction and experience of nature: perspectives of urban youths', *Tijdschrift voor Economische en Sociale Geografie,* 90: 3–16.

Kopoka, P.A. (1999) 'Human rights and child welfare in Sub-Saharan Africa', paper presented at the International Conference on Mainstreaming Democratic Governance in the Social Sciences and Humanities for the 21st Century, University of Dar es Salaam Institute of Development Studies, September–October.

Kraack, A. and Kenway, J. (2002) 'Place, time and stigmatised youthful identities: bad boys in paradise', *Journal of Rural Studies,* 18: 145–155.

Kristeva, J. (1982) *Powers of Horror. An Essay on Abjection*, translated by L. Roudiez. New York: Columbia University Press.

Kröhnert, S., Olst, N. V., and Klingholz, R. (2005) ,Mecklenburg-Vorpommern. Das wichtigste Kapital sind die Leere und die Landschaft', in *Deutschland 2020. Die demographische Zukunft der Nation*. Berlin: Berliner Institut für Bevölkerung und Entwicklung.

Kuleana Centre for Children's Rights (1999) *The State of Education in Tanzania: Crisis and Opportunity*. Mwanza: Kuleana.

Laegran, A.S. (2002) 'The petrol station and the Internet cafe: Rural technospaces for youth', *Journal of Rural Studies*, 18: 157–168.

Laegran, A.S. (2003a) *Connecting places. Internet cafes as technosocial spaces*, STS-report 64:2003. Trondheim: NTNU.

Laegran, A.S. (2003b) 'Escape vehicles? The Internet and the automobile in a global/local intersection', in Oudshoorn, N. and Pinch, T. (eds) *How Users Matter. The Co-construction of Technology and the User*. Cambridge, MA: MIT Press.

Lähteenmaa, J. (2006) 'Alueellisen eriarvoisuuden kokemukselliset ulottuvuudet suomalaisten maaseutunuorten elämässä [The experiential dimensions of regional inequalities in the lives of Finnish rural youth]' in Wilska, T-A. and Lähteenmaa, J. (eds) *Kultainen nuoruus? Tutkimuksia nuoruudesta 2000-luvun alun Suomessa* [Golden youth? Research on youth in Finland at the beginnings of the 2000s]. Helsinki: Youth Research Society.

Lake, M. (1985) 'Helpmeet, slave, housewife: women in rural families, 1870–1930' in Grimshaw, P., McConville, C., and McEwan, E. (eds) *Families in Colonial Australia*. Sydney: Allen and Unwin.

Lamvik, G. (1996) 'A fairy tale on wheels: The car as a vehicle for meaning within a Norwegian subculture', in M. Lie and K.H. Sørensen (eds) *Making Technology Our Own? Domesticating Technology into Everyday Life*. Oslo: Scandinavian University Press.

Latour, B. (1992) 'Where are the missing masses? The sociology of a few mundane artifacts', in Bijker, W. and Law, J. (eds) *Shaping Technology, Building Society: Studies in Sociotechnical Change*. Cambridge, MA: MIT Press.

Latour, B. (1993) *We Have Never Been Modern*, translated by C. Porters. Cambridge, MA: Harvard University Press.

Latour, B. (2004) 'Why has critique run out of steam? From matters of fact to matters of concern', *Critical Inquiry*, 30: 225–248.

Lawson, V.A. (2000) 'Arguments within geographies of movement: the theoretical potential of migrants' stories', *Progress in Human Geography*, 24: 173–189

Leckie G.J. (1996) '"They never trusted me to drive": farm girls and the gender relations of agricultural information transfer', *Gender, Place and Culture*, 3: 309–326.

Lefebvre, H. (1991a) *Critique of Everyday Life*, vol. 1. London: Verso.

Lefebvre, H. (1991b) *The Production of Space*. Oxford: Blackwell.

Levinson, B. and Holland, D. (1996) 'The cultural production of the educated person: an introduction', in B. A. Levinson, D. E. Foley, and D. C. Holland *The Cultural Production of the Educated Person: Critical Ethnographies of Schooling and Local Practice*. Albany, NY: State University of New York Press.

Lévi-Strauss, C. (1966) *The Savage Mind*. London: Weidenfeld and Nicolson.

Lewis, G. (1989) 'Counterurbanisation and social change in the rural south Midlands', *East Midlands Geographer*, 11: 3–12.

Lewis, G. and Sherwood, K. (1994) *Rural Mobility and Housing*, Working Papers 7–10. Leicester: Department of Geography, University of Leicester.

Leyshon, M. (2002) 'On being 'in the field': practice, problems and progress in research with young people in rural areas', *Journal of Rural Studies*, 18: 179–191.

Liechty, M. (1995) 'Media, markets and modernization: youth identities and the experience of modernity in Kathmandu, Nepal', in Amit-Talai, V. and Wulff, H. (eds) *Youth Cultures: A Cross-cultural Perspective*. London: Routledge.

Little, J. (1987) 'Gender relations in rural areas: the importance of women's domestic role', *Journal of Rural Studies*, 3: 335–342.

Little, J. and Austin, P. (1996) 'Women and the rural idyll', *Journal of Rural Studies*, 12: 101–111.

Little, J., Panelli, R., and Kraack, A. (2005) 'Women's fear of crime: A rural perspective' *Journal of Rural Studies*, 21: 151–165.

Liu, X. (2000*) In One's Own Shadow: An Ethnographic Account of the Conditions of Post-Reform Rural China*. Berkeley: University of California Press.

Liu, X. (2002) *The Otherness of Self: A Genealogy of the Self in Contemporary China*. Ann Arbor: The University of Michigan Press.

López Levy, M. (2004) *We are Millions: Neo-Liberalism and New Forms of Political Action in Argentina*. London: Latin America Bureau.

Lorimer, H. (2005) 'Cultural geography: the busyness of being "more-than-representational"', *Progress in Human Geography*, 29: 83–94.

Low, M. (2005) 'Power and politics in human geography', *Geografiska Annaler*, 87 B: 81–88.

Lucey, H. and Reay, D. (1999) Rationality and mastery: independent spatial mobility of middle class and working class urban children, unpublished paper, University College, London.

Lugalla, J.L.P. and Madihi, M. (2004) *Child Domestic Workers and Access to Education in Makete District, Tanzania*. Report submitted to UNICEF, Tanzania.

Lukes, S. (2005) *Power: A Radical View*, 2nd ed. Houndmills, Hants: Palgrave Macmillan.

Lundbye, H.I. (2005) 'The Stars of the Cars—kulturell produksjon og identitetskonstruksjon i rånemiljøet', unpublished master's thesis, University of Oslo.

Mabala, R. and Kamazima, S.R. (1995) *The Girl Child in Tanzania: Today's Girl, Tomorrow's Woman*. Dar es Salaam: UNICEF.

Macdonald, C. (1999) 'Too many men and too few women: gender's "fatal impact" in nineteenth-century colonies', in Daley, C. and Montgomerie, D. (eds) *The Gendered Kiwi*. Auckland: Auckland University Press.

Machacek, L. (1997) 'Individualisation of the first post-communist generation in the Slovak Republic', *Sociologia*, 29: 21–44.

Mackie, P.K. (2007) *'Children in Informal Trading: Cusco, Peru'*, unpublished Ph.D. thesis, Department of Geography, Swansea University.

Macnaghten, P. and Urry, J. (1998) *Contested Natures* London: Sage.

Magazine, R. (2003) 'Action, personhood and the gift economy among the so-called street children in Mexico City', *Social Anthropology*, 11: 303–318.

Martin, A.K. (1997) 'The practice of identity and an Irish sense of place', *Gender, Place and Culture*, 4: 89–119.

Martin, P.M. (2004) 'Contextualizing feminist political theory', in Staheli, L.A,. Kofman, E., and Peake, L.J. (eds) *Mapping Women, Making Politics: Feminist Perspectives on Political Geography*. London: Routledge.

Massey, D. (1991) 'A global sense of place', *Marxism Today*, June: 24–29.

Massey, D. (1993a) 'Politics and space/time', in Keith, M. and Pile, S (eds) *Place and the Politics of Identity*. London: Routledge.

Massey, D. (1993b) 'Power-geometry and a progressive sense of place', in Bird, J., Curtis, B., Putnam, T., Robertson, G., and Tichner, L. (eds) *Mapping the Futures: Local Cultures, Global Change*. London: Routledge.

Massey, D. (1998) 'The spatial construction of youth culture', in Skelton, T. and Valentine, G. (eds) *Cool Places. Geographies of Youth Cultures*. London: Routledge.

Matthews, H. (1984) 'Cognitive mapping abilities of young boys and girls', *Geography*, 69: 327–336.

Matthews, H. (1992) *Making Sense of Place: Children's Understanding of Large-Scale Environments*. London: Harvester-Wheatsheaf.

Matthews, H. (2003) 'The street as a liminal space: The barbed spaces of childhood', in Christensen, P. and O'Brien, M. (eds) *Children in the City*. London: Routledge Falmer.

Matthews, H. (2005) 'Editorial—Rising four: reflections on the state of growing up', *Children's Geographies*, 3: 271–273.

Matthews, H. and Limb, M. (1999) 'Defining an agenda for the geography of children: review and prospect', *Progress in Human Geography*, 23: 61–90.

Matthews, H., Limb, M., and Percy-Smith, B. (1998) 'Changing worlds, changing places: the microgeographies of teenagers', *Tijdschrift voor Economische et Sociale Geografie*, 89: 193–202.

Matthews, H., Limb, M., and Taylor, M. (2000) 'The street as thirdspace: class, gender and public space', in Holloway, S.L. and Valentine, G. (eds) *Children's Geographies: Living, Playing, Learning and Transforming Everyday Worlds*. London: Routledge.

Matthews, H., Taylor, M., Sherwood, K., Tucker, F., and Limb, M. (2000) 'Growing-up in the countryside: children and the rural idyll', *Journal of Rural Studies*, 16: 141–153.

Mayall, B. (1994) 'Action at home and at school', in Mayall, B. (ed) *Children's Childhoods: Observed and Experienced*. London: Falmer Press.

Mayall, B. (2002) *Towards a Sociology for Childhood: Thinking From Children's Lives*. Buckingham: Open University Press.

Mayo, M. (2001) 'Children's and young people's participation in development in the South and in urban regeneration in the North', *Progress in Development Studies*, 1: 279–293.

McAslan, E. (2002) 'Social capital and development', in Desai, V. and Potter, R.B. (eds) *The Companion to Development Studies*. London: Arnold.

McAuley, A. (1995) 'Inequality and Poverty', in Lane. D. (ed) *Russia in Transition: Politics, Privatisation and Inequality*. London and New York: Longman.

McCormack, J. (2000) Alta Vistas: An analysis of New Zealand children's cultural knowledges of 'rurality'. Unpublished Master of Arts thesis, University of Otago, Dunedin.

McCormack, J. (2002) 'Children's understandings of rurality: exploring the inter-relationship between experience and understanding', *Journal of Rural Studies*, 18: 193–207.

McDonald, P., Ruzicka, L., and Pyne, P. (1987) *'Marriage, Fertility and Mortality' in Australians, Historical Statistics*. Willoughby: Weldon & Syme.

McDowell, L. (2002) 'Masculine discourses and dissonances: strutting "lads," protest masculinity and domestic respectability', *Environment and Planning D: Society and Space*, 20: 97–119.

McEwan, I. (1988) *The Child in Time*. London, Pan Books Ltd.

McGrath, B. (2001) '"A problem of resources": Defining rural youth encounters in education, work and housing', *Journal of Rural Studies*, 17: 481–495.

McHugh, K.E. (2000) 'Inside, outside, upside down, backward, forward, round and round: a case for ethnographic studies in migration', *Progress in Human Geography*, 24: 71–89.

McIvor, C. (2001) '"Do not look down on us": child researchers investigate informal settlements in Zimbabwe', in Ashley, H. (ed) *Participatory Learning and Action (PLA) Notes*, 42: 34–38.

McKay, M. Diary 1890–1899, private collection of McKay family, Melbourne.

McKendrick, J.H. (2001) 'Coming of age: rethinking the role of children in population studies', *International Journal of Population Geography*, 7: 461–472.

McKenzie, A. Diaries Kept at Martin's Bay, Otago, MS Copy Micro 0227-1. Manuscripts and Archives Collection, Alexander Turnbull Library.

Meinert, L. (2003) 'Sweet and bitter places: The politics of schoolchildren's orientation in rural Uganda', in Olwig, K.F. and Gulløv, E. (eds) *Children's Places: Cross-cultural perspectives*. London: Routledge.

Mellström, U. (1995) *Engineering Lives. Technology, Time and Space in a Male-Centred World*. Linköping: Lindköping Studies in Art and Science, No 128.

Mizen, P., Pole, C., and Bolton, A. (eds) (2001) *Hidden Hands: International Perspectives on Children's Work and Labour*. London: Routledge Falmer.

Moore, R. (1986) *Children's Domain: Play and Play Space in Child Development*. London: Croom Helm.

Mormont, M. (1990) 'Who is rural? Or, how to be rural. Towards a sociology of the rural' in Marsden, T., Lowe, P., and Whatmore, S. (eds) *Rural Restructuring: Global Processes And Local Responses*. London: Wiley.

Morris, J. (1991) *Pride against Prejudice: Transforming Attitudes to Disability*. London: The Women's Press.

Moseley, M.J. (1979) *Accessibility: the Rural Challenge*. London: Methuen & Co.

Mosha, D. (2005) 'Elimination of child labour: A Luta Continua!' *Sunday Observer* (Tanzania), 20 February: 8.

Mouffe, C. (1996) 'Democracy, power and the "political",' in Benhabib, S. (ed) *Democracy and Difference: Contesting the Boundaries of the Political*. Princeton, NJ: Princeton University Press.

Murray, W. (2006) *Geographies of Globalization*. London: Routledge.

Myres, S. (1988) 'Victoria's daughters: English speaking women on nineteenth-century frontiers', in Schlissel, L., Ruiz, V., and Monk, J. (eds) *Western Women: Their Land, Their Lives*. Albuquerque: University of New Mexico Press.

Nairn, K., Panelli, R., and McCormack, J. (2003) 'Destabilising dualisms: young people's experiences of rural and urban environments', *Childhood*, 10: 9–42.

Nasution, M.A. (2001) *Orang Indonesia di Malaysia*. Yogyakarta: Pustaka Pelajar.

Nebraska Farmer (1907–1912).

Nespor, J. (1998) 'The meanings of research: kids as subjects and kids as inquirers', *Qualitative Inquiry*, 4: 369–389.

Neth, M. (1995) *Preserving the Family Farm: Women, Community, and the Foundations of Agribusiness in the Midwest, 1900–1940*. Baltimore: Johns Hopkins University Press.

New Zealand Farmer (1892–1896).

Nieuwenhuys, O. (1994) *Children's Lifeworlds: Gender, Welfare and Labour in the Developing World*. London: Routledge.

Ní Laoire, C. (2000) 'Conceptualising Irish rural youth migration: a biographical approach', *International Journal of Population Geography* 6: 229–243.

Northeast Midwest Institute (2005) *Rural Population as a Percent of State Total by State, 2000*. Online. Available at: <httpl/www.nemw.org/poprural.htm> (accessed 18 November 2005).

Norton, L. (1876–1895) Norton Family Diaries. By permission of Henry L. Norton. Manuscripts Division, Kansas State Historical Society, Topeka, Kansas.

Noyes, B. (2001) *Encounters, Georges Bataille*, Australian Broadcasting Corporation. Online. Available at: <http://www.abc.net.au/rn/relig/enc/stories/s281136.htm> (accessed on 13 February 2006).

Nugent, J.B. (1985) 'The old-age security motive for fertility'. *Population and Development Review*, 11: 75–97.

Nutini, H. and Isaac, B. (1974) *Los Pueblos de Habla Nahuatl de la Region de Tlaxcala y Puebla*. Mexico City: INI and SEP.

Nutley, S. and Thomas, C. (1995) 'Spatial mobility and social change: the mobile and the immobile', *Sociologia Ruralis*, 35: 24–39.

Nyanzi S., Pool R., and Kinsman J. (2001) 'The negotiation of sexual relationships among school pupils in south-western Uganda', *AIDS Care*, 13: 83–98

Onyango, P. (1988) 'Child labour policies and programmes in Kenya', in Bequele, A. and Boyden, J. (eds) *Combating Child Labour*. Geneva: International Labour Organisation.

Opitz-Karig, U. (2003) *Zur Spezifik der Situation Jugendlicher im ostdeutschen ländlichen Raum*. Rostock: Tagung "Socialer Wandel in ländlichen Räumen".

Orellana, M., Thorne, B., Chee, A., and Lam, W. (2001) 'Transnational childhoods: the participation of children in processes of family migration', *Social Problems*, 48: 572–591.

Otago Witness (1893–1899).

Oudshoorn, N., Saetnan A.R., and Lie, M. (2002) 'On gender and things: reflections on an exhibition on gendered artefacts', *Women's Studies International Forum*, 25: 471–483.

Owens, P. (1994) 'Teen places in Sunshine, Australia: then and now', *Children's Environments*, 11: 292–299.

Panelli, R. (2002) 'Editorial: young rural lives: Strategies beyond diversity', *Journal of Rural Studies*, 18: 113–122.

Panelli, R., Nairn K., and McCormack, J. (2002) '"We make our own fun": reading the politics of youth with(in) community', *Sociologia Ruralis*, 42: 106–130.

Panelli, R., Kraack, A., and Little, J. (2005) 'Claiming space and community: rural women's strategies for living with, and beyond, fear', *Geoforum*, 36: 495–508.

Parpart, J.L., Shirin, M.R., and Staudt, K. (2002) 'Rethinking em(power)ment, gender and development; an introduction', in Parpart, J.L., Rai, S.M., and Staudt, K. (eds) *Rethinking Empowerment in a Global/Local World*. London: Routledge.

Parr, H. and Philo, C. (1995) 'Mapping mad identities' in Pile, S. and Thrift, N. (eds) *Mapping the Subject: Geographies of Cultural Transformation*. London: Routledge.

Paulgaard, G. (2001) 'Ungdom, lokalitet og modernitet', unpublished PhD thesis, University of Tromsø.

Pavis, S., Platt, S., and Hubbard, G. (2000) *Young People in Rural Scotland: Pathways to Social Inclusion and Exclusion*. York: Joseph Rowntree Foundation.

Peirce, M.H. (1997) 'Introduction,' in Peirce, M.H. (ed) *Capitalization: A Bolivian Model of Social and Economic Reform*. Washington, DC: Woodrow Wilson Center.

Penn, H. (1999) 'Children in the majority world: is Outer Mongolia really so far away?' in Hood, S., Mayall, B., and Oliver, S. (eds) *Critical Issues in Social Research: Power and Prejudice*. Buckingham: Open University Press.

Penn, H. (ed.), (2005) *Unequal Childhoods: Children's Lives in Developing Countries*. London: Routledge Falmer.

Percy-Smith, B. (1999) *Multiple Childhood Geographies: Giving Voice to Young People's Experience of Place*, unpublished Ph.D. thesis, Centre for Children and Youth, University College, Northampton.

Philo, C. (1992) 'Neglected rural geographies: a review' *Journal of Rural Studies*, 8: 193–207.

Philo, C. (2000a) 'More words, more worlds: reflections on the "cultural turn" in human geography', in Cook, I., Crouch, D., Naylor, S., and Ryan, J.R. (eds) *Cultural turns/geographical turns*. Harlow, UK: Prentice Hall.

Philo, C. (2000b) 'The cornerstones of my world: introduction to special issue on the spaces of childhood', *Childhood*, 17: 243–256.

Pile, S. and Thrift, N. (1995a) 'Conclusions: spacing and the subject', in Pile, S. and Thrift, N. (eds) *Mapping the Subject: Geographies of Cultural Transformation*. London: Routledge.

Pile, S. and Thrift, N. (1995b) 'Introduction' in Pile, S. and Thrift, N. (eds) *Mapping the Subject: Geographies of Cultural Transformation* London: Routledge.

Pilkington, H. (1994) *Russia's Youth and Its Culture*. London/New York: Routledge.

Pilkington, H. (2004) 'Youth strategies for global living: space, power and communication in everyday cultural practice', in Bennett A. and Kahn-Harris, K. (eds) *After Subcultures. Critical Studies in Contemporary Youth Culture*. Basingstoke, UK and New York: Palgrave Macmillan.

Pilkington, H. and Johnson, R. (2003) 'Peripheral youth: relations of identity and power in global/local context', *European Journal of Cultural Studies*, 6: 259–283.

Pilkington, H., Omel'chenko, E., Flynn, M., Bliudina, U., and Starkova, E. (2002) *Looking West? Cultural Globalization and Russian Youth Cultures*. University Park, PA: Pennsylvania State University Press.

Postman, N. (1982) *The Disappearance of Childhood*. New York: Delacorte Press.

Potter, R., Binns, T., Elliot, J., and Smith, D. (2004) *Geographies of Development*, 2nd ed. Harlow: Pearson Education.

Pratt, G. (2000) 'Geographies of subject formation', in Johnston, R.J., Gregory, D., Pratt, G., and Watts, M. (eds) *The Dictionary of Human Geography*. Oxford: Blackwell.

Preston, D. (1994) *Bolivia: An Overview of Human Issues,* Unpublished Report for ODA, School of Geography, University of Leeds.

Pribilsky, J. (2001) '*Nervios* and "Modern Childhood": Migration and shifting contexts of child life in the Ecuadorian Andes', *Childhood*, 8: 251–273.

Punch, S. (2000) 'Children's strategies for creating playspaces: negotiating independence in rural Bolivia', in Holloway, S. and Valentine, G. (eds) *Children's Geographies: Living, Playing, Learning*. London: Routledge.

Punch, S. (2001a) 'Household division of labour: generation, gender, age, birth order and sibling composition', *Work, Employment & Society*, 15 (4): 803–823.

Punch, S. (2001b) 'Multiple methods and research relations with young people in rural Bolivia', in Limb, M. and Dwyer, C. (eds) *Qualitative Methodologies for Geographers*. London: Arnold.

Punch, S. (2001c) 'Negotiating autonomy: childhoods in rural Bolivia', in Alanen, L. and Mayall, B. (eds) *Conceptualising Child-Adult Relations*. London: Routledge Falmer.

Punch, S. (2002a) 'Research with children: the same or different from research with adults?' *Childhood*, 9: 321–341.

Punch, S. (2002b) 'Youth transitions and interdependent adult–child relations in rural Bolivia', *Journal of Rural Studies*, 18: 123–133.

Punch, S. (2003) 'Childhoods in the majority world: miniature adults or tribal children?' *Sociology*, 37: 277–295.

Punch, S. (2004) 'The impact of primary education on school-to-work transitions for young people in rural Bolivia', *Youth & Society*, 36: 163–182.

Punch, S. (2007) 'Negotiating migrant identities: young people in Bolivia and Argentina', *Children's Geographies*.

Qvortrup, J. (2000) 'Macroanalysis of childhood', in Christensen, P. and James, A. (eds) *Research with Children: Perspectives and Practices*. London: Falmer Press.

Rahman, N.A. (2002) 'Singapore Girl? Indonesian housemaids want to be heard', *Inside Indonesia*, January–March. Online. Available at: <http://www.insideindonesia.org/index.htm> (accessed 20 January, 2006).

Rahnema, M. (1992) "Participation", in Sachs, W. (ed.) *The Development Dictionary; A Guide to Knowledge as Power*. London: Zed Books Ltd.

Rajani, R. (1998) 'Child sexual abuse in Tanzania: much noise, little justice', *Sexual Health Exchange*, No. 1. Online. Available at: <www.kit.nl/ils/exchange_content/html/1998_1_child_sexual_abuse.asp?/ils/exch> (accessed 1 November 2005).

Rajani, R. (2000) 'Child rights in Tanzania: a political perspective', *International Children's Rights Monitor*, 13(1): 13–15.

Reboratti, C. (1996) *Sociedad, Ambiente y Desarrollo Regional en la Alta Cuenca del Río Bermejo*. Buenos Aires: Instituto de Geografía, Universidad de Buenos Aires.

Research and Analysis Technical Working Group (2005) *Tanzania: Poverty and Human Development Report 2005*, The Poverty Eradication Division at the Ministry of Planning, Economy and Empowerment. Dar es Salaam: Mkuki na Nyota Publishers.

Reynolds, P. (1991) *Dance Civet Cat: Child Labour in the Zambezi Valley*, Athens, Ohio: Ohio University Press.

Ridge, T. (2002) *Childhood Poverty and Social Exclusion: From a Child's Perspective*. Bristol: The Policy Press.

Riordan, J., Williams, C., and Ilynsky, I. (eds) (1995) *Young People in Post-Communist Russia and Eastern Europe*. Aldershot and Vermont: Dartmouth Publishing Company.

Roberts, K., Clark, S.C., Fagan, S., and Tholen, J. (2000) *Surviving Post-Communism. Young People in the Former Soviet Union*. Cheltenham: Edward Elgar.

Robinson, K. (1991) 'Housemaids: the effects of gender and culture on the internal and international migration of Indonesian women', in Bottomley, G. et al. (eds), *Intersexions: Gender/Class/Ethnicity*. Sydney: Allen and Unwin.

Robinson V., Hockey J., and Meah, A. (2004) '"What I used to do...on my mother's settee": spatial and emotional aspects of heterosexuality in England', *Gender, Place and Culture*, 11: 417–435

Robson, E. (1996) 'Working girls and boys: children's contributions to household survival in West Africa', *Geography*, 81: 403–407.

Robson, E. (2000) 'Invisible carers: young people in Zimbabwe's home-based healthcare', *Area*, 32: 59–70.

Robson, E. (2004a) 'Children at work in rural Northern Nigeria: patterns of age, space and gender', *Journal of Rural Studies*, 20: 193–210.

Robson, E. (2004b) 'Hidden child workers: young carers in Zimbabwe', *Antipode*, 36: 227–248.

Robson, E., Ansell, N., Huber, U., Gould, W.T.S., and van Blerk, L. (2006) 'Young caregivers in the context of HIV/AIDS in sub-Saharan Africa', *Population, Space and Place*, 12: 93–111.

Rodgers, G. and Standing, G. (1981) *Child Work, Poverty and Underdevelopment*. Geneva: International Labour Office.

Rogers, E.M. (1995) *Diffusion of innovations*. 4th ed. New York: Free Press.

Rose, G. (1997) 'Situating knowledges: positionality, reflexivities and other tactics', *Progress in Human Geography*, 21: 305–320.

Rowlands, J. (1995) 'Empowerment examined', *Development in Practice*, 5: 101–107.

Rowlands, J. (1997) *Questioning Empowerment: Working with Women in Honduras*. Oxford: Oxfam Publications.

Rubenson, B., Anh, T.V., Hojer, B., and Johansson, E. (2004) 'Child domestic servants in Hanoi: Who are they and how do they fare?' *The International Journal of Children's Rights*, 11: 391–407.

Ruddick, S. (1998) 'Modernism and resistance; how "homeless" youth sub-cultures make a difference', in Skelton, T. and Valentine, G. (eds) *Cool Places: Geographies of Youth Cultures*. London: Routledge.

Rudolph, M. (1997) 'Unterschiede auf dem Land. Landjugendliche in Ost- und Westdeutschland', *Berichte über Landwirtschaft*, 75: 486–497.

Rufo, K. (2003) 'Rhetoric and power: rethinking and relinking', *Argumentation and Advocacy*, 40: 65–84.

Rusman, R., Djohan. E., and Hull, T. (1999) *They Simply Die: Searching for the Causes of High Infant Mortality in Lombok*. Jakarta: PPT-LIPI.

Rwezaura, B. (1998) 'The duty to hear the child: a view from Tanzania', in W. Ncube (ed) *Law, Culture, Tradition and Children's Rights in Eastern and Southern Africa*. Aldershot: Ashgate.

Salamon, S. (1992) *Prairie Patrimony: Family, Farming and Community in the Midwest*. Chapel Hill: University of North Carolina Press.

Saldanha, A. (2002) 'Music, space, identity: geographies of youth culture in Bangalore', *Cultural Studies*, 16: 337–350.

Schefold, W. (1995) 'Das schwierige Erbe der Einheitsjugend: Jugendverbände zwischen Aufbruch und Organisationsmüdigkeit', in Rauschenbach, T., Sachsse, C., and Olk, T. (eds) *Von der Wertgemeinschaft zum Dienstleistungsunternehmen. Jugend- und Wohlfahrtsverbände im Umbruch*, 2nd ed. Frankfurt am Main: Suhrkamp.

Scheper-Hughes, N. (1992) *Death without Weeping: The Violence of Everyday Life in Brazil*. Berkeley: University of California Press.

Scheper-Hughes, N. and Sargent, C. (1998) *Small Wars: The Cultural Politics of Childhood*. London: University of California Press.

Scheyvens, R. (1998) 'Subtle strategies for women's empowerment; planning for effective grassroots development', *Third World Planning Review*, 20: 235–253.

Schildkrout, E. (1981) 'The employment of children in Kano (Nigeria)', in Rodgers, G. and Standing, G. (eds) *Child Work, Poverty and Underdevelopment*. Geneva: International Labour Organisation.

Scott, J. (1985) *Weapons of the weak: Everyday Forms of Peasant Resistance*. New Haven: Yale University Press.

Scott, J. (1990) *Domination and the Arts of Resistance: Hidden Transcripts*. London: Yale University Press.

Scott, J. (2001) *Power*. Cambridge: Polity.

Sechaba Consultants (2002) *The Border Within: The Future of the Lesotho-South African International Boundary*. Migration Policy Series No. 26, Southern African Migration Project. Canada: Queen's University Press,

Sharp, J.P., Routledge, P., Philo, C., and Paddison, R. (2000) *Entanglements of Power: Geographies of Domination/Resistance*. London: Routledge.

Shields, R. (1999) *Lefebvre: Love and Struggle, Spatial Dialectics*. London: Routledge.

Shipman, A. (2004) 'Lauding the leisure class: symbolic content and conspicuous consumption', *Review of Social Economy*, 62: 277–289.

Shoard, M. (1980) *The Theft of the Countryside*. London: Temple-Smith.

Short, J.R. (1991) *Imagined Country: Society, Culture and Environment*. London: Routledge.

Shucksmith, M. (2004) 'Young people and social exclusion in rural areas', *Sociologia Ruralis*, 44: 43–59.

Sibley, D. (1995a) 'Families and domestic routines: constructing the boundaries of childhood', in Pile, S. and Thrift, N. (eds) *Mapping the Subject: Geographies of Cultural Transformation*. London: Routledge.

Sibley, D. (1995b) *Geographies of Exclusion: Society and Difference in the West*. London and New York: Routledge.

Sibley, D. (1997) 'Endangering the sacred. Nomads, youth cultures and the English countryside', in P. Cloke and J. Little (eds), *Contested Countryside Cultures: Otherness, Marginality and Rurality*. London: Routledge.

Silvey, R. and Lawson, V. (1999) 'Placing the migrant', *Annals of the Association of American Geographers*, 89: 121–132.

Skelton, T. (2000) '"Nothing to do, Nowhere to go?" Teenage girls and "public" space in the Rhondda Valleys, South Wales', in Holloway, S.L. and Valentine, G. (eds) *Childrens Geographies*. London: Routledge.

Skelton, T. and Valentine, G. (eds) (1998) *Cool Places. Geographies of Youth Cultures*. London: Routledge.

Skelton, T. and Valentine, G. (2003) '"It feels like being Deaf is normal": an exploration into the complexities of defining D/deafness and young D/deaf people's identities', *The Canadian Geographer*, 47: 451–466.

Sklair, L. (1994) 'Capitalism and development in global perspectives,' in Sklair, L. (ed.) *Capitalism and Development*, London: Routledge.

Smith, F.M. (1998) 'Between East and West. Sites of resistance in East German youth cultures', in Skelton, T. and Valentine, G. (eds) *Cool Places. Geographies of Youth Cultures*. London: Routledge.

Smith, L.T., Smith, G.H., Boler, M., Kempton, M., Ormond, A., Chueh, H.C., and Waetford, R., (2002) '"Do you guys hate Aucklanders too?" Youth voicing difference from the rural heartland', *Journal of Rural Studies* 18: 169–178.

Soininen, A. (2001): '"To a town with a better future": Young people and their future orientations in the Barents region'. Finland: Youth Research Network. Online. Available at: < http://66.102.7.104/search?q=cache:rJYDAe4SfTcJ:www.alli.fi/nuorisotutkimus/julkaisut/barents.pdf+To+a+town+with+a+better+future+Finland&hl=en&gl=nz&ct=clnk&cd=1> (accessed 4 August 2006).

Soja, E. (1996) *Thirdspace: Journeys to Los Angeles and Other Real-and-Imagined Places*. Oxford: Blackwell.

Somers, M. R. (1994) 'The narrative constitution of identity: a relational and network approach', *Theory and Society*, 23: 605–649.

Spencer, C. (2005) 'How can we give "children's geographies" away?' *Children's Geographies*, 3: 265–266.

Spencer, C. and Woolley, H. (2000) 'Children and the city: a summary of recent environmental psychology research', *Child: Care, Health and Development*, 26: 1–18.

Statistisches Landesamt Mecklenburg-Vorpommern (2003) *Statistisches Jahrbuch Mecklenburg-Vorpommern*. Schwerin: Statistisches Landesamt Mecklenburg-Vorpommern.

Statistisches Amt Mecklenburg-Vorpommern (2006) *Statistischer Jahresbericht 2005—Entwicklungen in MV*. Schwerin: Statistisches Amt Mecklenburg-Vorpommern.

Stenning, A. (2005) 'Post-socialism and the changing geographies of the everyday in Poland', *Transactions of the Institute of British Geographers*, 30: 113–127.

Stephens, S. (1995) *Children and the Politics of Culture*. Princeton, NJ: Princeton University Press.

Storey, P. and Brannen, J. (2000) *Young People and Transport in Rural Areas*. Leicester: Youth Work Press.

Sukamdi, Haris, A., and Brownlee, P. (2000) (eds) *Labour Migration in Indonesia: Policies and Practice*. Yogyakarta : Population Studies Centre, Gadja Mada University.

Suryakusuma, J. (2004) *Sex, Power and Nation: An Anthology of Writings, 1979–2003*. Jakarta: Metafor Publishing.

TACAIDS (2003) *National Multi-Sectoral Strategic Framework on HIV/AIDS, 2003–2007*. Dar es Salaam: The Prime Minister's Office.

Tamtiari, W. (1999) 'Dampak Sosial Migrasi Tenaga Kerja ke Malaysia', *Populasi: Buletin Peneltian Kebijakan Kependudukun*, 10: 239–256.

Tapscott, D. (1998) *Growing Up Digital: The Rise of the Net Generation*. New York: McGraw-Hill.

Taracena, E. (2003) 'A schooling model for working children in Mexico: the case of children of Indian origin working as agricultural workers during the harvest', *Childhood*, 10: 301–318.

Taylor, C.C. (2004) 'More power to you, or should it be less?' *Social Analysis*, 48: 179–185.

Thomas, E. (1938) *The Childhood of Edward Thomas: A Fragment of Autobiography*. London: Faber and Faber.

Thomas, M. (2004) 'Pleasure and propriety: teen girls and the practice of straight space', *Environment and Planning D: Society and Space*, 22: 773–789.

Thomas, M. (2005) 'Girls, consumption space and the contradictions of hanging out in the city', *Social & Cultural Geography* 6: 587–605.

Thrift, N. (2003) 'Performance and...', *Environment and Planning A*, 35: 2019–2024.

Tienda, M. (1979) 'Economic activity of children in Peru: labor force behaviour in rural and urban contexts', *Rural Sociology*, 44: 370–391.

Toynbee, C. (1995) *Her Work and His: Family, Kin and Community in New Zealand 1900–1930*. Wellington: Victoria University Press.

Treacher, A. (2000) 'Children: memories, fantasies and narratives: from dilemma to complexity', in Radstone, S. (ed) *Memory and Methodology*. Oxford: Berg.

Tsang, A.K.T., Irving, H., Alaggia, R., Chau, S.B.Y., and Benjamin, M. (2003) 'Negotiating ethnic identity in Canada: the case of the "satellite children"', *Youth and Society*, 34: 359–384.

Tucker, F. (2003) 'Sameness or difference? Exploring girls' use of recreational spaces', *Children's Geographies*, 1: 111–124.

Tucker, F. and Matthews, H. (2001) '"They don't like girls hanging around there": conflicts over recreational space in Rural Northamptonshire', *Area*, 33: 161–168.

Tuhkunen, A. (2002) 'Ideal life and proud feelings in the north', *Young*, 10: 42–60.

Turner, J.C. (1991) *Social Influence*. Milton Keynes: Open University Press.

UNAIDS (2004) *Epidemiological Fact Sheets on HIV/AIDS and Sexually Transmitted Infections: 2004 Update United Republic of Tanzania*, UNAIDS.

UNDP (2005) *Human Development Report*. Online. Available at: <http://hdr.undp.org/reports/global/2005/>) (accessed 4 August 2006).

UNICEF (1997) *The State of the World's Children*. Oxford: Oxford University Press.

UNICEF (2006) "The State of the World's Children: Excluded and Invisible", Available at: <http://www.inicef.org/sowc06/index.php>.

UNICEF (1999) *International Child Development Centre (Innocenti) Digest: Child Domestic Work*. Florence: UNICEF.

UNICEF and United Republic of Tanzania (2001) *Situation Analysis of Children in Tanzania*. Tanzania: UNICEF.

United Nations (1994) *The Salamanca Statement and Framework for Action on Special Educational Needs*. Paris: UN Educational, Scientific and Cultural Organisation.

United Nations (2004) *Draft Articles for a Comprehensive and Integral International Convention on the Protection and Promotion of the Rights and Dignity of Persons with Disabilities*. New York: United Nations.

United Nations Economic and Social Council (2005) 'Tackling Emerging Issues in International Migration. International Migration in the ESCAP Region', Committee on Emerging Social Issues. Online. Available at: <http://www.unescap.org/esid/committee2005/English/CESI2_2E.pdf> (accessed 1 March 2006).

United States–Indonesian Society (USINDO) (2005) 'About Indonesia'. Online. Available at: < http://www.usindo.org/ai.htm> (accessed 20 February, 2006).

Urassa, M., Boerma, J., Ng'weshemi, J., Isingo, R., Schapink, D., and Kumogola, Y. (1997) 'Orphanhood, child fostering and the AIDS epidemic in rural Tanzania', *Health Transition Review*, 7: 141–153.

Urry, J. (1995) *Consuming Places*. London.: Routledge.

U.S. Census Bureau (2005) *Quick Facts*. Online. Available at: <http://quickfacts.census.gov> (accessed 18 November 2005).

U.S. Census Office (1902) *Census Reports*, vol. 2, *Twelfth Census of the United States, Taken in the Year 1900, Population, Part II*. Washington, DC: United States Census Office.

Usher, R. (2002) 'Putting space back on the map: globalisation, place and identity', *Educational Philosophy and Theory*, 34: 41–55.

Utomo, I. (1998) 'State ideologies and provision of reproductive health education and services: a case study of Indonesian youth', paper presented to seminar on Gender Inequalities and Reproductive Health; Changing Priorities in and Era of Social Transformation and Globalization, Campus de Jordao, Brazil, November.

Vaaranen, H. and Wieloch, N. (2002) 'Car crashes and dead end careers: Leisure pursuits of the Finnish subculture of the kortteliralli street racing', *Young Nordic Journal of Youth Research*, 10: 42–58.

Valentine, G. (1996) 'Angels and devils: moral landscapes of childhood', *Environment and Planning D: Society and Space*, 14: 581–599.

Valentine, G. (1997a) 'A safe place to grow up? Parenting, perceptions of children's safety and the rural idyll', *Journal of Rural Studies*, 13: 137–148.

Valentine, G. (1997b) '"Oh yes I can". "Oh no you can't". Children and parents' understanding of kids' competence to negotiate public space safely', *Antipode*, 29: 65–89.

Valentine, G. (1997c) '"My son's a bit dizzy". "My wife's a bit soft": gender, children and cultures of parenting', *Gender, Place and Culture*, 4: 37–62.

Valentine, G. (1999) '"Oh please, mum. oh please, dad": Negotiating children's spatial boundaries', in McKie, L., Bowlby, S., and Gregory, S. (eds) *Gender, Power and the Household*. Basingstoke: Macmillan.

Valentine, G. (2000) 'Exploring children and young people's narratives of identity', *Geoforum*, 31: 257–267.

Valentine, G. (2003) 'Boundary crossings: transitions from childhood to adulthood', *Children's Geographies*, 1: 37–52.

Valentine, G. (2004) *Public Space and the Culture of Childhood*. London: Ashgate.

Valentine, G. and Holloway, S.L. (2001) 'A window on the wider world? Rural children's use of information and communication technologies', *Journal of Rural Studies*, 17: 383–394.

van Blerk, L. (2005) 'Negotiating spatial identities: mobile perspectives on street life in Uganda', *Children's Geographies*, 3: 5–22.

van Blerk, L. and Ansell, N. (2006) 'Imaging migration: placing children's understanding of 'moving house' in southern Africa', *Geoforum*, 37: 256–272.

Vanderbeck, R. and Dunkley, C.M. (2003) 'Young people's narratives of rural-urban difference,' *Children's Geographies* 1: 241–259.

Vanderbeck, R. and Johnson, J. (2000) "That's the only place where you can hang out': urban young people and the space of the mall,' *Urban Geography*, 21: 5–25.

van Hoven, B. (2001) 'Women at work—experiences and identity in rural East Germany', *Area*, 33: 38–46.

van Hoven, B. (2002) 'Experiencing democracy: women in rural East Germany', *Social Politics: International Studies in Gender, State Society*, 9: 444–470.

Van Vliet, W. (1983) 'Exploring the fourth environment: an examination of the home range of city and suburban teenagers', *Environment and Behavior*, 15: 567–588.

Verdery, K. (1999) *The Political Life of Dead Bodies: Reburial and Post-Socialist Change*. New York: Columbia University Press.

Vermont Agency of Human Services (2003) *2003 Vermont Community Profiles*, Online. Available at: <http//www.ahs.state.vt.us> (accessed 26 February 2004).

Vickers, A. (2005) *A History of Modern Indonesia*. Cambridge: Cambridge University Press.

Victorian Yearbook (1900–1930). Melbourne: Victorian Government Printer.

Vlassoff, M. (1985) 'Labour demand and economic utility of children: A case study in rural India', *Population Studies*, 33: 415–428.

Waara, P. (1996) *Ungdom I gränsland (Youth in Borderland)*. Smergraf: Smejdbacken.

Waara, P. (2002) 'At the end of the world: young people in the Barents area'. *Young* 10: 2–11.

Wajcman, J. (1991) *Feminism Confronts Technology*. Cambridge: Polity Press.

Waksler, F. (1996) *The Little Trials of Childhood and Children's Strategies for Dealing with Them*. London: Falmer Press.

Wallace, C., Dunerley, D., Cheal, B., and Warren, M. (1994) 'Young people and the division of labour in farming families', *Sociological Review* 42: 501–530.

Ward, C. (1978) *The Child in the City*. London: Architectural Press.

Ward, C. (1990) *The Child in the Country*. London: Bedford Square Press.

Werz, N. (2001) 'Abwanderung aus den neuen Bundesländern von 1989 bis 2000', *Aus Politik und Zeitgeschichte*, B 39–40: 23–31.

Westwood, S. (2002) *Power and the Social*. London: Routledge.

Wiborg, A. (1999) 'Place, nature and migration: students' attachment to their rural home places', *Sociologia Ruralis*, 44: 416–432.

Widodo, A. (2002) 'Consuming passions: millions of Indonesians must watch soap operas', *Inside Indonesia*, Oct-Dec. Online. Available at: <http://www.insideindonesia.org/edit72/Theme%20-%20Amrih.htm> (accessed February 2006).

Wilkinson, J. (2000) *What is Child Poverty? Facts, Measurements and Conclusions*. London: Save the Children.

Williams, C.P. (2005) 'Knowing one's place': gender, mobility and shifting subjectivity in Eastern Indonesia', *Global Networks*, 5: 401–417.

Williams, R. (1985) *The Country and the City*. London: The Hogarth Press.

Willis, P.E. (1977) *Learning to Labour: How Working Class Kids Get Working Class Jobs*. Farnborough: Saxon House.

Wilson, G. and Wilson, O. (2001) *German Agriculture in Transition. Society, Policies and Environment in a Changing Europe*. Basingstoke, Hants and New York: Palgrave.

Wilson, O. and Klages, B. (2001) 'Farm restructuring in the ex-GDR: towards a new farm model?' *Journal of Rural Studies*, 17: 277–291.

Wimshurst, K. (1980–1981) 'Child labour and school attendance in South Australia, 1890–1915' *Historical Studies*, 19: 388–411.

Winchester, H.P.M. and Costello, L.N. (1995) 'Living on the street: Social organisation and gender relations of Australian street kids', *Environment and Planning D: Society and Space*, 13: 329–348.

Wolf, E. (1957) 'Closed corporate peasant communities in Mesoamerica and Java', *Southwestern Journal of Anthropology*, 13: 1–18.

Woodhead, M. (1998) *Children's Perspectives on Their Working Lives: A Participatory Study in Bangladesh, Ethopia, The Philippines, Guatemala, El Salvador and Nicaragua*. Stockholm: Rädda Barnen.

Woods, M. (2005) *Rural Geography: Processes, Practices and Experiences in Rural Restructuring*. London: Sage.

Woodward, (2005) 'Introduction', *Picture of Innocence: Portraits of Children from Hogarth to Lawrence*, catalogue to the exhibition. Holbourne Museum of Art, Bath, and the Lakeland Arts Trust.

Wyatt, S. (2003) 'Non-users also matter: The construction of users and non-users of the Internet' in Oudshoorn, N. and Pinch, T. (eds) *How Users Matter: The Co-construction of Users and Technology*. Cambridge, MA: MIT Press.

Wyn, J. and Dwyer, P. (1999) 'New directions in research on youth in transition', *Journal of Youth Studies*, 2: 5–21.

Wyn, J. and White, R. (1997) *Rethinking Youth*. London: Sage.

Young, C. and Light, D. (2001) 'Place, national identity and post-socialist transformations: an introduction', *Political Geography*, 20: 941–955.

Young, L. and Ansell, N. (2003) 'Fluid households, complex families: the impacts of children's migration as a response to HIV/AIDS in southern Africa', *Professional Geographer*, 55: 464–479.

Zourabichvili, F. (1996) 'Six Notes on the percept (on the relation between the critical and the clinical)', in Patton, P. (ed) *Deleuze: A Critical Reader*. Oxford: Blackwell.

Index